THE NEW
INTERNAL
AUDITING

THE WILEY/RONALD-INSTITUTE OF INTERNAL AUDITORS PROFESSIONAL BOOK SERIES

Gil Courtemanche • The New Internal Auditing

THE NEW INTERNAL AUDITING

Gil Courtemanche

A RONALD PRESS PUBLICATION
JOHN WILEY & SONS
New York • Chichester • Brisbane • Toronto • Singapore

Library of Congress Cataloging in Publication Data:

Courtemanche, Guilbert W., 1932–
   The new internal auditing.

   "A Ronald Press publication."
   Includes index.
   1. Auditing, Internal.   I. Title.

HF5668.25.C68   1985   657'.458   85–12059
ISBN 0–471–82885–8

Printed in the United States of America

10 9 8 7 6 5 4 3 2 1

Foreword

The New Internal Auditing is a unique addition to the list of outstanding books on internal auditing which have appeared in recent years: it is the only book currently in existence which is devoted entirely to an analysis of the contemporary audit environment and the formulation of a success-oriented audit philosophy.

In a style that is clear, forthright and highly readable, the author addresses all the issues of concern to the internal audit profession at this pivotal point in its history. Readers will encounter a host of bold, intriguing and useful insights into such matters as audit independence, the Code of Ethics, audit relations, audit disclosure, management support and audit report writing. The book is particularly interesting and refreshing in that it was wholly inspired by actual internal audit practice. As the author readily concedes, few readers will find themselves in full agreement with all aspects of the book. Nevertheless, the book will have a profound influence on the future direction of the internal audit profession and on how each of us approaches our work.

The New Internal Auditing will be a very practical aid to audit directors, managers and supervisors seeking to promote a progressive and consistent audit philosophy within their organizations. It will also be an invaluable resource for the individual internal auditor striving to achieve mastery over the emerging audit environment.

JAMES A. HOOPER, CIA
Past Chairman of the Board, 1983–84
The Institute of Internal Auditors, Inc.

Preface

After receiving their initial training, many internal auditors spend much of their later careers reeducating themselves. Internal auditors' self-reeducation involves much more than extending and enriching their early knowledge or modifying their youthful idealism. It involves the actual correction of ideas which either were never true or have been invalidated by time and changing circumstances. This book was originally intended as a polemic addressed principally to practitioners, researchers, teachers and students in the field of internal auditing. Its purpose was to test certain commonly held notions about internal auditing by the litmus of actual experience and, when the notions were found to be defective, to propose ideas more nearly in conformance with reality.

As the writing progressed, the book showed signs of increasing relevance to independent accountants, accounting and financial executives, corporate counsels, chief executives, members of board audit committees and others interacting with the internal auditing profession. These groups also need to reconsider certain notions about internal auditing which they may have picked up in their early business training.

It is unlikely that the progress envisioned by this book for the internal auditing profession can be achieved by internal auditors alone. The fate of internal auditing is bound up with that of its clients and associated professions. Internal auditing is looking for friends—indeed, it can't continue to progress without the help of friends. Its single most important objective in the years ahead will be to increase the number of people willing to say that they have benefited from their interaction with internal auditing.

Those needing to make their association with internal auditing more predictable, more profitable and more satisfying will find the means to do so interwoven in the pages of this book. The book should be particularly useful to chief executives, board audit committee chairpersons and others to whom the audit function reports. More often than not, these officials misunderstand the IIA's intended meaning of audit independence and unknowingly contribute to the problems so often found at the interface between internal auditing, senior management and the board. Also, corporate officials need to be made more aware of the contribution they can make toward reshaping the internal audit environment of the future.

GIL COURTEMANCHE

Rosemead, California
November 1985

Acknowledgments

Few books are written alone. This is especially true of first books. Without the encouragement and assistance of the individuals mentioned below, this first book would almost certainly never have been written.

My daughter Cherie was the first to suggest that her dad "do something creative" like writing a book. Later, during her faculty residency at Southern California Edison in the summer of 1982, Professor Lois M. McClain, of California State University at Los Angeles, urged me to write a book about internal auditing. When I later consulted with John Dattola, Director of Research for the IIA, he encouraged me to undertake this project and subsequently played a key role in steering the manuscript through the prepublication review process.

My greatest debt is owed to Jim Hooper, who has been my principal mentor in the field of internal auditing since 1975. Thanks to his unfailing generosity, I was exposed to the theory and practice of internal auditing, and to the deliberations of The Institute of Internal Auditors, in a manner and to an extent accorded to very few. Although Jim can in no way be blamed for any defects contained in this book, it remains that the book could not have been written had I not had the benefit of his example and his support these many years.

Early versions of the manuscript were first read by Ed Kain, Manager of Project and Construction Audits at Southern California Edison. To Ed I owe thanks for the benefit of many insightful discussions on the audit process and the first professional opinion of the merits of my manuscript. Since Ed is the kind of person whose opinion is respected by all who know him, his early favorable verdict was a real morale booster.

The manuscript was put together by Karen Lizarraga, whose many admirable qualities include a cheerful nature and an effortless virtuosity in transforming a barely legible scrawl into sparkling word processing copy.

Last but not least, I wish to thank my wife Prose, my daughter Janine, Mark Ulloa and Steve Doyle for never showing any doubts concerning the outcome of this project.

G. C.

Contents

PART 3   THE AUDIT

PART 4   THE AUDIT REPORT

APPENDICES

THE NEW
INTERNAL
AUDITING

Introduction

The test of a first-rate intelligence is the ability to hold two opposed ideas in mind at the same time and still retain the ability to function.

F. Scott Fitzgerald

The field of internal auditing is much more complex and challenging than is generally perceived by those outside the profession. Because of the sensitive nature of his work, the internal auditor has traditionally shunned publicity and seldom discusses professional matters outside the internal audit community. This self-imposed obscurity was partially lifted with the passage of the Foreign Corrupt Practices Act (FCPA) in December 1977.* As was widely reported in business journals and periodicals at the time, the accounting provisions of the FCPA focused responsibility on boards of directors and senior management for the maintenance of adequate systems of internal accounting control. Publicly held corporations had long been encouraged by the New York Stock Exchange, the American Institute of Certified Public Accountants (AICPA) and the Securities and Exchange Commission (SEC) to estab-

*The act is reproduced in its entirety in Appendix A.

1

lish board audit committees to oversee matters relating to financial reporting and corporate governance. In response to the FCPA, independent accountants urged board audit committees and management to undertake special reviews of internal accounting controls and to strengthen the role of the corporate internal auditor.

Almost overnight, the internal auditor was taken from his anonymous post in the wings and pushed onto center stage. He was told to improve the quality of his staff. His reporting relationship was changed. Many auditors found themselves reporting to the chairman or the president and meeting with the board audit committee on a regular basis. At first, the auditor was exhilarated by his sudden change of fortune. Later on, however, he had reason to suspect that his past training and experience had not prepared him adequately for the frequent and sensitive interaction with management that his new role required.

The problems he was experiencing were similar to those he had had for some time as he and his staff were striving to expand beyond accounting into operations. Internal auditing was perceived as a critical, disclosure-oriented activity posing a threat to those unfortunate enough to be selected for review. This perception was not entirely invalid. Disclosure and criticism was more or less the name of the game when internal auditing was restricted to the accounting area and reports seldom went higher than the controller. Internal auditors schooled in the traditional methods of financial audits did tend to carry an adversary style into their operational audits and few managers welcomed the visits of these aggressive perfectionists. Now, the internal auditor was seeing in senior management and the board audit committee the same fear and mistrust that he had perceived in middle management during his early operational audits. Was this the inevitable fate of the internal auditor— to be despised as the bearer of bad tidings?

The growth of internal auditing since the middle to late seventies has created a veritable boom in the field of auditor training. The profession has been swamped by new entrants having little or no formal education or practical experience in internal auditing. Even those with many years of experience have felt a need for more training, both to sharpen their technical skills and to better understand the new audit environment. The profession's educational accomplishments to date have been truly impressive but they have taken place mainly in three areas: principles of internal auditing, internal auditing techniques and the administrative aspects of internal audit management.

As internal auditors assimilate the principles of their profession, master its varied techniques and implement sound administrative practices, they are becoming increasingly aware of what must be provided in the next phase of their education. They will require both a broad perspective and an in-depth understanding of the managerial and human processes underlying the internal audit function. To use a medical analogy, internal auditing is failing to help many of its patients in spite of the technical tools at its command. What is needed is a holistic approach that recognizes managers and auditees as complex personalities striving to cope with an environment that generates all manner of professional and personal stress.

This book was conceived as a practitioner's attempt to inquire into internal auditing as the subtle and complex phenomenon it truly is. The strategy of the book was to let the audit environment speak for itself in the hope that it might provide clues to the future direction of the internal audit profession. This approach has produced an interesting result. On the one hand, the body of basic pronouncements of The Institute of Internal Auditors (IIA) survives largely unscathed. On the other hand, new interpretive notes are struck which are in close harmony with ideas expressed by many speakers and writers both in the United States and abroad. What is emerging are the outlines of a new internal auditing which, while preserving much of what has been inherited from the past, is seeking to adapt itself to a changing world. The new internal auditing is based in part upon the premise that what the world needs now is not an internal version of external auditing but a true *internal* audit profession peculiarly adapted to serving its clients under conditions of close association.

It is unlikely that any one reader will find himself in full agreement with every aspect of this book. In fact, the book may suggest a number of useful lines of inquiry for researchers in academia and in professional institutes. Researchers wishing to compare positions taken in the book to those of the IIA will find Appendices B through E useful since they contain all of the basic pronouncements of the Institute which were available at the time of publication.

Since the book makes no claim to infallibility, it is hoped that readers will exercise forbearance if certain passages do not appear to jibe with their own experience or strongly felt convictions. What makes internal auditing such a fascinating field of study is its capacity for irony and even contradiction. Things can be true, or not true, depending upon the circumstances. Things which were true yesterday may no longer be true today; and things which are still true today may not apply tomorrow. Some things may even be true and not true in the same company, at the same time.

Until recently, there were two basic conceptions of internal auditing: the traditional and the modern. The traditional conception of internal auditing views accounting as its true discipline,* accounting control as its true concern and the board audit committee as its true client. The modern conception of internal auditing does not reject the substance of the traditional conception but seeks to extend it beyond its narrow confines. Modern internal auditing claims an unlimited scope, reserves the freedom to borrow from many disciplines and recognizes senior management as an additional client more or less distinct from the board audit committee.

What emerges from the inquiry undertaken by this book is still a third conception of internal auditing. From an analytical standpoint, the new internal auditing might be termed "neo-modern." It too preserves the essential substance of traditional auditing. In addition, it retains the unlimited scope and varied disciplines of modern internal auditing and acknowledges senior management as a principal client. As will be seen in this book, the new internal auditing has a number of distinguishing features developed in specific response to perceived inherent limitations of the strictly modern conception. Its main distinguishing feature, however, is a reaching out to the *entire* organization for potential clients and for general support.

Individual practitioners, academics, researchers and public accountants are certainly entitled to their opinions as to which conception of internal auditing is "right." As a practical matter, however, it will be prudent for none of the three conceptions to attempt to squelch the other two. Given the diversity in styles of organization and management among companies, industries, the private and public sectors and even countries, it is highly unlikely that any one internal audit prescription will do for all. Experience teaches that "right" and "wrong" have only limited relevance in the everyday world of business. Those who would make a contribution soon learn to think in terms of what works and what doesn't.

In keeping with our own advice, we will not argue that the new internal auditing is right so much as that it is valid. It is valid because its various elements already exist and are seen to work well in certain environments. The best environment for the new internal auditing is found in medium to large corporations where considerable authority and discretion have been delegated downward into the organization and where senior management and the board are strongly dedicated to the ideal of excellence. Such organizations are most apt to allow internal auditing considerable latitude in identifying problem areas, accepting clients any-

---

*In a computerized environment, electronic data processing (EDP) must be viewed as a necessary auxiliary discipline.

where in the organization and working out solutions at whatever level appears most suitable.

The historical and logical validity of the new internal auditing makes it of interest to *all* internal auditors—even those who are bound by present choice or circumstance to the traditional or modern approach. Intellectual categories such as traditional, modern and neo-modern are abstract constructs not actually found in the real world. Few things in the real world are purely of one type or another and few internal audit organizations are purely traditional, modern or neo-modern. The basic forces tending to impel certain organizations toward a neo-modern solution to the internal audit problem are being felt in other organizations destined to remain traditional or modern for many years to come. An understanding of the new internal auditing will permit these other organizations to selectively borrow some of its elements to make traditional or modern internal auditing work better. This judgment must be made by those who bear the responsibility for results. No one else can make the judgment for them.

In any case, if a reader considers that a point made in this book is simply not true under any circumstance, he is warmly urged to pursue the point with the author by writing to him.

PART 1

The Profession

CHAPTER 1

Role of
Internal Auditing

To be, or not to be, that is the question . . .

WILLIAM SHAKESPEARE, *Hamlet*

The Institute of Internal Auditors, headquartered in Orlando, Florida, has more than 28,000 members located in 102 different countries. Actually, the Institute serves many more internal auditors than it appears since a single member may represent a staff ranging anywhere from two or three to 100 or more auditors.

THE ROLE DEBATE

The IIA has many outstanding accomplishments to its credit, but most important among these has been the maintenance of a *Statement of Re-*

sponsibilities of Internal Auditing first issued in 1947 and updated four times through December 4, 1981.* The reason this *Statement* is so important is that there is a great deal of diversity among internal audit organizations. Even within the same industry and among companies of the same size, internal audit organizations vary widely in the number and qualifications of their staffs as well as in what they do and do not do. For example, the profession had considerable difficulty in deciding upon a suitable response to the advent of the computer during the 1950s and 1960s. Later, there was vigorous discussion concerning whether computerized information systems should or should not be audited while still in the developmental stage. To this day, many internal auditors hesitate to claim jurisdiction over the review of management processes and controls. And they certainly shake their heads in disbelief when informed that certain audit departments are hiring industrial engineers to perform work sampling and productivity measurement studies.

In view of the divergence of opinion concerning the role of internal auditing, the IIA has felt it necessary to periodically hammer out an official concensus on the subject. However, the IIA's repeated formulations of the responsibilities of internal auditing have not quelled the role debate entirely, and perhaps never will.

IMPORTANCE OF ROLE DEFINITION

Most discussions of organizational effectiveness and employee performance tend to revolve around matters of technical proficiency. But when something else is amiss, it is usually blamed on "poor attitude." Both of these diagnostic biases can overlook a third possible reason for unsatisfactory work performance: outdated role definition.

According to a recent survey, the profession most highly respected by the general public is nursing. And yet, consider the following true story which happened to an internal auditor in early 1983:

The auditor received a call at the office from his daughter. She had taken her mother to the hospital because of severe headaches, nausea and high blood pressure.

Since everything appeared to be under control, the auditor finished his workday before going to the hospital. When he finally arrived at the hospital, he decided to check with the nursing station before going to his wife's room. He identified himself and inquired about his wife's condition. There were three nurses at the station, obviously engaged in rou-

*See Appendix B.

tine administrative tasks. All three declined to offer any information whatsoever concerning the patient's condition. When the auditor insisted, one nurse volunteered to try to contact the doctor in charge of the case but was not very hopeful that he could be reached at that time.

A confrontation ensued and the auditor demanded to see his wife's medical chart. Someone buzzed for the supervising nurse who promptly escorted the auditor to a small conference room. Among other things, the supervisor explained that nurses were not permitted to engage in diagnosis and that their duty was to the patient and not to visitors.

Since the supervising nurse appeared to be a reasonable person, the auditor asked her a few questions: Had a doctor seen his wife? Had treatment been prescribed for her headaches, nausea and blood pressure? Was she resting comfortably or was she in pain? Had tests been ordered? The supervising nurse was obviously well informed concerning the status of the patients in her ward because she readily answered all of these questions and more.

When the supervising nurse was finished, the auditor asked her two more things: In answering his questions, had she engaged in diagnosis or violated any ethical rule or hospital procedure? The answer was "no." In her absence, were the nurses at the ward station authorized to communicate with him just as she had? The answer was "yes."

The supervising nurse smiled feebly when she realized the implications of her own answers to two simple questions. It was obvious that the nurses under her supervision either did not understand the desperate need for information felt by members of a patient's immediate family, or did not view it as their role to provide information to the family even when the absence of their supervisor had left them in charge.

Apart from the professional, ethical or legal aspects of this story, two things came through clearly to our internal auditor. First, he was not on the nurses' list of important people. He certainly wasn't a patient, and his relationship to the patient did not appear to accord him any special status. Second, since the auditor had seen nurses behave differently elsewhere under similar circumstanes, he resolved to patronize another hospital the next time around.

Our story illustrates very well how a profession's traditional role definition can become outdated as circumstances change. It may have been appropriate for nurses to define their role mainly in terms of the patient at a time when doctors were easily accessible. However, given the work patterns of doctors today, and the fact that nurses provide the only continuing professional presence in most hospital wards, it seems inevitable that nurses will have to take on increasing responsibility for dealing with visitors. Most nursing supervisors are aware of this and work accordingly. But the idea is probably not systematically discussed in training programs for junior nurses.

There are interesting similarities between our story concerning nursing and the status of the internal auditing profession today. Internal auditing need not feel embarrassed by its ongoing role debate. Such debates have occurred, and continue to occur, in many other professions. They are almost always a positive sign of growth and change as a profession moves from a limited self-image to a new vision of its role in society.

IDENTITY CRISIS OF THE AUDITOR

"Identity crisis" may be too strong a term, but the fact remains that many individuals are less than fully comfortable in their role as internal auditors. The typical internal auditor was educated to be an accountant, and the college department where he pursued his major was heavily oriented toward *public* accounting. His first job was with a public accounting firm. His early concerns had to do with commonly accepted accounting principles, internal accounting control, consistency, materiality and the like. His nontechnical concerns revolved around the public trust vested in the external auditor and the independence required for him to fulfill this trust. Chances are that he left public accounting without acquiring an in-depth understanding of the techniques used by CPA firms to reconcile their duty to the public with the imperatives of successful client relations.

In any case, our young CPA was eventually attracted to a job in internal auditing. His technical knowledge and skill, his excellent work habits and his prestigious professional license propelled him quickly to supervision in the specialized area of financial audits. By this time, our typical internal auditor has had ten years or so of exclusive preoccupation with accounting. He views his company's external auditors as professional peers to be emulated. His experience in internal financial audits has brought him into contact with only a limited number of company managers. He continues to attend meetings of the local CPA society and conscientiously fulfills the continuing education requirement to maintain his license. He has been too busy to take a certified internal auditor (CIA) review course and has no firm plan to sit for the CIA examination. He is vaguely fearful that his prestige as a CPA will suffer if he takes the CIA exam and fails to pass it. When he attends an IIA function, he finds much of the subject matter alien, irrelevant to his present work and vaguely suspect. Does he hear that some audit departments are providing internal consulting services to their employers? What, he asks himself, does this have to do with auditing?

So far, we have been discussing the typical internal auditor. But what of the atypical auditor? Is he fully comfortable in his role? Interestingly, the atypical auditor does not necessarily dispute the view of internal auditing maintained by the CPA. If he is an engineer, an economist, an EDP expert or a former management consultant, he is apt to emphasize those credentials and to acknowledge his connection with internal auditing in words designed to make a cock crow. In other words, internal auditors with CPA backgrounds tend to restrict the scope of *true* internal auditing to those things falling roughly within the technical purview of public accounting. Engineers and other professionals, on the other hand, will confide that they do not think of themselves as auditors and will thereby concede to the CPA his narrow definition of "true" internal auditing. What bothers engineers and other professionals, of course, is how to include under a single professional label the tasks of "checking up on people" and helping them. They want to be helpers and want no part of the traditional image of the internal auditor.

CONFUSION IN MANAGEMENT

It might help internal auditing to establish its true identity if it received clear and consistent signals from its principal clients: top management and the board audit committee. But this is not very likely. Who hasn't met the vice-president who fully supported the audit function until it proposed to do an audit in his area? A corporate counsel advised her company's newly appointed director of audits to audit anything he wanted but to stay out of management. An executive vice president sternly told his company's manager of audits to inform him immediately if anyone under him declined to be audited. Yet, he was the first to complain when auditing undertook a sensitive review ordered by the president. Another director of audits carried out an assignment requested by the board audit committee. When she was done, she was informed that half the board liked what she did and the other half didn't. So what's the answer? What is the proper role of the internal audit function?

GETTING DOWN TO BASICS

To answer our question, we have to get down to basics and work up from there. Prior to passage of the FCPA in 1977, it was possible for even a good-sized corporation to have no internal audit function at all. This tells us something. Prior to 1977, internal auditing had no role at all in many companies. It didn't exist! After the FCPA, most public accounting firms concluded that it would be imprudent to have a corporate client of any significant size which did not have a board audit committee supported by a qualified internal audit staff. This is why some wags have labeled the FCPA as the "Internal Auditors Full Employment Act of 1977."

Given the above, any director of internal auditing can draw some fairly reliable conclusions about his basic role. First, his role is to be there—to exist. Second, his role is to develop and maintain a reasonably qualified internal audit staff of a size adequate to the nature and size of his company. Third, his role is to implement a credible audit program designed to ensure the adequacy of his company's systems of internal accounting control. Finally, his role is to report periodically to the audit committee concerning the adequacy of the company's systems of internal accounting control. Unfortunately, this is all there is to the role of the internal auditor from a purely defensive and legal standpoint. His role is to evaluate the adequacy of internal accounting controls and to report his conclusions to management and the board audit committee. Stripped down to its bare essentials, the scope of internal auditing is roughly coextensive with that of public accounting. Take away all that is discretionary, and internal control boils down to internal accounting control as defined by the public accounting profession and the FCPA. In a sense, the accounting-oriented auditor has been right all along in his limited definition of the role of internal auditing.

INTERNAL AUDITING IS INTERNAL

It should be clearly noted that whether one refers to management or the board of directors as the primary client of an audit activity, the client is *internal* to the organization. Nowhere in the law, or in IIA pronouncements, does it say that the internal auditor is the instrument of any entity apart from his employer. The internal auditor is an employee of his company. He is paid by his company, and he can be reassigned or dismissed by his company. The internal auditor has no intelligence-gathering, regulatory or law enforcement responsibility of any kind. Nor, up to now, has the work of the internal auditor been established as being invested with the public trust.

The internal auditor is not open for business with the general public. He is not licensed by the state for public practice. The internal auditor does not issue opinions upon which the public relies in making decisions. To the author's knowledge, no member of the public has ever successfuly sued an internal auditor.

OFFER AND ACCEPTANCE

Since internal auditing's clients are exclusively internal, and since in most cases the board's claim to its services will be limited to the evaluation of internal accounting controls, it is clear that the residual role of the internal auditor is essentially what management wishes it to be. And management is bound to no one in arriving at decisions in this matter— not even the pronouncements of the IIA. This is why internal auditing's role debate has been so persistent. Internal auditing is what internal auditing does, and what it does is decided by thousands of employers throughout the country and the world, all of whom are independent of each other. This is not to say that convergence has not taken place. It has, but convergence has not yet brought uniformity.

Apart from the review of internal accounting controls, what internal auditing does in a particular company is ultimately the result of offer and acceptance as between the internal auditor and management. The auditor offers to perform certain services and management either accepts or rejects the offer. Conversely, management suggests that the internal auditor perform certain duties, and the internal auditor either agrees or declines. Even when mutual agreement is reached, an activity may turn out to be nonviable and may have to be dropped or transferred elsewhere. After all, management and the internal auditor are not entirely free to define anything they wish as falling within the scope of internal auditing. Principles of sound organization require that functions be combined or separated in a coherent manner so as to maximize the synergetic benefits of specialization and to avoid the stresses set off by functional schizophrenia.

STATEMENT OF RESPONSIBILITIES

Again, we find ourselves returning to the IIA's *Statement of Responsibilities*. The usefulness of the *Statement* consists in the fact that it represents the current consensus based on experience and informed judgment. The *Statement* serves as a guide both to the internal auditor and management in their ongoing effort to optimize the role of the internal audit function.

The current *Statement*, published in December of 1981,* describes internal auditing as "an independent appraisal activity established within an organization as a service to the organization." The *Statement* goes on to say that the objective of internal auditing is "to assist members of the organization in the effective discharge of their responsibilities. To this end, internal auditing furnishes them with analyses, appraisals, recommendations, counsel and information concerning the activities reviewed."

The *Statement* mentions the following areas as falling within the scope of internal auditing:

Adequacy of internal controls (as broadly defined by the IIA).†
Quality of performance in carrying out assigned responsibilities.
Reliability and integrity of financial and operating information.
Compliance with policies, plans, procedures, laws and regulations.
Verification and safeguard of assets.
Economy and efficiency in the use of resources.
Effectiveness of operations and programs.

It should be clear from the above, and from a careful reading of the *Statement* itself, that the IIA envisions a broad and flexible role for the internal auditing function consistent with the needs and wishes of management. The *Statement* is not in agreement with those who would limit internal auditing services exclusively to the area of accounting or internal accounting control.

WHAT INTERNAL AUDITING DOES

What internal auditing does is best summarized in three key words:

1. Ascertaining (determining, verifying)
2. Appraising (evaluating, assessing)
3. Recommending (consulting)

When one clears away the fog surrounding the issue of internal auditing's role, we find that most auditors spend their workdays *determining,*

---

*The *Statement* is reproduced in Exhibit 1. All five historical versions of the *Statement* are included in Appendix B.
†The IIA's definition of "internal control" is much broader than the AICPA's definition of "internal accounting control."

EXHIBIT 1. STATEMENT OF RESPONSIBILITIES OF INTERNAL AUDITING

The purpose of this statement is to provide in summary form a general understanding of the role and responsibilities of internal auditing. For more specific guidance, readers should refer to the *Standards for the Professional Practice of Internal Auditing.*

Nature

Internal auditing is an independent appraisal activity established within an organization as a service to the organization. It is a control which functions by examining and evaluating the adequacy and effectiveness of other controls.

Objective and Scope

The objective of internal auditing is to assist members of the organization in the effective discharge of their responsibilities. To this end, internal auditing furnishes them with analyses, appraisals, recommendations, counsel, and information concerning the activities reviewed. The audit objective includes promoting effective control at reasonable cost.

The scope of internal auditing encompasses the examination and evaluation of the adequacy and effectiveness of the organization's system of internal control and the quality of performance in carrying out assigned responsibilities. The scope of internal auditing includes:

Reviewing the reliability and integrity of financial and operating information and the means used to identify, measure, classify, and report such information.

Reviewing the systems established to ensure compliance with those policies, plans, procedures, laws, and regulations which could have a significant impact on operations and reports, and determining whether the organization is in compliance.

Reviewing the means of safeguarding assets and, as appropriate, verifying the existence of such assets.

Appraising the economy and efficiency with which resources are employed.

Reviewing operations or programs to ascertain whether results are consistent with established objectives and goals and whether the operations or programs are being carried out as planned.

Responsibility and Authority

Internal auditing functions under the policies established by management and the board. The purpose, authority and responsibility of the internal au-

EXHIBIT 1. (continued)

diting department should be defined in a formal written document (charter), approved by management, and accepted by the board. The charter should make clear the purposes of the internal auditing department, specify the unrestricted scope of its work, and declare that auditors are to have no authority or responsibility for the activities they audit.

The responsibility of internal auditing is to serve the organization in a manner that is consistent with the *Standards for the Professional Practice of Internal Auditing* and with professional standards of conduct such as the *Code of Ethics* of The Institute of Internal Auditors, Inc. This responsibility includes coordinating internal audit activities with others so as to best achieve the audit objectives and the objectives of the organization.

Independence

Internal auditors should be independent of the activities they audit. Internal auditors are independent when they can carry out their work freely and objectively. Independence permits internal auditors to render the impartial and unbiased judgments essential to the proper conduct of audits. It is achieved through organizational status and objectivity.

Organizational status should be sufficient to assure a broad range of audit coverage, and adequate consideration of and effective action on audit findings and recommendations.

Objectivity requires that internal auditors have an independent mental attitude, and an honest belief in their work product. Drafting procedures, designing, installing, and operating systems, are not audit functions. Performing such activities is presumed to impair audit objectivity.

The *Statement of Responsibilities of Internal Auditors* was originally issued by The Institute of Internal Auditors in 1947. The current *Statement,* revised in 1981, embodies the concepts previously established and includes such changes as are deemed advisable in light of the present status of the profession.

verifying or ascertaining whether something is or is not; *appraising,* assessing or evaluating controls and/or operations on the basis of appropriate criteria; and *recommending* corrective actions to management—all from a position of independence within the organization. This common-sense view of internal auditing's role encompasses everything from checking the accuracy of accounting records, to reviewing the controls of a computerized information system, to providing internal consultation.

SOME MISLEADING NOTIONS

Once we accept the above as an accurate and comprehensive description of what internal auditing is and does, we immediately see how we are subject to being misled by certain fashionable, but simplistic, statements concerning the nature of internal auditing. Take, for example, the popular aphorism: "Internal auditing is the eyes and ears of management." This statement does describe a certain aspect of internal auditing, but it also has the potential to mislead individuals who know little else about the subject. "Eyes and ears" connotes spying, or intelligence gathering. Although internal auditing is a very useful source of information for management, its methods of gathering information, and its purpose in doing so, bear little or no resemblance to spy operations. Only a very small percentage of internal audit examinations are sensitive in nature or covert in approach.

Descriptions of internal auditing as simply "an appraisal activity" are also potentially misleading. Such descriptions, if taken too literally, appear to exclude the work of a large segment of the internal audit community. What about the auditors whose assignments involve mainly ascertainment, or verification, and very little "appraisal?" Are we to exclude from internal auditing all of the work being done to verify balance sheet values, job costs, contract payments and the like? Taken literally, "appraisal" could also be interpreted as excluding the recommending function. Are we to exclude from internal auditing all of the hours spent in assisting auditees to identify and select viable solutions to the problems pinpointed in our appraisals?

Internal auditing is often described as "a control which functions by examining and evaluating the adequacy and effectiveness of other controls." This idea of internal auditing as a control over other controls is valid and very useful. It serves to explain much of internal auditing today and also provides a central concept around which to construct a vision of the profession's principal role in the future.* However, the fact remains that the idea has caused considerable confusion among practicing internal auditors today. The notion that internal auditing consists exclusively in the review and evaluation of other controls leads to the

---

*For an excellent discussion of internal control broadly defined, refer to *Criteria For Management Control Systems*, by R. K. Mautz and James Winjum, (Research Foundation of Financial Executives Institute, 1981). Refer also to the IIA's *Statement on Internal Auditing Standards No. 1* which is reproduced in its entirety in Appendix E. The *Statement* is reproduced from *The Internal Auditor*, December, 1983, published by The Institute of Internal Auditors, Inc., P.O. Box 20099, Orlando, Florida 32889-0003.

mistaken impression that controls are the only target of internal audit activity. When management asks internal auditing to verify a cash fund or a parts inventory, its objective is to determine whether all of the company's assets are actually there. Only if the assets are not all accounted for will management ask "why?" And only if the "why" is amenable to cost-effective control will management want to take corrective action. This is only one example of the fact that internal auditing is very often found to review operations themselves—either directly or through basic records. It is usually when operations are found to be unacceptable that the matter of control comes up. In other words, controls are evaluated as inadequate *after* operations are judged to be unsatisfactory. Poor control is an inference drawn from poor operations.

There is another way in which the idea of a control over other controls does not fit the facts exactly. There are many areas where internal auditing is simply a "control of last resort." It is the last in a whole string of internal controls. The auditing of cost-plus contracts is a good example of this. The controls in effect to ensure compliance with contract terms, and the correctness of amounts billed by contractors, are many and varied. They extend all the way from the development of clear bid specifications and the selection of reputable contractors to careful management of the project and the systematic certification of materials consumed, labor utilized and work performed. This long string of controls constitutes a control system. The fact that a control is situated farther down the string than other controls does not necessarily make it an evaluation of previous controls. The detailed audit review of contractor billings, including verifying the correctness of contractors' overhead calculations, must realistically be viewed as a basic control in and of itself. It is the final control in the string—the control of last resort. It is not merely an evaluation of all preceding controls.

The idea of internal auditing as a control of last resort probably needs to be more clearly acknowledged by the profession since it accounts for so much work being done by internal auditors today. Such acknowledgement is needed to produce a more complete theory of internal auditing. Some will resist this suggestion because they are attempting to rid themselves of such last-resort control tasks as reconciling checking accounts and verifying invoice payments prior to mailing. This should not pose a problem. A proper theory of internal auditing would include provision for the progressive migration of certain controls from internal auditing downward into the organization. The ultimate resolution of this migratory process would leave internal auditors with few remaining duties as a direct control of last resort, thus permitting them to focus mainly on the evaluation of other controls. As a practical matter, however, this day will be a long time in coming for most of us.

THE RECOMMENDING FUNCTION

Much of the current debate surrounding the role of internal auditing centers on the "recommending" function. Views on this function of internal auditing have run to wide extremes. The most conservative position is that internal auditing should limit its activity to ascertaining and appraising and should eschew recommendations altogether. Few people uphold this view today. Most internal audit organizations, and the IIA, support the middle position that internal auditors may, and should, include recommendations in their reports. However, there is considerable disagreement where what is recommended is not a general course of action but a relatively specific solution or plan of action developed by the auditor. The proposal of specific and detailed plans extends the role of internal auditing into the gray area of internal consulting.

The profession is not so much against including internal consulting within the scope of internal auditing as it is unprepared to do so at this time. In other words, it will take time to secure a consensus on the question. Interestingly, the profession appears to have become more conservative on the recommendation question in its most recent revision of the *Statement of Responsibilities* dated December 1981. The June 1971 *Statement** specifically listed "recommending operating improvements" in the list of activities falling within the scope of internal auditing. The same item was included again in the June 1976 *Statement* but was dropped in the December 1981 *Statement*. However, *SIAS No 2: Communicating Results*, approved in early 1984, gave some emphasis to the recommendation function and may signal a return to a more progressive view.†

Whether and when the profession will accept internal consulting as falling within its scope remains to be seen. In a recent survey of internal auditing distributed to all IIA members, one of the questions posed had to do with so-called "nonaudit functions" currently performed by internal audit organizations. Specifically included among the nonaudit functions to be checked (if performed) was internal consulting. For the time being, this author freely admits that he inclines toward the broad view of

---

*See Appendix B.
†*SIAS No. 2* is reproduced in Appendix E.

internal auditing and that he shares Larry Sawyer's* attitude that internal consulting represents the highest expression of the profession's role.

Internal consulting does not come about as a result of a deliberate decision to create, staff, and promote a new and separate activity. Rather, internal consulting emerges as an unplanned outgrowth of the full maturation of the individual auditor, the audits organization as a whole and their relationship with management and auditees. The ability to recommend solutions to problems is based squarely on years of experience and organizational wisdom acquired in the performance of ascertainment and appraisal tasks. When an organization has a highly competent, loyal and dedicated audits department, calling on it for assistance in solving a problem is the most natural thing in the world. No amount of objection from purists concerned about a possible loss of objectivity will prevent management from making such requests and auditors from accepting them. The actual benefit to all concerned is too great and the potential disadvantage is too speculative to do otherwise.

INTERNAL AUDITING AS A ROLE

Many difficulties in defining the role of internal auditing come as a result of overlooking the obvious: that internal auditing is simply a *role!* Internal auditing is not tied to a particular academic degree nor to a particular functional aspect of the company such as accounting. Being an internal auditor is like being a manager. No one would attempt to tie the label "manager" to a specific academic background or to a specific functional area in business. The title "manager" denotes a role, and so does the title "internal auditor." An individual may have an engineering degree and it may be his (or her) intention to return to engineering work at a later time. But if he is assigned to the auditing department, and if his duties involve ascertaining, appraising or recommending from a position of organizational independence, he is performing the role of an internal auditor.

INTERNAL AUDITING AS A PROFESSION

How can one refer to internal auditing as a profession having a common body of knowledge if anyone can be an internal auditor? The answer is

---

*Lawrence B. Sawyer, CIA, noted author and speaker on internal auditing. He is best known for his comprehensive and authoritative work *The Practice of Modern Internal Auditing*, published by the Institute of Internal Auditors, Inc., Altamonte Springs, Florida, and currently in its second edition.

not all that difficult when it is considered that the essence of any profession lies principally in its role and only secondarily in its underlying body of knowledge. A doctor heals the sick and a nurse cares for them. An engineer designs structures and machines. A pharmacist prepares and dispenses drugs. An attorney represents clients. The distinction between a body of knowledge and a profession can be illustrated by pointing to the difference between a law professor and an attorney. A professor of law shares the same body of knowledge as the attorney but if she (or he) is not licensed to the bar of any state and does not practice law, she is not an attorney. Her actual profession is that of an educator. It is her role, rather than her mastery of a body of knowledge, which determines her profession.

What distinguishes a profession from other ordinary roles in life is largely the need to adhere to a basic standard of excellence and to a code of ethics. In the business environment, the quality that distinguishes internal auditors from other employees are scrupulous devotion to honesty, loyalty, objectivity and diligence. Other people can be self-serving, can deceive, can engage in dirty politics and can even do shoddy work and get away with it. An internal auditor can't. People expect more from the internal auditor and they hold him to the standards of his profession.

COMMON BODY OF KNOWLEDGE

The common body of knowledge of the internal auditing profession is comprised mainly of two things:

1. A basic set of assumptions, concepts and techniques revolving around the nature, role and process of internal auditing.
2. A combination of various disciplines, techniques and skills related to business management which, if possessed, ensure the ability to perform the ascertainment, appraisal and recommendation functions over a fairly broad area.

An individual may be able to perform adequately as an internal audit specialist without having the knowledge necessary to pass the CIA examination. But chances are that his usefulness to the internal audit organization will be limited in scope and that he will not be viewed as eligible for supervision or management within internal auditing. It is likely that internal auditing will always need such specialists, either on a permanent or temporary basis, and their lack of a CIA certificate need in no way detract from the unique value that they bring to the audits organization. But one cannot define the common body of knowledge of a profession in terms of the specialist no matter how valuable his contribution may be. If, in fact, the specialist wishes to become a full-fledged member of the internal auditing profession, he will probably find that preparing for the CIA examination does not present an insurmountable difficulty. In most cases, the gaps in his formal education can be filled with the completion of only one or two years of additional college work.

SUMMARY

The *Statement of Responsibilities of Internal Auditing,* promulgated by the IIA, reflects the current consensus of the profession concerning its role. This consensus is subject to change over time.

Internal auditing is internal. The most basic function performed by the internal auditor is to provide assurance to the board of directors concerning the adequacy of internal accounting controls. Activities beyond this limited scope will usually derive their primary support from management rather than from the board of directors.

The potential scope of internal auditing is practically unlimited. What internal auditing does in a particular company, apart from the review of accounting controls, is ultimately the result of free offer and acceptance between the internal auditor and management. This explains the high degree of diversity among companies with respect to the internal audit function.

The role of the internal auditor is to *ascertain* whether something is or is not, to *appraise* or evaluate an activity on the basis of appropriate criteria and to *recommend* courses of action to management—from a position of independence within the organization. Internal consulting will someday be accepted as a valid activity of internal auditing.

Capsule descriptions of internal auditing, if not put in perspective, have the capacity to mislead. Internal auditing is not a spying activity. Nor is internal auditing exclusively a control over other controls. Too many attempts at defining internal auditing border on the reductionist and fail to encompass its full richness and variety.

Internal auditing is a profession having a defined role, upholding a basic standard of excellence and adhering to a code of ethics. Certification as a *professional* internal auditor requires one to have mastered the common body of knowledge judged essential for satisfactory performance over a reasonably broad area.

Beginners and specialists working in the field of internal auditing are true internal auditors by virtue of the role that they play within the organization. An individual does not have to be certified to be a true internal auditor. The nature of an individual's academic credentials, or his ultimate plans for the future, have no bearing on his current status as an internal auditor.

DISCUSSION

The issues addressed in this chapter relate mainly to the distinction between the traditional and modern conceptions of internal auditing. Prior to passage of the FCPA in 1977, internal auditing had relatively low status and found its principal support in the controller. Modern internal auditing sought to enhance the mission and status of the profession by giving it a broader scope.

Internal auditing received a major boost with the advent of the FCPA. The mission of financial auditing was elevated to that of ensuring the adequacy of internal accounting controls. The status of the internal audit activity as a whole was raised by transferring functional responsibility for the activity from the controller to the board audit committee. The task of fulfilling the requirements of the FCPA attracted significant numbers of certified public accountants into the internal audit profession. It also attracted the attention of numerous educators and researchers in accounting.

The view of internal audit traditionalists today is that their position has been vindicated by the events of recent years. It is the traditional component of internal auditing which has achieved greater status, recognition, acceptance and compensation for the entire profession.

Internal audit modernists are no less gratified than traditionalists by the profession's good fortune in recent years. Modernists welcome the greater support being provided by audit committees and senior management in the area of internal accounting control. The difference between traditionalists and modernists is that the latter view internal accounting control as only one item, albeit an extremely important item, in the overall scope of the internal audit profession.

It is becoming increasingly clear to many internal auditors that the board audit committee is not in a position to effectively sponsor and support the full range of activities advocated by modern internal auditing.

For this reason, internal auditors are making a clearer distinction between activities sponsored by the audit committee and those sponsored mainly by management. At an IIA symposium in Baltimore in 1982, no less an authority than Dr. Victor Z. Brink remarked that "the temptation of a total allegiance to the audit committee is not in the best interest of the organization and, ultimately, not in the best interest of internal auditors."*

Neo-modernists would certainly agree with Dr. Brink, since they see the profession's next breakthrough as occurring *below* the level of senior management itself. If this breakthrough is to occur on a wide scale, the IIA must continue to issue pronouncements on the role and scope of internal auditing which provide the latitude needed by the profession to fully explore its destiny.

The Internal Auditor, June, 1984, p. 31; published by The Institute of Internal Auditors, Inc., P.O. Box 20099, Orlando, Florida, 32889-0003.

CHAPTER 2

Audit Independence

One of a kind isn't much of a poker hand.

ANONYMOUS

"Audit independence" is a term often used but seldom defined with any precision. Of all the issues surrounding internal auditing, independence is the most basic and the most difficult to handle. If there is a heavenly reward for internal auditors, it almost certainly is a place where the auditing function has unlimited scope, no resource constraints, the prerogative to review anything at any time, the freedom to tell it like it is and the unfailing support of the head of the organization. This chapter has little to say to the internal auditor whose circumstances even remotely approach this ideal picture. Most of us, unfortunately, must be content to live in a world that is less than perfect. Our charters may say that we have unlimited scope, but we are conscious of resource and other constraints which effectively prevent us from doing many things which we would like to do.

NOT A RIGHT BUT A PRIVILEGE

It is typical of the average internal auditor that he starts his career with a wholly unrealistic concept of audit independence. His first mistake is to define audit independence as somehow attaching to himself personally. After failing to obtain the support of his superiors in a controversy, he then progresses to the more advanced view that independence resides in the audits function as a whole rather than in the individual auditor. Only later, when he has occasion to observe the director of audits exercise extreme caution in a difficult matter of auditee relations, does he begin to suspect the real truth that independence is not so much a right to be asserted as a privilege to be managed.

STYLES OF AUDIT INDEPENDENCE

There are many styles of audit independence. One wishes that there were actual schools of thought on the subject so that practicing internal auditors could more clearly understand their differences, weigh their relative merits and judge their suitability for specific audit environments. There being no schools of thought or open debates, audit practitioners are left to adopt styles of independence based on vague assumptions, inclinations of temperament, the example of predecessors or the influence of peers outside the organization.

The Outsider

One style of audit independence might be termed the "outsider." This style is based on the conscious or unconscious assumption that the internal audit function somehow represents an outside interest or point of view. The style reflects an emotional position taken by individuals who, for one reason or another, have difficulty in identifying with the goals and values of their employers. By reason of temperament or personal background, such individuals prefer the point of view of the independent accountant, the regulatory agency, the IIA or some other outside entity. This type of audit independence is almost always self-limiting. It has the effect of turning off both the auditee and management. Management may concede it a certain usefulness in limited areas but it never allows it to expand beyond those areas.

The Management Proxy

Another style of audit independence might be termed the "management proxy." This style is based on the assumption that internal auditing serves as an agent of senior management and/or the board of directors. There is no questioning the fact that most internal auditors act in support of the goals and objectives of senior management and the board. But this fact of itself does not confer to the auditor the status of special agent or representative. Any tendency to take on the role of management proxy is bound to create resentment among auditees. Eventually, the tendency will be repudiated by management itself. If the tendency persists, management will again react by restricting the scope of internal auditing to those areas where it will do the least harm to organizational morale.

The Autonomist

The "autonomist" style of audit independence reflects the assumption that internal auditing possesses a special wisdom and a special mission that make it answerable principally to itself. Internal audit organizations which follow this style of independence in effect assert their independence from management itself without, however, maintaining any conscious or unconscious allegiance to outside entities. Their allegiance is to a paradigm—an ideal mental construct of what ought to be.

The autonomist style of audit independence is wrong in that it is based on bad theory. The style may work for a while but only because of a carefully engineered (or fortuitous) congruence between the actions of the internal audit organization and the needs of management at the time. The moment that this congruence is lost, the flaw in the autonomist style of audit independence becomes painfully evident: management and the internal auditors have a falling out and the illusion of independence from management is quickly dispelled.

The Absolutist

The "absolutist" style of audit independence is based on the view that the auditor has an ethical obligation to "tell it like it is" and to "stick to his guns no matter what." The error in this view is that it is a distortion of the admirable qualities of honesty and integrity.

People who derive too much satisfaction from calling a spade a spade are not so much truthful as they are mischievous. In a word, they are troublemakers who enjoy sowing consternation and discord. They exempt themselves from the obligation to consider other people's sensibilities—an obligation which even senior management, with its much greater power, usually feels it must observe. The trouble with the absolutist style of audit independence is that it sooner or later wears down management's inclination to support the audit function. The burden of support becomes too great for management, which has many other concerns to deal with. No matter how meritorious audit findings may be, if they create too much unhappiness management will sooner or later place a check upon the audit department.

People who insist upon always being right, and who reject all compromise, are motivated less by integrity than by pride. They are interested less in beneficial change than in personal or organizational vindication. They define the management process as an intellectual debate rather than as the exercise in leadership which it really is. They add to the problem rather than help to solve it.

When confronted with an absolutist audit style, management's usual response is to clip its wings—to teach it a lesson. Absolutism is, again, a self-limiting style. It does not foster the growth and the advancement of the profession.

Need for a Better Way

We have described four styles of audit independence: the outsider, the management proxy, the autonomist, and the absolutist. All of these styles work, in the sense that they have been used by various internal audit organizations at one time or another. The styles may even have been appropriate under the circumstances which led to their initial adoption. However, many internal audit organizations today suffer considerable frustration from their inability to expand into new areas and to improve their status within the company. Such organizations will sooner or later have to face up to the possibility that their style of audit independence may have become obsolete.

Enactment of the FCPA has exacerbated the problem of independence for the internal auditor. Defective styles of audit independence could be tolerated when their adverse effects were felt mainly at the lower levels of the organization. But when the FCPA caused the internal auditor's status to be raised, an awareness grew that defective styles of audit independence could affect the very highest levels of the organization.

Enactment of the FCPA has so changed the environment that internal auditors will have to undergo a psychic metamorphosis within a very short time in order to survive. Warning signs are already being posted to the effect that the next generation of audit directors may be enlisted from general management instead of from the ranks of the profession itself.

INDEPENDENT OF WHAT?

In what sense is the internal auditor independent? What is he independent of? Is he independent of his own sense of integrity and personal honor? No. Is he independent of the IIA Code of Ethics? No. Is he independent of generally accepted accounting principles, of laws, regulations, policies, procedures and other rightful criteria by which he conducts his audits? Hardly. Is he, finally, independent of the objectives, goals and plans promulgated by management? No, again. He may be permitted a certain objectivity toward some of the things we've just mentioned, but independence is hardly the correct word to describe his essential relationship to them.

As we have said, the internal auditor is usually hired by management, and he is subject to reassignment or even dismissal by management. He is bound to carry out management's rightful instructions and requests and, ultimately, he is bound by management's express or implied limitations upon his scope. Is, then, the internal auditor independent of management? The answer must be that he is not!

DEPENDENCE ON MANAGEMENT

If management is defined as including the board of directors, there can be little doubt concerning the internal auditor's essential *dependence* on management. The question of independence becomes only slightly more complex if a distinction is made between the board of directors and management in the narrow sense. In certain organizations, the internal auditor may be appointed by the board. Or appointment or removal of the internal auditor may require concurrence by the board. In these cases, the internal auditor may enjoy a certain independence from management in matters falling under the jurisdiction of the board audit committee. But, as we will see later in this book, any supposed independence from management on the part of the internal auditor is so fraught with difficulties and risks that any auditor in his right senses would exhaust all possible alternatives before putting it to the test. Most internal auditors prudently conjoin management and the board of directors into a single, unified authority in their minds and readily concede their essential dependence upon this authority.

In matters not related to internal accounting control or corporate governance, there should be no doubt concerning the internal auditor's independence from senior management. It doesn't exist, except perhaps as a polite myth—until internal auditing chooses to confront senior management on a significant issue. The intensity of senior management's wrath will quickly dispel any illusion the internal auditor may have entertained concerning his status.

Up to this point, we have managed to describe the internal auditor not so much in terms of independence but in terms of a strong and complex web of dependencies.

INDEPENDENCE FROM THE AUDITEE

Careful and systematic reflection on the matter of independence leads inexorably to the conclusion that the internal auditor's independence refers not to his relationship to the board of directors or senior management but to the *activity being audited*. Management (in the broad sense, as including the board of directors) is the source and not the object of the auditor's independence. Independence is a privilege granted by management to the auditor so that he may perform his work effectively. Management does not intend that the auditor turn this privilege against management itself. Put another way, audit independence is a type of special status within the organization. The internal auditor is independent *because* of management. Without management, he would have little or no independence whatsoever. This is not to say that management is entirely free to deal arbitrarily or capriciously with the internal auditor. The internal auditor derives considerable strength from the FCPA, the policies of the SEC, the pronouncements of the IIA, commonly accepted business practice and management's own desire to maintain a reputation for decency and fairness. But these sources of strength hardly make the auditor independent of management. They merely serve to qualify his dependence on management.

The *Statement of Responsibilitites of Internal Auditing* describes independence in the following terms:

> *Internal auditors should be independent* of the activities they audit. *Internal auditors are independent when they can carry out their work freely and objectively. Independence permits internal auditors to render the impartial and unbiased judgments essential to the proper conduct of audits. It is achieved through organizational status and objectivity.*

To properly understand the nature of independence, it is useful to recognize that independence is not peculiar to the internal auditor. Many, if not most, staff organizations enjoy varying degrees of independence vis-à-vis the organizations they serve: personnel, corporate security, building services and other similar functions are able to perform their duties in an impartial manner consistent with policies and procedures only to the extent that they are immune to undue pressure from users. Outside consultants enjoy a type of temporary independence which is very similar to that of internal auditors. In fact, their independence may be greater since they won't be around to pay the price of independence which auditees often exact from the internal auditor.

INSTRUMENT OF MANAGEMENT

If internal auditing is to reach it full potential and maximize its contribution to the welfare of the organization, it will have to resolve all ambiguity in its relationship with senior management. Independence from senior management must be recognized as the nonsense notion that it is. Senior management is, along with the board of directors, a client of the internal audit function. It is not the auditee. In matters other than internal accounting control, internal auditing is an instrument of senior management to be used as it sees fit. "Unlimited scope" is not so much a right to be exercised autonomously by the auditor as it is a statement of management's own intended use of the audit function. In other words, when management speaks of unlimited scope, it is serving notice to all concerned that *it* may use the audit function to review any area in the corporation. It is not necessarily telling auditing that it may, on its own initiative, launch a review of a highly sensitive area without first seeking senior management's concurrence. This idea is implicit in the common practice of having management review and approve the internal audit plan.

CONFLICT WITH MANAGEMENT

Any in-depth inquiry into the nature of audit independence must ultimately address the question of possible conflict with management over a matter of personal or professional ethics. Does the fact that the internal auditor may feel compelled to reject instructions from management prove that he is in fact independent of management? Does the theoretical possibility that the internal auditor may be required to divulge misdeeds of the president to the chairman of the board mean that he is independent of the president? The answer is no to both questions.

The possibility of conflict with management over a serious question of principle is not a problem peculiar to internal auditing and should not be considered in the definition of the internal auditor's normal relationship to management. A company doctor could be given instructions diametrically opposed to the Hippocratic oath. Or an engineer could be given orders in the design of a structure which might endanger the lives of thousands of people. Neither of these theoretical possibilities argues in favor of an independent relationship between doctor or engineer and their employers in the normal course of affairs. Such tragic conflicts effectively cancel normal relationships and sweep those involved into a different realm altogether. In a majority of such cases, the result is not effective independent action by the employee but a severing of the employee-employer relationship.

NATURE OF AUDIT INDEPENDENCE

Independence, in the context of internal auditing, is essentially an organizational concept. Audit independence has two aspects: organizational separation from the activity being audited, and adequate status within the overall organization.*

The purpose of *organizational separation* is to shield the internal auditor from the biases, fears, loyalties and ambitions affecting the activity being audited. For the auditor to be affected by these same factors is to lose all ability to appraise the activity objectively. The purpose of *organizational status*, on the other hand, is to confer sufficient "power" to the auditor to enable him to perform his work effectively. As will be seen in Chapter 4, power is needed in any organization in order to overcome resistance and to secure cooperation.

Noteworthy of audit independence is that it is not an end in itself. The danger in an excessive preoccupation with the concept of audit independence is that one can lose sight of the *purpose* of it. Also, excessive preoccupation with independence can prevent the auditor from pursuing his analysis of the audit process to a deeper level. If one should ask what the essential conditions for a successful audit are, what would the answer be? Tentatively, this author has identified five:

Access
Objectivity
Freedom
Diligence
Responsiveness

*Refer to Appendix B, *Statement of Responsibilities of Internal Auditing, Independence.*

All five of these concepts are discussed in some detail under the following subheadings, and the reader is invited to ponder two questions during the discussion: do the concepts in fact represent the essential conditions for a successful audit? And, how does each concept relate to the idea of audit independence?

Access

Every auditor knows what access is. Access has to do with the availability of the information needed by the auditor to perform his audit. Access is broken down into three generic sources of information: facilities, records and people. The word "facilities" encompasses all physical reality which might provide information to the auditor through direct observation. For example, the auditor may never know whether a protective fence is truly secure unless he personally inspects the fence. To do his job, he requires access to facilities.

Records are a representation of reality rather than the reality itself. In many cases, the auditor does not have the means or the time to ascertain or evaluate the "hard" reality which is the ultimate object of the audit.* Instead, he tests the accuracy of records reflecting the reality and, if the records are adequate, he bases his evaluation on the records themselves. In order to do this, he must have access to records.

It often happens that the auditor knows of no record which might provide the information he requires. This is why he needs access to people. People can provide records which the auditor was not aware even existed or which are not generally available because they are closely controlled by the people in question. Or, people can provide extremely valuable information which exists only in their minds.

What, then, is the connection between access and independence? Is it organizational separation which provides the auditor with access to facilities, records and people? The answer, of course, is no. Anyone doubting this need only approach any organization to which he does not belong and request access to its records on the theory that he is not a member. He will receive short shrift. Is it organizational status which provides the internal auditor with access to facilities, records and people? The answer is yes, but the answer forces us to enrich our definition of status. Status becomes much more than the simple notion it is usually made to be. Status becomes a whole complex of things which are needed

---

*Where the purpose of an audit is to evaluate the accuracy and integrity of management information, the records themselves become the object of the audit and "hard reality" the criterion by which the records are assessed. Either way, the auditor requires access to records.

to secure access from organizations systematically trained to deny information to anyone not specifically authorized: an audit charter, a sufficient reporting relationship and visible management support.

Can access be obtained without audit independence? Significantly, the answer is yes. If the answer were no, it would mean that an auditor could never perform an audit involving senior management and the board. Here is a case where it is useful to distinguish between the ends and the means. There is no way that the board or senior management can grant independence to the auditor from themselves. As we said earlier, independence is an organizational concept designed in part to secure from others what might not otherwise be forthcoming from them. It is inconceivable that internal auditing could possess the type of organizational status that would "compel" the board and senior management to do what they do not wish to do. But what is conceivable is that the board and senior management may grant access to the auditor *willingly*. In other words, nothing prevents senior management or the board from

EXHIBIT 2. THE GRANTING OF ACCESS

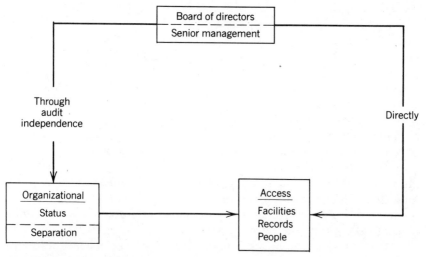

Comment: In regular audits, the board of directors and senior management secure access for the auditor through the privilege of audit independence (specifically, organizational status). There is no cause-and-effect relationship between organizational separation and access.

In audits involving themselves, the board and senior management grant access directly.

freely granting access to the internal auditor in a particular instance where it suits their purpose. In effect, the auditor secures the access he requires without benefit of audit independence.

Exhibit 2 is an illustration of the concept of access.

Objectivity

The words "independence" and "objectivity" are so often used together that many internal auditors can barely distinguish between the two. Even the *Statement of Responsibilities* comes close to defining one in terms of the other when it says that "objectivity requires that internal auditors have an independent mental attitude."*

What is objectivity? Objectivity is a state of mind permitting someone to perceive reality as it truly is. Let us bypass the troublesome epistemological question posed by this definition and simply accept that there exists an objective reality which most qualified internal auditors would agree upon. What, then, are the attributes of the human mind which would enhance its ability to see reality correctly? The following attributes immediately suggest themselves:

Intelligence

Formal knowledge (education)

Experiential knowledge (experience)

Absence of emotional bias (love, loyalty, hate, fear, self-interest, and so forth)

A person who is highly intelligent, has had the benefit of a good education and rich experience (both relevant to the area under review) and whose judgment is not impaired by love, loyalty, hate, fear, self-interest or other forms of emotional bias, has a good chance of understanding reality correctly as defined by current social consensus. On the other hand, a person who lacks intelligence, has had no education and little experience and whose emotional biases border on the neurotic would have little chance of arriving at the objective truth—again, as defined by current social consensus.

What is the connection between independence and objectivity for the internal auditor? Clearly, there is no necessary connection between audit independence (which is an organizational concept) and intelligence, formal knowledge or experiential knowledge. These three qualities can only be provided by the auditor himself. Audit independence relates to

*Refer to Appendix B.

objectivity mainly with respect to emotional bias. Organizational separation and organizational status can and do free most internal auditors from the biases of the auditee which make it difficult for him to "see" his own activity in a completely objective manner.

Does audit independence always produce objectivity? The answer is no. If the auditor lacks intelligence and knowledge, it is unlikely that he will arrive at an adequate understanding of audit reality solely by virtue of his lack of emotional bias.

Can there be objectivity without audit independence? Another way to pose this question would be: is it conceivable that a member of the auditee organization could perform as good a review of an activity as the auditor? Most people would say that this is indeed conceivable for two reasons:

The auditee organization may be relatively free of emotional biases;* and/or

The individual concerned may have sufficient intelligence and knowledge to remain relatively unaffected by whatever emotional biases do exist. Intelligence and knowledge can, in fact, provide a defense against emotional bias. A person who knows little of mathematics and who is under pressure to conform may accept the proposition that one is the square root of two. But no amount of social pressure could persuade the skilled mathematician to accept this error in the privacy of his own mind.

Therefore, can the internal auditor maintain his objectivity with respect to management even though he is not organizationally independent from management? If we accept the definition of objectivity as a state of mind permitting the auditor to perceive reality as it truly is, then it should be possible for the competent internal auditor to maintain a minimal degree of objectivity, in the privacy of his own mind, with respect to management. But here again, management and/or the board are free to bypass the problem of audit independence and to enhance the auditor's objectivity directly by creating circumstances, giving instructions and providing assurances that permit the auditor to think as freely as he can.

The concept of audit objectivity is illustrated in Exhibit 3.

Freedom

There is a distinction between the internal state of one's mind (objectivity) and the truthfulness of one's written or oral communications (frank-

*Changes in an organization's leadership can often provide "windows of objectivity" permitting cooperative audits of a particularly fruitful nature.

EXHIBIT 3. THREE ASPECTS OF OBJECTIVITY

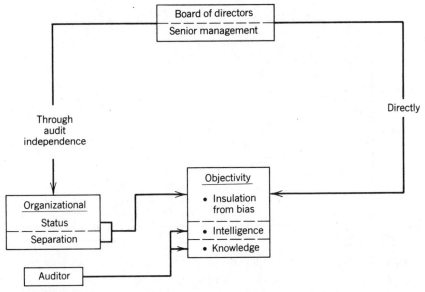

Comment: In regular audits, the board of directors and senior management insulate the auditor from bias through the privilege of audit independence. Both organizational status and organizational separation promote insulation from bias.

In audits involving themselves, the board and senior management can promote insulation from bias directly by creating circumstances, giving instructions and providing assurances that permit the auditor to think as freely as he can.

Note that two out of the three factors making up objectivity (intelligence and knowledge) can only be provided by the auditor.

ness or candor). An auditor may understand the truth very well and yet be fearful of expressing it. The condition permitting an auditor to communicate what he knows, without fear of adverse consequences, we shall call "freedom." In internal auditing, freedom is the ability to speak, or write, freely and without fear. The concept is illustrated in Exhibit 4.

There is no doubt that independence promotes freedom; that it enhances the auditor's ability to communicate his findings, conclusions and recommendations in a forthright manner. Both aspects of audit independence work in favor of the auditor in this regard. His organizational separation from the auditee serves to insulate him, at least in part, from the consequences of the auditee's disapproval. Also, the status of the

EXHIBIT 4. FREEDOM

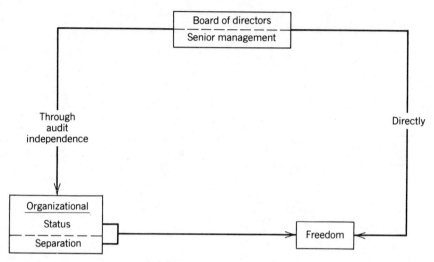

Comment: Freedom is the ability to speak, or write, freely and without fear. Both aspects of audit independence promote freedom.

The board and senior management can grant freedom to the auditor directly, either on an ad hoc or ongoing basis, by giving the auditor appropriate (and credible) instructions.

audit department within the overall organization effectively inhibits the auditee from engaging in intimidating behavior. The auditee is aware that he cannot effectively challenge internal auditing's charter and that senior management has rejected such challenges in the past. If he abuses the auditor, he knows that the auditing department has immediate access to the very highest levels of the corporation and that he might receive a prompt reprimand for his behavior. Of course, all of this assumes that senior management truly supports the audit function and does not treat the audit charter merely as a token document to impress itself, the board, the independent accountants, regulatory examiners and the SEC.

How does "freedom" enter into internal auditing's relationship with management? As was the case with access and objectivity, senior management may grant freedom of expression to the internal auditor on an ad hoc or ongoing basis without granting him organizational independence (which it cannot do). All that management has to do is tell the auditor that it wants him to speak freely—and mean it. If management ever grants this privilege and then shows the slightest displeasure at the result, it may be sure that the internal auditor will think twice before accepting the invitation again. If management "punishes" the internal auditor, the lesson will not be lost on his successors. Management will have thrown away a precious resource as a result of its bad faith.

Diligence

Even with access, objectivity and freedom, the internal auditor may fail to perform adequately because of lack of diligence. Objectivity and freedom are essentially states of mind, whereas diligence is a quality of the will.

Diligence may be viewed as relating somewhat to objectivity and freedom in the sense that diligence may overcome conditions tending to reduce objectivity and freedom. Every manager and every internal auditor has encountered individuals who, although not necessarily superior in knowledge or experience, have a rare ability to determine and to express the truth. Clearly, this ability is traceable more to qualities of character than of intellect.

Generally, diligence is a quality contributed by the auditor himself. However, diligence can be influenced, for better or for worse, by the degree of status accorded to the audit function.* Meaningful status can materially strengthen the auditor's determination to do a good job. In a sense, too much emphasis has been given to the relationship between audit staff qualifications and audit results. Every military commander knows that victory does not always go to the best trained and the best equipped. Superior morale has often tipped the scales of battle in favor of the weaker side. In the same manner, managements and boards of directors sincerely interested in developing an effective internal auditing function will do well to look beyond well-drafted audit charters, prestigious diplomas and impressive professional certificates. Like soldiers, internal auditors instinctively look for credible signs of earnest purpose from their commanders. When the signs are there, performance can exceed all expectations. When the signs are lacking, actual performance is usually far short of potential.

In audits involving senior management and the board of directors,

*Audit committees in particular should take heed of what follows. It can be safely predicted that, sooner or later, a significant weakness in internal accounting control will elude a highly qualified staff of internal auditors. Press accounts will tend to blame the auditors. But all insiders, and all experienced internal and external auditors, will suspect the real truth: diligence of the internal audit staff was diluted by lack of a strong mandate from the top.

EXHIBIT 5. DILIGENCE

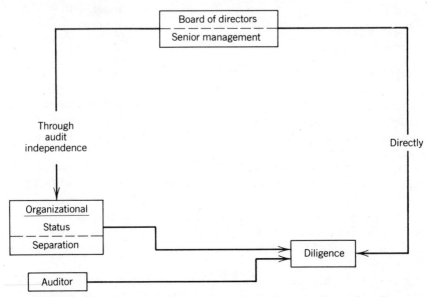

Comment: Even with access, objectivity and freedom, the internal auditor may fail to perform adequately for lack of diligence.

Diligence is provided mainly by the auditor.

Diligence can be reinforced by signs of earnest purpose on the part of management and the board. Meaningful organizational status promotes diligence in the auditor. In audits involving themselves, management and the board can promote diligence directly through the display of unity and serious intent.

diligence cannot be influenced through audit independence. But it can be directly influenced by the unity and resolve displayed by the officials concerned. A review wanted by the audit committee but resisted by management, or vice versa, will not elicit the same degree of diligence from internal auditors as one which is unreservedly desired by both. Exhibit 5 is an illustration of the concept of diligence.

Responsiveness

The presence of all the conditions previously discussed will not result in a successful audit unless the auditee considers the auditor's findings, responds to them and takes corrective action when appropriate. This condition we will call "responsiveness." It is illustrated in Exhibit 6.

EXHIBIT 6. RESPONSIVENESS

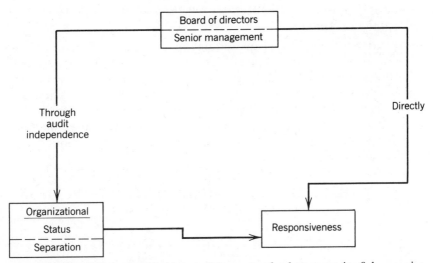

Comment: Auditee responsiveness is promoted when meaningful organizational status is accorded to the audit function.

There is no cause-and-effect relationship between organizational separation and auditee responsiveness.

In audits involving themselves, the board and management determine the degree of their own responsiveness.

Organizational separation contributes little or nothing to the auditor's ability to secure a proper response from the auditee. Rather, organizational status makes all the difference in this area.

Again, internal auditing cannot use organizational status (clout) to secure responsiveness from senior management and the board in a project involving those levels. Responsiveness must be given freely. As a practical matter, management and the board will feel an obligation mainly to consider the auditors' findings. They may or may not "respond" to the findings and they may or may not accept the auditors' recommendations.

SUMMARY

Audit independence is not so much a right to be asserted as a privilege to be managed. Auditing is not independent *of* management. It is independent *because* of management.

Audit independence is achieved through organizational separation and organizational status. Independence applies only to internal auditing's relationship to the operations under review. Management can't provide independence from itself.

Audit independence is a means and not an end in itself. Exhibit 7 shows the nine essential requirements for effective internal auditing and identifies the contribution made to the satisfaction of these requirements by the two components of audit independence: organizational status and organizational separation. Three requirements are seen to be satisfied mainly by the auditor. In audits involving themselves, management and the board can satisfy many of the requirements directly without the intermediacy of audit independence.

EXHIBIT 7. ESSENTIAL REQUIREMENTS OF EFFECTIVE AUDITING

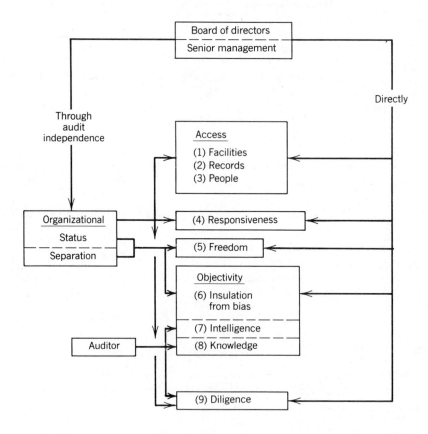

Certain styles of audit independence are becoming obsolete. Their obsolescence has been accelerated by the enactment of the FCPA, which has brought the entire internal audit function into close contact with senior management and the board of directors. Internal auditing will have to develop new modes of audit independence which will permit effective interaction at the highest levels of the organization.

DISCUSSION

The special value of opinions rendered by public accountants derives from their presumed independence. This presumption of independence is based upon the organizational separation between accountants and clients such that accountants will value their professional reputations more than their association with any one client.

There is no way that licensed CPAs can carry the presumption of independence with them when they leave a CPA firm for employment with a corporation. The presumption may be operative when the CPAs do public accounting work on the side, but it is not operative when they review the accounts of their own employers.

There is considerable evidence that internal auditors' efforts to simulate the independence of their external counterparts threatens to limit their effectiveness by alienating them from their own organizations. Both traditional and modern internal auditors need to do some fresh thinking about internal audit independence. Theories and styles of audit independence borrowed from the public accounting profession are a poor fit for an internal audit profession seeking to realize its full potential by working within the firm.

The problem is not that the IIA has issued defective pronouncements concerning audit independence. Rather, it is that the IIA's pronouncements have not been detailed and emphatic enough. This has left both traditional and modern internal auditors free to entertain notions about audit independence which are either of questionable validity or lacking in depth and sophistication.

The internal audit profession is unlikely to fulfill its mission to be of "service to the organization" if a significant number of its practitioners are immobilized by the false ethical imperative to remain independent of senior management. Ironically, senior management itself may be contributing to internal auditors' confusion concerning audit independence. Although management has raised internal auditing's reporting relationship, it has too often failed to acknowledge its sponsorship of internal audit activities—especially those activities not sponsored directly by the board audit committee. In too many cases, internal auditing has been cut loose from its moorings in the controller's organization and set adrift without a flag. Senior management's misguided efforts to respect internal auditing's "independence" have resulted in inadequate communication between management and the internal audit function. By declining to tell internal auditing what is on its mind, management has not so much promoted internal audit objectivity as it has compelled internal auditing to engage in a perpetual guessing game. Through a remarkable quirk of false signals and self-deception, internal auditing has been induced to affirm its independence from management while trying desperately to find out what management wants it to do.

Unless senior management assumes proper responsibility for the audit function, one or more predictable problems will surely arise. First, there is an excellent chance that internal auditing may simply play it safe and never seek to engage in meaningful operational or management audits. Such an outcome should not be desired by any management determined to maintain a competitive edge in the world economy of the 1980s and 1990s. Or, internal auditing may muster up the necessary courage and venture forth on the basis of its best assessment of management's intent. The trouble is that it may take only one mistake for management's plans to be disrupted and for internal auditing's usefulness to be jeopardized. Finally, internal auditing may act correctly and in line with management's intent and yet appear to be preempting management's initiative and authority in the eyes of the organization at large. It would be tragic if, in such cases, management had no choice but to punish a friend and damage a valuable corporate asset.

The new internal auditing proposes to actively promote the extension of its services well below the level of the chairman and the president by seeking clients among vice presidents, department heads and other members of management. To do this successfully and effectively, it will have to maintain adequate communications with senior management to ensure against mistrust and misunderstanding. Also, it will have to concentrate on audit independence at the level of the individual audit engagement. An engagement will be deemed acceptable if the client explicitly or implicitly agrees to conditions which are compatible with the furtherance of corporate goals and objectives, the specific intentions of senior management, the production of a quality audit product and observance of the IIA Code of Ethics. More will be said about this in the chapters to follow.

CHAPTER 3

Code of Ethics

Expedients are for the hour, but principles are for the ages.

Reverend Henry Ward Beecher, *Proverbs from Plymouth Pulpit*

MORALITY

There is a difference between morality and ethics. Generally, morality is perceived as having to do with fundamental right and wrong. Moral codes are usually associated with religions and/or philosophies commanding the loyalty of nations and even of entire civilizations. Moral codes tend toward the universal and claim applicability to all people for all time. On the other hand, the claims made by codes of ethics are usually much more modest. For example, if, a few years ago, an American dentist had attempted to expand his practice by advertising, the American Dental Association (ADA) would have declared his conduct to be unethical. If the dentist had failed to respond to the warnings of his peers, his ability to practice his profession would have been severely curtailed. Serious as the dentist's breach of professional ethics would have been, however, no one would have claimed that he had been "immoral" in the sense that he had violated a fundamental rule of human conduct.

CODES OF ETHICS

Despite their lower status, codes of ethics can be extremely important. They are usually compatible with a society's moral code and are often an extension of moral principles as they are believed to apply under very specific circumstances. The doctor's Hippocratic oath enjoins her (or him) to do all in her power to preserve human life. Since a doctor has a special ability to save lives, her failure to exercise that ability is viewed as tantamount to murder. Where ethical rules are congruent with basic moral principles in this manner, they must be taken very, very seriously. In lesser matters, however, ethical rules are designed to regulate individual behavior according to the needs of society. To violate such lesser ethical rules is to break faith with one's fellow being. The punishment may not be eternal, but it can last a lifetime.

THE IIA CODE OF ETHICS

The IIA Code of Ethics* is a code of conduct prescribed by The Institute of Internal Auditors. An examination of the nature, origin, and purpose of the Code leads to the following conclusions:

> The Code is not applicable to all people. It is not even addressed to all internal auditors. It is set forth specifically for the guidance of *members of the Institute*.†
>
> Although the Code does not so state, it is generally understood that the Institute stands prepared to revoke an individual's membership for any serious violation of the Code.
>
> Loss of membership is the only sanction which the Institute can impose for violation of the Code. There are no provisions for government-imposed sanctions such as revocation of a state-issued license.

---

*The Code is reproduced in its entirety in Appendix C.
†The Certified Internal Auditor Code of Ethics, whose provisions are similar to the IIA Code, applies specifically to CIAs. See Appendix C.

Employers are free to endorse the IIA Code of Ethics and may add sanctions of their own to those imposed by the IIA. Or employers may cite the Code in further support of rules imposed by their own internal policies.

Certain provisions of the Code are congruent with Judeo-Christian morality. At least one provision is specifically congruent with civil law. No part of the Code is inconsistent with concepts of correct behavior as upheld in most modern, democratic societies.

Many provisions of the Code uphold a higher standard of behavior than is ordinarily expected of the general employee population. The Code views the auditor as holding the *trust* of his employer and thereby having an obligation to maintain strict standards of honesty, loyalty, objectivity and diligence in the performance of his duties.

Principal Thrust of the Code

The IIA Code of Ethics specifically states that members may have to use judgment in the application of the principles covered in the Code. The application of judgment in complex situations involves weighing diverse, and sometimes conflicting, considerations. How does the Code envision that this will be done by the internal auditor? Clearly, the auditor has little choice but to identify the principal thrust of the Code and to give this thrust foremost consideration in the resolution of any conflict.

The Code has eight articles. The first seven are mainly a description of the obligations of the internal auditor toward his employer. Only part of Article II, and all of Article VIII, describe obligations other than those due to the employer. However, even Article VIII could be viewed as ultimately benefiting the employer.

An objective appraisal of the IIA Code of Ethics can only lead to the conclusion that its thrust is heavily weighted in the direction of *loyalty to the employer*. The IIA Code of Ethics was not conceived as a shield to protect internal auditors' so-called independence from management which, as was argued at length in Chapter 2, is a nonsense notion held over from former connections with another profession. Quite to the contrary, the IIA Code of Ethics was devised to create a special bond between internal auditors and their employers: a bond compounded of the resin of the employer's trust and the hardener of the auditor's loyalty. The creators of the IIA Code of Ethics understood that the internal auditor could never expand his horizons unless he enjoyed the trust of management. And they also knew that management could not give its trust unless it possessed a *special* loyalty from the internal auditor. In a word, the IIA Code of Ethics was constructed as a monument to the extraordinary loyalty offered by the internal auditor to his employer.

As was explained earlier, codes of ethics are not codes of morality. Codes of professional ethics are not so much written in heaven as etched in the hearts of people. The IIA Code of Ethics is a special code which describes and regulates a unique relationship between fallible and imperfect human beings in a particular organizational environment. The IIA Code of Ethics is a code of correct behavior with a special bias comprised of trust and loyalty. Once we accept this interpretation of the Code of Ethics, it becomes clear how obsolete styles of audit independence can pose serious obstacles to the advancement of the internal auditing profession. The nonsense notion of independence *from* management causes the internal auditor to qualify his loyalty such that management is induced to limit its trust. The special bond envisioned by the Code of Ethics is never established. Management is denied the full resources of the internal auditor and the internal auditor is denied the full realization of his talents.

Let us now examine the specific articles of the Code in the light of our foregoing comments:

Article I

Members shall have an obligation to exercise honesty, objectivity, and diligence in the performance of their duties and responsibilities.

This article enjoins the internal auditor to exercise three specific qualities *in the performance of his duties*. Since the duties and responsibilities of the internal auditor are established by management and/or the board of directors, it follows that the Code is specifically concerned that the auditor should:

Be truthful, straightforward and undeceitful (honest) in his dealings with his employer; and

Exercise care and thoroughness, and avoid conscious bias, in all of the things that he ascertains, appraises and recommends to his employer.

The specific point to be stressed in an appraisal of Article I is that the qualities mentioned are recommended in the context of *the auditor's service to his employer.*

Article II

Members, in holding the trust of their employers, shall exhibit loyalty in all matters pertaining to the affairs of the employer or to whomever they may be

rendering a service. However, members shall not knowingly be a part of any illegal or improper activity.

"Trust" is a special relationship whereby a person places his welfare in the hands of another. "Loyalty" is the quality of being faithful to a person to whom fidelity is held to be due. Article II of the Code envisions a trust-loyalty relationship *between the internal auditor and his employer.* The article mentions no limitation to the auditor's obligation of loyalty other than that he must not knowingly be a part to any illegal or improper activity. Illegal activity requires no interpretation since it is defined by law. Improper activity may be taken to mean any activity which, although not necessarily subject to legal penalty, would be seriously condemned by society for reasons transcending the law.

It is relevant to note that the Code, in its introduction, states that "members must maintain high standards of conduct, honor and character in order to carry on proper and meaningful internal auditing practice." The combination of the words "honor" and "character" added to "loyalty" and "honesty" places the internal auditor in a position where he can't have it two ways: he cannot accept his employer's trust *and* compromise his loyalty to him. He can't excuse his disloyalty to his employer by appealing to a "higher loyalty." There is an old tradition in Western culture that no matter how unworthy one's superior may be, one may not betray his trust while still deriving benefit from that trust.

If an internal auditor cannot maintain an unqualified loyalty to his employer, honor and integrity require that the internal auditor disengage from his trust relationship. He should seek an assignment outside the internal auditing department or, if necessary, he should resign from his employment altogether. But it would be dishonorable for him to continue to hold his employer's trust, and to accept compensation and other benefits from his employer, all the while being unfaithful to that same employer.

The obligation to be honorable and honest also enjoins the internal auditor from being deceitful in his loyalty to his employer. He must be loyal as *employers* normally understand loyalty and not as he, the auditor, may define it in the privacy of his own mind.

Article III

Members shall refrain from entering into any activity which may be in conflict with the interest of their employers or which would prejudice their ability to carry out objectively their duties and responsibilities.

Article IV

Members shall not accept a fee or a gift from an employee, a client, a customer, or a business associate of their employer without the knowledge and consent of their senior management.

Since Articles III and IV are specific and self-explanatory, no comment will be provided other than to point out that the two articles clearly reflect the main thrust of the Code, which is the trust placed in the internal auditor by the employer and the auditor's obligation to display loyalty in all matters pertaining to the affairs of his employer.

Article V

Members shall be prudent in the use of information acquired in the course of their duties. They shall not use confidential information for any personal gain nor in a manner which would be detrimental to the welfare of their employer.

Internal auditors are not like other employees. The type of work which they do, and their special access to facilities, records and personnel, bring them into contact with information not readily available to others. Some of this information may be confidential or sensitive. In addition, the sheer scope and variety of the information available to the internal auditor provide a view of the organization as a whole rivaling that enjoyed by many senior executives. The individuals who drafted the IIA Code of Ethics understood full well that the internal auditor's access to information offered considerable opportunity for mischief. Article V of the Code was written specifically to remind the internal auditor of his duty and obligations in the use of information acquired in the course of his employment.

Internal auditors have, in fact, established an admirable record of prudence and discretion in the handling of audit information. One often reads, or hears, about disgruntled employees who have sought to embarrass their employers through the release of inside information. Most people have never heard of such a case involving an internal auditor. However, internal auditors will have to exercise special care if society continues on its present path of increasing regulation and litigation. Auditors who would never consider betraying the privacy of their employers could become the unwitting allies of outsiders with hostile designs against their companies. Auditors must be sensitized to the security risk posed by the sheer concentration of analytical and evaluative information in their audit files. Information selected for permanent retention should be assessed on the basis of probable future value to the organization. Documents and reports which no longer have value should be discarded, if only to minimize the cost of storage.

The internal auditing community needs to sort out its thoughts and feelings concerning the retention of information in audit files. Discussions of this area almost always disclose unwarranted assumptions and errors of fact. One unwarranted assumption is that internal auditors must somehow stand ready to defend their audit findings in detail years after these have been reported to management. The truth of the matter is that management seldom, if ever, has occasion to inquire concerning years-old audit findings; and when it does, it is not for the purpose of challenging the auditor's prior work.

Another unwarranted assumption is that audit files must be preserved for possible users other than management. If one asks who these possible users might be and how internal auditing is obligated to them, the answer is less than fully clear. Again, internal auditing appears to be under the influence of ideas inherited from another profession which was instituted for an entirely different purpose.

Working papers compiled by public accountants are held to be the property of the public accountants. However, the theory producing this result in the case of public accountants does not apply to internal auditing. Documents prepared or compiled by internal auditors are the property of the employer. The retention of internal audit documents is governed mainly by three considerations:

1. Statutory requirements, if any.
2. Regulatory requirements, if any.
3. The needs of the employer—including the needs of the internal audit department as recognized by the employer.

Compliance with Article V of the Code requires that the internal auditor manage his files according to the considerations listed above. It should be noted that statutory requirements will seldom apply to internal auditing since these relate to basic business records presumed to be filed and retained by other departments having primary jurisdiction over the records.

As a practical matter, internal auditors have no reason to retain information in their files which might later prove embarrassing to their employers. If such information was mistakenly retained in the files and is later requested by outsiders, the internal auditor should not release the information except under the advice of counsel.

Article VI

Members, in expressing an opinion, shall use all reasonable care to obtain sufficient factual evidence to warrant such expression. In their reporting, members shall reveal such material facts known to them which, if not revealed, could either distort the report of the results of operations under review or conceal unlawful practice.

This article enjoins internal auditors to be both *diligent* and *honest* in their reports to their employers. The article specifically addresses the duty of internal auditors to bring unlawful practices to the attention of responsible authority within the organization. Internal auditors have a duty to do this in spite of any natural reluctance to damage the careers and lives of fellow employees. Under Article VI of the Code, internal auditors are prevented from ignoring unlawful practices uncovered in the course of their internal audit assignments. Interestingly, the language of Article VI does not appear to require internal auditors to report unlawful acts suspected or observed under conditions entirely separate from their work as auditors. Equally of interest is the manner in which Article VI qualifies auditors' obligation to disclose unlawful practices. Auditors must disclose the facts known to them "which, if not revealed, could either distort the report of operations under review or conceal unlawful practice."

Given the general thrust of the Code, distortion and concealment have meaning only in the context of the employer's right to the information known to the internal auditor. Nothing in the Code, or in the law, establishes a right of access to audit information on the part of anyone other than the employer (except in cases of subpoena). Given this, the internal auditor's duty under Article VI is to protect his employer from being deceived concerning illegal activities taking place within the area under review. The Code does not state that the internal auditor is bound to report illegal activity to authorities outside the organization itself. In other words, the internal auditor's professional duty is entirely discharged when he advises responsible authority within the organization (presumably up to the board of directors, if necessary) that illegal acts have been, or are being, committed. Neither the Code nor the law imposes any obligation upon the auditor beyond this point.

All American citizens with an elementary knowledge of civics understand that no one can be compelled to incriminate himself. The constitutional protection against self-incrimination applies equally to individuals and to legal persons such as corporations. No individual or corporation is obligated to step forward and declare his guilt under the law.

Not only are individuals under no legal obligation to declare their own guilt, they are also not obligated to step forward and declare the guilt of others. Under American law, failure to report the unlawful act of another is not unlawful. One is not an accessory to an unlawful act merely by virtue of one's undisclosed knowledge of the unlawful act.

Readers with highly developed ethical sensibilities may be surprised, and even mildly scandalized, by the viewpoint expressed above. Isn't it one's duty, on general principle, to seek the punishment of the guilty? Doesn't the knowledge of wrongdoing, undisclosed, infect us with the guilt of the wrongdoer? One tends instinctively to answer "yes" to these two questions. And yet, there is a wise and profound tradition, both in Christian morality and in Western cultural history, which argues to the contrary. Christian morality teaches us to avoid passing judgment lest we also be judged; that our verdict on others will be the verdict passed on us; that the measure with which we measure others will be used to measure us; and that we should not point to the speck in the eye of another and overlook the plank in our own. In *The Gulag Archipelago*, Aleksandr I. Solzhenitsyn describes the Stalinist tyranny as having consisted not so much in the punishment of innocents as in the wholesale and unrestrained condemnation of the guilty. Western jurisprudence understands that no society can long remain free unless it maintains a benign tolerance of human frailty. Most of us are slow to condemn others for fear of promoting an atmosphere of unbending justice which would sooner or later find us guilty as well. If it were a crime not to disclose one's own guilt, as well as the guilt of others, most of us would end up behind bars.

The immunity accorded to spouses from having to testify against each other is a reflection of our culture's inclination to respect the sanctity of close relationships. Most nations reacted with genuine outrage to accounts that Nazi youth members were being urged to report on the political opinions of their own parents. Many internal auditors would argue that their relationship with their employers is a special relationship which exempts them from reporting the misdeeds of their employers under all but extraordinary circumstances.

The ultimate purpose of systems of justice is not so much to punish the guilty as to protect society from rule by internal predators. The maintenance of an orderly society can normally be achieved through the routine efforts of law enforcement specialists with the moral support and occasional assistance of the general citizenry. There is nothing in the IIA Code of Ethics to suggest that internal auditors should act as self-appointed watchdogs over the behavior of their employers. Society will be much better served if, by rejecting special social-control functions, internal auditors are enabled to form a closer partnership with management and to broaden the scope of their beneficial services. In summary, Article VI of the Code must be understood as requiring internal auditors to protect the employer from the consequences of his lack of knowledge concerning illegal acts committed within the organization.

Article VII

> *Members shall continually strive for improvement in the proficiency and effectiveness of their service.*

The significant thing about this article is not what it says but the context in which it says it. The article does not suggest that the auditor should improve his proficiency and effectiveness for reasons of ambition, monetary gain, pride, intellectual satisfaction or self-realization. The article poses self-improvement simply as an *ethical obligation* to one's employer. Viewed in this light, Article VII is a fascinating departure from the "what's in it for me" school of motivation and represents a reversion to the old-fashioned idea of competence as an ethical duty in its own right.

Article VIII

> *Members shall abide by the by-laws and uphold the objectives of The Institute of Internal Auditors, Inc. In the practice of their profession, they shall be ever mindful of their obligation to maintain the high standard of competence, morality, and dignity which The Institute of Internal Auditors, Inc., and its members have established.*

Given the overall thrust of the Code of Ethics, this article should not be viewed as presenting the internal auditor with competing loyalties. Conformity with Article VIII is more realistically viewed as reinforcing the auditor's obligations to his employer as specified in the preceding seven articles.

SUMMARY

The IIA Code of Ethics was designed to promote trust in the internal auditor on the part of the employer and loyalty toward the employer on the part of the internal auditor.

Consistent with the avoidance of all illegal and improper activity, the Code enjoins the internal auditor to support the interests and welfare of his employer in the performance of his duties. In a manner consistent with the *Statement of Responsibilities of Internal Auditing*, the Code does not view the internal auditor as "independent" of his employer. Accordingly, the Code does not enlist the internal auditor in any duty or responsibility to entities apart from his employer. The internal auditor does not possess a special mandate to assist law enforcement agencies independently of his employer.

DISCUSSION

As in the case of audit independence, there is considerable diversity of opinion among internal audit practitioners concerning professional ethics. Again, the reason for this does not lie with defective pronouncements by the IIA. Rather, it probably has to do with lack of emphasis. Ethics appears to be a neglected subject within the profession. There are no official or unofficial interpretations of the Code of Ethics. IIA-sponsored seminars on internal auditing seldom address the Code except in passing, and one never reads commentaries on the Code in *The Internal Auditor* or in other IIA publications. A recent research study specifically mentioned the dearth of materials on the ethical aspects of internal audit practice.*

The new internal auditing has an interest in the ethics of internal auditing for the same reason that it has in audit independence. Internal auditors' relationship with management and auditees can be significantly influenced by their assumptions and attitudes concerning professional ethics. Practitioners who would consider it their duty to report unlawful practices to outside agencies are not likely to seek, or to welcome, the type of close involvement with management at all levels that is contemplated by the new internal auditing.

The point we are making is mainly one of psychology since there is no evidence that unlawful practice is particularly prevalent in American corporations. However, the belief that one's profession makes him a moral and legal watchdog for society produces an aloofness that is not conducive to close rapport with pragmatic and hard-driving managers.

If certain internal auditors are to roll up their sleeves with management to improve operations and profits, they must first discard the false robes of justice which have been impeding their movements for so long. We are not suggesting that internal auditors should give up their ideal-

---

*M. A. Dittenhofer and R. J. Klemm, *Ethics and the Internal Auditor*: (Institute of Internal Auditors, Altamonte Springs, Florida, 1983), p. 1.

ism. Quite to the contrary, internal auditors need a goodly amount of idealism in their makeup if they are to perform effectively. What we are suggesting is that internal auditors should understand the limits of their role and not violate those limits. Given his own code of ethics, it is as inappropriate for an internal auditor to act as a policeman as for a policeman to act as a prosecutor, a prosecutor to act as a judge, or a judge to act as a jury. It's a question of knowing one's role and sticking to it.

Despite all of the arguments that have been made against the concept of the internal auditor as policeman, there will undoubtedly be some readers who remain unconvinced. Some of these readers may be highly trained, highly ethical CPAs steeped in the traditions of public accounting and unremitting in their hostility toward breaches of honesty, accountability and legality. "What about our ethical duty as CPAs?" such people might ask. Anticipating this quite valid objection, the author interviewed a number of full-time practicing CPAs—some of whom were associated with Big-Eight firms. The result? Not a single interviewee stated that his firm would feel compelled by ethical considerations to notify the authorities concerning a client's breach of the law. What they all said was that if the client persisted in his actions despite their advice, and if the actions in question were sufficiently grave or repugnant, they would simply withdraw from their engagement.* All interviewees also stressed that they would decline to certify financial statements known to them to contain material misrepresentations.

*It is customary for CPAs taking on a new client to confer once with the client's former CPAs. Some interviewees told this author that they might feel obligated to inform their successors concerning the unlawful behavior of the client if they were specifically asked what circumstances led to the termination of their engagement. Conceivably, such a pattern of disclosure among peers could make it impossible for a company to secure the services of a prestigious CPA firm.

PART 2

The Environment

CHAPTER 4

Power

All power is of one kind, a sharing of the nature of the
world.

RALPH WALDO EMERSON, "Power"

Several generations ago, power was an obsession and was often wielded with a heavy hand. Perhaps as a reaction, today's young generation has a mistrust of power almost to the point of wishing it out of existence. The heavy-handed, arbitrary and cruel use of power is wrong, stupid and usually counterproductive in the long run. On the other hand, to wish power out of existence is an intellectual error of the first order. Anarchy is not a viable alternative to the abuse of power. In fact, it usually leads right back to the abuse of power.

The internal auditor needs to understand power and specifically power as it exists in the business organization. Every company has problems relating to power—what some people refer to as "politics." Discussions concerning politics usually tend toward the cynical and unless the auditor develops a positive and constructive view of power, he will sooner or later be infected by the cynicism around him and become less effective as an auditor.

The purpose of this chapter will be to propose such a positive and constructive view of power in the organization and to suggest a success-oriented approach to the question of power.

PHYSICAL POWER

First of all, what is power? In the physical sciences, power has been defined as the capacity to do work. A 100-horsepower motor has the capacity to perform twice as much work as a 50-horsepower motor. No one would assert that physical power is bad. Physical power is essentially a cosmic good since it underlies all flow of energy—all movement, change, life, growth and development. A universe without power would be a dead universe. It's true that physical power can be misused. Someone who uses a weapon to harm an innocent person is misusing physical power. But the evil is not in the weapon: it is in the one misusing the weapon.

SOCIAL POWER

The notion of social power closely parallels that of physical power: it is the capacity to do "social work." Social power is also a cosmic good. The creative work of intelligent beings can properly be viewed as an expression of the creative power of the universe. To those having a religious orientation, man's creativity can be viewed as an extension of the creativity of the godhead. Either way we look at it, social power of itself is morally neutral. Its rightness or wrongness depends upon its use and application.

Social power is capable of producing highly organized, highly concentrated, and highly purposive energy flows. Organization, concentration and purposiveness appear to be built into the universe. The dilute energy of the sun is captured, organized and concentrated by living plants. Plant energy is in turn harvested, organized and further concentrated by animals which utilize the energy in an even more purposive way. The energy in both plants and animals is then assimilated by individual men and women whose capacity to organize and concentrate energy for special purposes exceeds that of anything else mentioned up to this point. However, there remains one thing which has an even greater capacity for purposive energy organization and concentration than the individ-

ual man or woman, and that is society. Society has the capacity to organize and concentrate physical, mental and emotional energy such that it
can produce wonders that would be absolutely unattainable by individual men and women.

NO MAN IS AN ISLAND

No man or woman has ever achieved a high standard of living by virtue
of individual productivity alone. No man or woman, if isolated from society, could ever duplicate the comfortable circumstances of his or her
present life. In this very real sense, no one can "succeed" by his or her
own merits alone. Most of the accomplishments in which we take inordi-
nate personal pride bear the unseen fingerprints of millions of our fellow beings. Despite all of the rivalries, jealousies, disputes and wars, the
entire human race is bound in an indissoluble partnership for the pursuit of collective security and the common good.

How, then, does society produce such wonders as ample and varied
food supplies; reliable access to pure water; shelter from heat, cold,
wind and rain; the mending of limbs and protection from disease; and
literature, art, music and theatre? Society produces all of these things
and more through a vast network of mutual cooperation.

Without mutual cooperation, a good part of human energy would be
canceled through strife and destructive competition. Through mutual
cooperation, society directs human energy and causes it to flow in the
same direction such that tremendous force can be generated. When
human beings organize themselves and agree upon a course of action,
things begin to happen. When, for example, investors, managers and
workers organize into a corporation, an enormous energy potential is
created.

The social power contained in the corporation produces tremendous
personal benefits for the internal auditor. The internal auditor has no
choice but to view all members of the corporation as friends and economic allies whose individual and combined efforts synergize with his
own efforts to produce an extraordinary harvest for all. Let us assume,
for the sake of argument, that an auditor had succeeded in reviewing
every activity in his company over a period of thirty-five years. If the
auditor had taken a consistently negative and critical attitude toward all
the auditees he had met, he would in effect have found fault with the
very people whose efforts had been most responsible for his economic
achievements throughout his career and into retirement. If the auditor
needs a good reason why he should offer the hand of friendship to every
organization he audits, let him ponder this.

CORPORATE POWER

Power in a corporation can be viewed as deriving from all of the cooperative agreements which promote the performance of the corporation's work. The work of a typical business corporation is extremely complex. Products must be designed and manufactured, materials must be ordered, customers must be persuaded to buy, policies must be adhered to and procedures must be complied with. There is no way that thousands of people could be made to come to work regularly, and to perform their duties in a uniform and disciplined manner, unless something was acting upon those people to subordinate their individual wills to the needs of the collective enterprise. That "something" is the thousands of agreements to cooperate—to give and to take orders in the pursuit of an economic objective.

COOPERATIVE AGREEMENTS

A basic characteristic of cooperative agreements is that they are reciprocal in nature. Let us take a typical manager and assume that he (or she) and his subordinates were all strangers to each other. If he met one of them on the street and asked him to do something, would the stranger comply? Not likely. Let us now take a typical employee and assume that he and his manager were strangers. If he met the manager on the street and said, "This is Friday and I would like to be paid $1000," would the manager agree to pay the money? Again, probably not. The reason there was no compliance in either case is that no one had a claim upon the other. Or, to put it differently, no one had "power" over the other.

In a sense, the word "power" is misleading in that it focuses on only one side of what is essentially a two-sided phenomenon. Power can be viewed as the presentation of a claim. The trouble with the one-sided view of power is that it overlooks the fact that claims between people are almost always the result of an exchange. If we now assume that the manager and her (or his) employees do know each other and work together, we see clearly that the manager's claim to the cooperation of her subordinate is matched by the subordinate's claim to a weekly paycheck.* The subordinate's power over his manager, with respect to a weekly pay-

---

*This discussion of mutual claims between people in a business environment is necessarily simplistic. Much more is exchanged than work for money. For example, an executive on the rise may "claim" cooperation in the present from certain individuals over whom he has no formal authority in return for an implied promise of favored treatment in the future. The individuals who do cooperate acquire a future claim (power) upon the executive.

check, is so absolute that he could take the manager to court to compel her to pay what was rightfully owed. It is clear, then, that it is not just the manager who has power over the subordinate but that each has power over the other. The employee and the corporation each have claims on the other—but for different things. Ultimately, however, the claims all have the same goal, which is to make a living far superior to what employees, management or the stockholders could achieve alone.

THE RECIPROCAL NATURE OF POWER

Social power, including power within a corporation, can be likened to the action of a magnet. It's a mistake to perceive a magnet as simply "pulling" something toward itself. If, in fact, a magnet is placed close to another piece of metal which is held fast, it is the magnet which will be "pulled." In other words, magnets create other magnets in formerly unmagnetized pieces of metal. The force between the permanent and temporary magnet is mutual such that each attracts the other.

Social power, including power within the corporation, is also reciprocal in nature. Power does not simply originate at the top and flow downward. Whenever a corporate chairman or president exercises power over a vice-president, he (or she) automatically imparts to the vice-president some degree of power over him. Since power is reciprocal in nature, it follows that everyone who feels the impact of power automatically receives the ability to exert power. Everyone has power and no one is powerless unless he lives in complete isolation from society.* Since everyone has power, social power must be viewed as a type of force field in which each individual is like a bit of metal simultaneously being influenced by the field and influencing others within the field. Saying that everyone has power and that no one is powerless is not saying that we can all have our way in all things. One can have power and yet be "overpowered." For example, most employees working at the lower levels of an organization mistakenly view the president mainly as a wielder of power. The truth of the matter is that the president is himself strongly influenced by powerful forces above, around and below him. If he should fail to resonate in harmony with these forces, he can experience stress and uncertainty the likes of which employees at the lower levels can scarcely imagine. Readers of the *Wall Street Journal* can find in almost any issue at least one account of a chief corporate executive involuntarily ousted from his post.

*It is interesting to consider that an individual could not succeed in denying society any power over him whatsoever without ultimately giving up all power that he himself may possess over others.

POLITICS

For purposes of this discussion, the word "politics" will be defined as the process of acquiring, retaining and exercising power. It may be possible to think of power in the abstract but the word politics immediately draws attention to people—the specific individuals actually engaged in the mobilization of social power.

Since, hopefully, we have conceded the point that social power is absolutely necessary in order to get the world's work accomplished, it follows that *someone* must be in a position to ensure that the work is performed as planned. The trouble with this is that the decisions society makes seldom receive the wholehearted support of everyone affected. There is always someone who not only disagrees but wants to do something about it. The result is politics, or the struggle for power.

There are even people who seek power not because they believe they know a better way but simply because they yearn for the privileges which go with power. Everyone knows that corporate politics can produce capricious, arbitrary and even harmful results. But, providing these results do not prevent the organization from surviving and prospering in the competitive market, more good than bad is done. Nothing this book can say will protect the auditor, or anyone, from the consequences of having zigged politically when he should have zagged. The problem is ages old and will always be with us. The best the auditor can do is to sharpen his skills, maintain his personal integrity, view the world's imperfections with benign tolerance and display a sense of humor that will enable him to carry on. The latter is perhaps the most important. People who can laugh are still on track. And the track will lead somewhere sooner or later.

THE POWER OF THE INTERNAL AUDITOR

Corporate staff people, including internal auditors, are prone to complain about their "lack of power." This is an understandable reaction, at the emotional level, to the many frustrations experienced by internal auditors. At the intellectual level, however, the proposition remains true that no one is without power and that no one's power is absolute. Anyone wishing to operate effectively in an organization must learn to correctly assess the nature, extent and limits of his own power as well as the power of others. The internal auditor must neither overestimate nor underestimate his power or the power of the board, management or auditees.

Persons who view internal auditors as powerless base their view on the fact that internal auditing is not located within the corporate "chain of command." Any line manager having such a simplistic view of power runs a serious risk of sooner or later making career-limiting errors of judgment. Practically every corporation has experienced cases of damaged careers resulting from ill-advised clashes with the audit department. Internal auditors are like everyone else. They are not without power. They may not command, but they often have considerable influence over those who do.

The influence of internal auditors qualifies as "power" in the generic sense. Internal auditors can and do affect how the social energy of the corporation is organized and concentrated. Internal auditors are in a position to influence the setting of goals, the development of plans, the use, allocation and preservation of resources, the integrity of information and the design of controls. In fact, the notion of "control" is closely related to that of power, and internal auditing's jurisdiction in matters of control places it very close to the use and application of power in the corporation.

The best way to appreciate the power of internal auditing is to review any comprehensive report of its activities over, say, a period of a year. Yearly activity reports to the board audit committee make it amply clear how internal auditing influences the manner in which the corporation performs its work.

INTERNAL AUDITING AND POLITICS

Because internal auditors are so intent on maintaining their objectivity, they delude themselves into believing that they are uninvolved in politics. Politics was defined earlier as the process of acquiring, retaining and exercising power. It takes only a little reflection to come to the conclusion that internal auditing is involved in politics in at least three ways.

First, internal auditing is continually engaged in efforts to maintain and increase its own influence. In this sense, internal auditing is much more political than many functions in the corporation whose roles were defined, and clearly delimited, many years ago. Auditing's "unlimited scope" and newly elevated reporting relationship will make its power within the corporation an open question for years to come.

Second, internal auditing's appraisal and recommendation functions often place it in direct competition with others seeking to influence how the organization is managed in specific areas. Even here, internal auditing is more political than most by virtue of the sheer number, scope and variety of issues it can get involved in.

Third, the appraisals and recommendations of internal auditing can have an impact on the image and status of individual managers. Every power seeker within the organization is extremely sensitive to factors which may enhance or damage his image and status. Since internal auditors have that ability, it is impossible for the corporate power seeker to view the audit organization in nonpolitical terms. Whether the audit department takes a position on a purely objective basis or not is beside the point. If the position constitutes an advantage or a threat to someone, the position is "political" in its potential impact: it may help or hinder someone's rise to power. In other words, the audit department's carefully cultivated objectivity may make it relatively nonpartisan with respect to personalities; but its equally carefully cultivated competence and diligence prevent its being nonpartisan with respect to issues. And, more often than not, specific individuals perceive themselves as being benefited or harmed depending on how issues are decided.

THE PULSING NATURE OF POWER

The power intensity of individuals and organizations is not dependent solely on their status and personal attributes. It can also depend to a large degree on specific circumstances. Since circumstances can change, power intensity can change. Close observers of power understand that power pulses up and down and this is why "timing" can be so critical in the use of power. The tactical principle is to time an initiative when one's power is at a high and the power of likely sources of resistance is at a low.

There is nothing unethical in the use of such tactical principles. Tactical principles in the use of power are ethically neutral in the same fashion that power itself is ethically neutral. It all depends on the ethical merits of the goals pursued. For example, let us assume that a department is well overdue for its first operational audit and that it has made it abundantly clear on a number of occasions that it does not want to be audited. For reasons of its own, senior management may, in the past, have cautioned the auditors not to press the matter. The worst time to propose an unwanted audit upon such an organization would be when it is busy at a critical corporate task. Organizations tend to wield unusual amounts of power when given important, time-critical assignments. They become so aligned with the short-term interests or perhaps even the survival of the corporation that everyone feels compelled to cooperate with them. When experiencing a power "high" of this kind, organizations will have no difficulty in declining an audit no matter what internal auditing's charter may say about unlimited scope, independence and access. Again, as we said in an earlier chapter, audit independence is not so much a right to be asserted as a privilege to be managed.

The power or influence of the internal audit function tends to fluctuate around a mean established by its status, reputation and the quality of its personnel. The power or influence of the individual internal auditor can also be said to vary around a "normal" value reflecting his personal qualities, competence and performance track record. Given the general support enjoyed by the audit department, that support can increase significantly when the department is in possession of a material audit finding. An audit finding having a significant impact on the organization has the capacity to mobilize forces from many quarters and to focus a very high level of power on the problem. Conversely, a minor finding may not enlist special support of any kind and may even generate negative support in the form of impatience or resentment. It follows from this that internal auditing should seldom permit disputes to develop over issues which management will deem of little relevance to the welfare of the organization. If stiff resistance is given by the auditee, support will not be forthcoming from other quarters. The audit department will lose and its general power level will ebb when word spreads of its defeat.

It is in the nature of internal auditing that it performs its function on other people's home ground. The inherent power of internal auditing is always weak as compared with that of the auditee. Minor findings can, at best, only raise internal auditing's power to a par with the auditee's. If minor findings are not accepted willingly, management will almost always decide disputes in favor of the auditee. In trivial matters, it is an axiom of corporate leadership that the line must prevail over staff. Internal auditing must be aware of this and must avoid inviting embarrassment by allowing disputes to develop over the wrong issues, in the wrong place and at the wrong time.

ALLIANCES INCREASE POWER

Social power was described earlier as deriving from cooperative agreements between people. The power of a corporation is created when its members agree to work together toward a common objective. Special alliances within a corporation represent a further extension of the same principle, creating "power pockets" within the overall power field. Internal auditors need to be more sensitive to the phenomenon of special alliances. Unless auditors are careful, they can cause special alliances to coalesce around the desire to resist the thrust of the internal audit function. It is almost always a tactical mistake to permit the audit program to appear to threaten a number of key personel at the same time. The threatened individuals will combine forces and present a consensus to senior management which senior management will find extremely difficult to ignore. The general rule is that internal auditing should address no more than one major issue at a time in order to better predict, manage and isolate its psychological impact upon the organization.

GOING WITH THE FLOW

Although necessary, some of the previous discussions about the nature and uses of power may have created the unfortunate impression that we view internal auditing as an adversary function. The world being what it is, and people being what they are, even the most benign activity can be turned into conflict through mistrust, rivalry or simple competition. However, internal auditing is not inherently adversarial. In fact internal auditing can and should be a thoroughly positive, constructive and helpful activity. The internal auditor's ultimate purpose in studying the workings of power is not to produce conflict but to prevent it or minimize it.

Internal auditors are generally nice people. Nice people have a tendency to eschew power considerations and to act simply on the basis of principle. The fact of the matter is that principle is often much more conducive to conflict than power. The principle-oriented personality is apt to initiate conflict over very trivial matters simply because right and wrong appear to be involved. The power-oriented personality, on the other hand, is more likely to negotiate differences based upon the probable outcome of an outright conflict if one were permitted to occur. If the negotiations are successful, conflict is avoided.

As stated earlier, the world of the internal auditor is changing very rapidly. The auditor's broader scope and higher reporting relationship are bringing him into contact with people who will expect him to display leadership and to integrate considerations of both principle and power in the solution of practical problems. The auditor's new reporting relationship will in fact provide the opportunity to solve many more problems than he could before. However, taking advantage of this opportunity will require a complete reorientation of the auditor with respect to his relationship with corporate power.

When internal auditing had little status and was situated deep in the organization, selling its audit findings too often involved swimming upstream against the prevailing power flow. Years of working under these conditions conditioned internal auditors to expect the organization to resist their audit findings more often than not. Auditors must forget their early conditioning and must now view the situation afresh. With their new status and reporting relationship, they are in a position to step into the power stream at its headwaters and to achieve many of their rightful objectives simply by going with the flow. The trick will be to involve upper management more directly in audit planning and to consult with upper management before difficulties arise. If this can be done successfully, internal auditing will have the advantage of knowing where management stands before making critical moves. To the extent that internal auditing is correctly perceived as being aligned with corporate power, most prudent auditees will be inclined to accept internal auditing's offer to engage in a cooperative relationship.

I WIN—YOU WIN

An adversary relationship between the auditor and the auditee runs the risk of damaging one or the other or, more likely, both. The energy expended in the conflict is lost as friction and diminishes the power output of the corporation as a whole. On the other hand, a cooperative power relationship makes winners of both the auditor and the auditee. Each gives more power to the other and both add to the output of the corporate engine. The auditee increases the force of the auditor's recommendation when he concurs with it—especially when he does so voluntarily and with enthusiasm. Conversely, the auditor adds to the force of the auditee's opinion when he picks up on a long-standing problem, investigates it, agrees with the auditee that the problem should be corrected and says so in his report.

SUMMARY

Physical and social power are both cosmic goods.

The social power contained in the corporation produces tremendous personal benefits for the internal auditor. The internal auditor must view all members of the corporation as friends and economic allies whose individual and combined efforts synergize with his own efforts to produce extraordinary benefits for all.

Social power is reciprocal. Everyone has power and no one is without power. Everyone's power is limited.

Politics is the process of acquiring, retaining and exercising power. Since politics is a necessary aspect of power, its occasional capricious and arbitrary results must be viewed with benign tolerance and a sense of humor.

Internal auditors have power. Internal auditors must understand the extent and limits of their own power as well as the power of others.

Internal auditing is political. It seeks to expand its influence; its activities have a bearing on how the organization is managed; and its findings have an impact on the image and status of power seekers within the organization. The audit department's carefully cultivated objectivity makes it relatively nonpartisan with respect to personalities but prevents it from being nonpartisan with respect to issues.

Power intensities are not constant but tend to pulse up and down with changes in circumstances. Auditors' normal power level is low as compared to that of the auditee. Significant findings can materially increase auditors' power level.

Alliances increase power. Auditors should avoid creating circumstances leading to the formation of contrary power alliances.

Internal auditing's new reporting relationship has increased its overall leadership responsibility within the corporation.

Effective leadership requires competence in the understanding and use of power. The internal auditor must use power wisely to achieve beneficial ends and to avoid unnecessary conflict. An adversary power relationship with auditees is highly undesirable. Conflicts between auditors and auditees are almost always mutually harmful. On the other hand, cooperation between auditors and auditees is almost always beneficial to both.

DISCUSSION

The jurisdiction and work patterns of the financial auditor have been established and honored for so long that his right to audit is not often challenged. A young woman once remarked that she had been an auditor for a number of years without ever suspecting that she caused fear in others until she happened to overhear two auditees in conversation. "I was amazed," the young woman told this author, "Those people were actually afraid of me."

It is typical in most corporations that operational and management auditors work in a more politically turbulent environment than do financial auditors. It is not unusual for auditees to question auditors' qualifications and, on occasion, to take violent exception to their findings. For this reason, operational and management auditors must often cite their audit charters and must appeal for management support in dealing with recalcitrant auditees.

The modern internal auditor has been led by circumstance to view himself as engaged in a battle on behalf of senior management against stubborn adversaries who refuse to recognize the rightness of the audit department's cause. And yet, the modern internal auditor is continually baffled and frustrated by senior management's reluctance to support him to the extent that it should. The modern internal auditor is in a sense tilting against the corporate windmill and bemoaning his lack of power to overcome the adversary.

The new internal auditing is looking for an alternative conception of power and its role in the internal auditing process. The new internal auditing views it as largely unproductive to tilt against the apparent negative aspects of corporate power. As an alternative, it is seeking to identify the *positive* elements of corporate power in an effort to ally itself with these elements for the benefit of the enterprise. As will be seen in later chapters, tapping the positive elements of corporate power will involve new concepts of audit relations, audit disclosure and management support.

CHAPTER 5

Auditees and Auditors

If the labor is mean, let him by his thinking and character make it liberal.

RALPH WALDO EMERSON, "Spiritual Laws"

The field of business management has produced many theories and a vast literature. Since every internal auditor needs to be a student of management on an ongoing basis, this book assumes that the reader already has at least a nodding acquaintance with scientific management, theories "X," "Y" and "Z," Maslow's hierarchy of needs, and all of the other useful constructs that have been built in an attempt to explain that complex human activity called "management." This and subsequent chapters will therefore not repeat ideas about management which have already been given wide distribution. Rather, the focus will be on specific aspects of the corporate environment which are not often discussed and which have special relevance to the work of the internal auditor.

THE INDIVIDUAL MANAGER

Large organizations have many managers, and internal auditors get to know very few of these on more than a casual basis. It follows that auditors must quard against the tendency to view individual managers as one-dimensional figures.

When an internal auditor is given a new assignment, one of the first things he does is to look up an organization chart identifying the key people he will be dealing with. If his audit relates to the procurement cycle, he will identify the names and titles of various people concerned with the purchasing, accounts payable and treasury functions. The tendency will be to view these individuals mainly in terms of their jobs. Subsequent meetings and observations will only tend to reinforce the auditor's perception of the managers and supervisors as being exclusively preoccupied with their duties and responsibilities as described in the tables of organization. The auditor will be misled into believing that since the individuals concerned spend most of their time managing and supervising operations, this must be uppermost in their list of priorities. If the auditor believes this to be the case, he is dead wrong!

What is overlooked in the one-dimensional view of the manager is the fact that the manager is almost always engaged in an extracurricular activity which takes higher priority than his official duties. What are we referring to? The fact that he is engaged in the management of his own career. Priority has no necessary correlation with time spent. The egocentric nature of the manager's top priority does not prevent him from working at his official duties most of the time. And the corporation, being realistic, does not consider the manager's attitude as posing a conflict of interest. Such a standard of loyalty would eliminate all but canonized saints from eligibility to the ranks of management, and saints would decline a career in management in favor of a higher calling anyway. This is why it has been said that the essence of management is the skillful alignment of the individual interests of subordinates with the interests of the organization as a whole. One arranges matters in such a way that the manager can only advance his interests by advancing those of his employer. This last thought provides a key concept for the successful management of the internal audit function as well as for the conduct of the individual audit. The skillful audit director manages his activity in such a manner that auditees will see it as being in their best career interest to cooperate with the audit department. And the skillful auditor conducts his individual audit on the same principle.

The primacy of career interest in the mind of the manager or supervisor is readily observable when a career threat presents itself. Work which can be deferred is deferred. Delegation to others is increased. Time and energy is conserved to deal with the threat. At stake are career advancement, financial growth and security, self-esteem, health, welfare of the family, prestige in the community, and so forth. No one can say that these are trivial matters for any man or woman. In fact, to the extent that the manager or supervisor represents a long-term asset to his organization, the value of that asset is now being threatened with sudden and severe depreciation.

If the threat to the manager or supervisor comes from an internal audit, he will tap every resource at his command to resist the troublesome findings. He will enlist the support of subordinates, superiors and other associates and, if necessary, he will initiate ad hominem attacks against the auditor. The auditor should try to prevent such situations from arising whenever possible. If they do arise nonetheless, he should decide quickly whether to defuse the situation or to press on. And the auditor should never press on alone. In the corporate environment, the individual seldom wins in a squabble against the group. The merits of the case notwithstanding, senior managers will almost always sacrifice the morale of the individual to preserve the morale of the group—and especially when the individual is an outsider. The auditor must consult with his supervisor and manager who will determine whether the issue is sufficiently material to warrant taking a firm position and whether adequate management support will be forthcoming to permit the auditing department to prevail. Auditing management must also judge whether the situation is one where it may win the battle but lose the war. As we said earlier, it is almost always best for staff, including internal auditing, to avoid bitter disputes with operating management.*

TWO EXCEPTIONS

There are only two cases when it is clearly in internal auditing's interest to engage in a serious dispute with an auditee. First, when a dispute is

*Internal auditors must be wary of senior management's unfortunate tendency toward pragmatism when resolving disutes. Senior management will act decisively to defend its own dignity and authority. But it can't always be depended upon to do so to protect others —even when they are in the right. Faced with an angry line organization, management may take the path of least resistance by faulting an auditor's "judgement" or writing him off as having no further value to the organization.

necessary to establish auditing's jurisdiction. In this case, internal auditing should choose its target carefully and should line up senior management's unqualified support before making its move. The ideal target for a jurisdictional dispute is an organization which is visible, not too powerful and one which management earnestly wants to reform. Properly handled, a successful jurisdictional dispute will serve notice to the rest of the organization that management fully intends to support internal auditing's charter. The second case is when senior management has signaled to the audit organization that it should take on an auditee whom it (management) wishes to "turn around" or to dismiss. Almost always, in this case, word that the auditee is out of favor with management will have spread throughout most of the organization. The resulting isolation will render the auditee virtually powerless, and his efforts to resist the audit function will only make matters worse for him. The auditing department will gain in two ways by not backing away from disputes in such cases: it will have carried out senior management's wishes; and, it will have fostered respect for its organizational status on the part of everyone on the sidelines. However, auditing will be well advised not to be the one to provoke a dispute and to behave professionally in every way in order to avoid being viewed as an unpredictable predator by the organization at large.

DISTINCT CULTURES

The psychology of disputes between auditors and auditees can go well beyond such simple matters as the technical merits of a particular audit finding or the posing of a threat to the auditee. In addition to having their individual personalities, auditees have a group personality which can determine a good part of their behavior. Auditees are members of an organization of people. As such, they share the assumptions, beliefs, prejudices, likes and dislikes of a social group. Auditees are therefore capable of reacting adversely to an audit, or an auditor, for reasons which might be termed "cultural." For example, an auditor may have worked a considerable time on an audit without having acquired or displayed any sympathy for the attitude, values and concerns of the group being audited. If the auditor produces a report draft which fails to acknowledge the positive accomplishments of the group, and which focuses on points of internal control never before brought up by management, the reaction may well be anger and resentment. The auditor will be viewed as an enemy seeking to find fault with the group and to make a name for himself at their expense. Protestations by the auditor that he is merely attempting to "help" will do little to correct a bad situation brought on by a poor auditing strategy, a defective audit program and an outdated report-writing style based on the exception principle.

Audit failures of the type described above are often laid at the feet of the individual auditor whereas they are in fact a failure of audit philosophy. An operating group may be working earnestly with inadequate resources to achieve specific goals set by management. The pressures created by management may have induced the operating group to concentrate on certain high-priority matters to the exclusion of practically everything else. On the other hand, the internal audit organization may itself be under pressure to conserve resources and to concentrate its efforts on known or suspected areas of control weakness. The result will most likely be an audit plan designed not to produce fair and balanced appraisals of the effectiveness and efficiency of operations, but to disclose control weaknesses peripheral to the central mission of the auditee organization. A better prescription for poor auditee relations could not be devised.

THE DOERS

By the term "doers," we refer to those individuals whose principal function is to *do* as opposed to plan, organize, direct and control. Internal auditors owe it to themselves to understand what makes doers tick. Doers are found at every level of the organization and are distinguished not so much by their rank as by their role and orientation. Doers see their role as performing actions in accordance with instructions. Doers are relatively unconcerned with social and economic trends, developments in their industry, competitive pressures or corporate goals and objectives. Ask them why things are done in a certain way and they answer by quoting procedures and instructions passed on to them by their supervisors and managers.

Doers are absolutely essential to an organization. Doers comprise the "bureaucracy" which was brilliantly described by Max Weber, the nineteenth century sociologist, in his *Essays in Sociology*. Properly instructed, doers provide assurance to management that things will be done according to plan. Doers provide the order and predictability which every organization requires for 95% of its activities. The internal auditor should not fault doers for their disinclination to think through the implications of what they do. He shouldn't do so even in the privacy of his own mind. Doers are not being paid to think. Much to the contrary, they are being very well paid *not* to think, and it would be perverse of the auditor to expect someone to do what he has specifically been told not to do.

Doers are tribal in outlook and are extremely protective of themselves and their superiors. Theirs is the strength of numbers and the knowledge that the organization could not function without them. Management has a great deal of respect for doers, especially as a class, and it immediately brands anyone who upsets them as "lacking in judgment."

The internal auditor can be certain that every document he requests, every question he asks and everything he says will be dutifully discussed by doers, and reported more or less accurately to supervision and management. Doers may have a sense of irony about other things but never about their work. Doers are not objective. In fact, they are the most subjective people in the world—judging people as friends or foes and evaluating events as favoring or threatening the security of their employment.

Doers can only be influenced by persons situated in the legitimate chain of command above them. The function of supervision is to provide direction to doers and they are the only ones able to perform that function.

The new and inexperienced internal auditor must understand how different the intellectual and emotional processes of the doer are from his own. For this reason, he must be very prudent in his contact with doers. At the personal level, the key is to be friendly and sympathetic in every way. In audit matters, the auditor should limit himself to requests for documents and other information, and interpretations thereof. The thing he must avoid above all else is to offer gratuitous comments or opinions about what he sees. If an adverse interpretation can be attached to such comments and opinions, doers will invariably attach such an interpretation. The word will spread concerning the auditor's "hostile" remark and supervision will be confronted with a morale problem. If the problem can be controlled, the consequence of the auditor's error in judgment will be merely an unmistakable drop in the level of friendliness and cooperation. If the problem is serious, the auditor may have to be recalled. The moral to all of this is clear and straightforward: restrict discussions with doers to questions of fact. Discuss all else with supervision and only with supervision!

THE PURSUIT OF PERFECTION

It happens to every internal auditor sooner or later. After a particularly hectic week when nothing has gone right, he finds himself having a beer with a small group of his fellow auditors and it all comes out: this is the messiest audit he's ever had; the auditee is messed up; in fact, the whole company is messed up. Such venting of one's frustrations is quite common among internal auditors and it does no real harm providing it happens privately among friends. But the regularity of such outbursts serves to remind us that it takes more than technical proficiency to go the distance as an internal auditor. It also takes a peculiar attitude of mind that enables the auditor to behave graciously in the midst of imperfection.

Every auditor needs to cultivate a sense of humility. An auditor who is not aware of his own limitations has no business evaluating the performance of others. Such an auditor wanders the corridors of his company brandishing a ten-foot yardstick and expressing continual amazement that no one seems to measure up. The pursuit of perfection may or may not be management's mandate, but it is certainly not the mandate of the internal auditor. The proper yardstick for the internal auditor is not perfection but adequacy. Let the perfectionist internal auditor change his yardstick and he will find that things will almost immediately change for the better. He will be happier with himself and with the auditee. The findings in his report will come across better and his suggestions for improvement will be more readily accepted.

AUDIT PHILOSOPHY

There is something almost misleading in the expression "audit environment." Most auditors view this term as describing something apart from the auditor. They only see management and the auditee in the audit environment. They don't see themselves. How strange this is, since there can't be an audit environment without an audit, and there can't be an audit without an auditor.

Granted that some audit environments are clearly better than others, quite apart from the auditor, the fact remains that the environment is seldom neutral with respect to the auditor. The auditor does make a difference. He can make the environment better or worse than it might otherwise be. It's important for all auditors to understand that their audit philosophy is a major determinant of the audit environment. The auditor who seeks to contribute to the success of the activity he is reviewing is fostering an environment very different from that fostered by the auditor who frantically searches for weaknesses that he can use to embarrass the auditee and to score points with his superiors, associates and senior management. The difference between these two types of auditors cannot be dismissed as just a question of personality. The modern internal auditor is usually a well-educated person with considerable psychological flexibility. This is to say that the typical auditor can be trained to adopt any one of a whole range of attitudes and to play a variety of roles. In fact, auditors can do just about anything they are asked to do. If internal audit departments are unhappy with their poor auditee relations, they should look beyond personalities and ask themselves whether they are perhaps suffering the predictable effects of an obsolescent audit philosophy.

THE DISCLOSURE SYNDROME

Internal auditors are like other people. They tend to behave in accordance with the expectations of their superiors and their peers. If, in the past, the glory and the promotions have gone to the aggressive show-and-tell auditors, then these are the auditors who will be emulated. If, in other words, the name of the game is "disclosure," that is the game that will be played.

Here is how the disclosure cycle often goes:

1. The smart manager never asks for an audit.
2. When an audit is forced on her (or him), the manager instructs her staff to volunteer no information, provide only those documents that are requested, answer only direct questions and answer in as brief a manner as possible.
3. The auditor senses the lack of willing cooperation and increases his (or her) efforts to come up with significant findings.
4. The auditor has difficulty in writing his exception report for lack of supporting information. His findings may be valid but they are not well documented.
5. The auditee manager disputes most of the findings in the draft report. The auditor redoubles his efforts. He withdraws certain findings but builds a stronger case for the others.
6. The final report is sent up the management chain. The report discloses a number of cases of simple human error.
7. Management comes crashing down on the auditee.
8. The auditee relates her experience to all her friends.
9. The cycle repeats itself with the next audit.
10. Three or four years later, the auditor is burned out, has few friends outside of auditing and is transferred to a routine supervisory position offering little chance for further promotion.

Internal auditing's "disclosure syndrome" probably traces its origins to public accounting where full disclosure of all material information is rightfully viewed as an ethical duty in the public interest. Young CPAs brought this disclosure tradition with them when they moved out of public accounting and accepted employment as corporate internal auditors. They also brought an impressive capacity for detailed review, verification and appraisal. Since internal auditors were originally placed in the service of corporate controllers, the CPAs were encouraged to give full expression to both their disclosure instinct and their capacity for detailed work.

When internal auditing expanded into the compliance area, disclosure continued to be a viable modus operandi. Since management did not attach too much importance to minor accounting discrepancies and violations of clerical procedure, auditees did not feel unduly threatened by internal auditors' habit of reporting all audit exceptions up the chain of command. But as internal auditors began to inquire into operational matters, auditee attitudes underwent a change. Auditing began to be perceived as posing a career threat. Middle managers who had been insensitive to the complaints of junior managers in the past began to take notice as the impact of audit findings reached progressively higher levels in the organization. As the audit director's reporting relationship was adjusted ever upward, even senior management began to wonder if it didn't have a loose cannon on the decks.

TIME FOR A CHANGE

Every operational auditor knows that change does not necessarily take place immediately after its need has been recognized. A good percentage of all operational audit findings are known to the auditees themselves well before the auditor ever steps through the door. In fact, it happens quite often that operating organizations will request an audit simply to secure support for a needed change.

Operating managers often find it dificult to implement change on their own. They have become prisoners of the status quo, unable to improve their own operation without setting off negative reactions among their superiors, their subordinates or other people with whom they interact. This can also happen to the internal audit department. Many audit directors have long suspected that their disclosure practices are standing in the way of better audit relations. But they have become prisoners of past management attitudes and expectations concerning disclosure. Management has been led to believe that auditors are supposed to disclose, and has made budgetary support of the audit function contingent upon well-publicized audit "results." What is beginning to happen is that both the audit director and management realize that something is wrong but neither is talking to the other for fear of being misunderstood. Neither wants to appear to be suggesting a cover-up of audit findings which would appear to be inconsistent with the ethics of internal auditing and, for that matter, the ethics of good management.

With the audit director now reporting to the board audit committee, the moment has arrived for a basic reexamination of internal auditing's disclosure processes. More will be said about this later, but it does appear that if internal auditing persists in viewing full and immediate disclosure as its primary function, forces will mobilize to ensure that internal auditing has little to disclose. The implications of this with respect to the full development of the scope of internal auditing need to be pondered by every audit director.

A NEW SPIRIT

Somebody has to say it: the internal auditing profession is caught up in the most impressive growth phase of its entire history; and yet, it may also be heading toward a fundamental reexamination of some of its most basic assumptions. There is a new spirit in the air which may end up invalidating certain things about internal auditing which most of us would never have thought of questioning just a few years ago.

Historians tell us that internal auditing received a healthy boost as a result of the New Deal legislation passed in the 1930s. Corporations had to conduct extensive analyses to demonstrate their compliance with the new legislation. Since independent accountants were not in a position to do all of this work, many internal auditors were added to corporate staffs. However, by the time the present generation of internal auditors came upon the scene, the effects of the auditing boom of the 1930s had completely dissipated. It's as if it never happened.

History may be in the process of repeating itself with the enactment of the FCPA. What auditors should ask themselves now is whether the effects of the FCPA will also eventually dissipate and leave them little better off than they were before. It's a good question, and although one cannot claim to know the answer with certitude, one is at least entitled to speculate on the matter. In fact, all internal auditors should feel it their duty to do so. The future of their profession may depend on it.

Consider when the FCPA was passed: in December of 1977. And what happened in 1980? At the polls the voters supported a radical shift away from the economic policies established during the Great Depression.* The country decided to give American business the freedom it needed to compete effectively in world markets. Was the FCPA a last gasp in an attempt to control and hinder corporate America? If the new industrial policies now in place continue to succeed, will their success cause an even speedier dissipation of the effects of the FCPA? Have internal auditors been hitching their wagon to a star or to a falling meteor?

There seems little doubt about the new spirit in the land. Some call it "industrial cooperation." It's based on the realization that government, controls and regulation are not capable of producing wealth. In our economy, the ability to produce wealth is to be found mainly in the energy, creativity and strivings of the private sector. The new spirit of industrial cooperation is also based on the realization that America, as a society, may have pursued the adversary principle beyond the point of net positive return.

THE ADVERSARY PRINCIPLE

It's amazing how we Americans love to fight. We will pay scalpers a week's wage to get a couple of ringside seats to a boxing match. We pass safety laws to protect ourselves from even minor injuries and yet encourage athletes to break each other's bones for possession of an inflated piece of pigskin. We drag each other off to court at the slightest pretext to engage in what has become a vast national sweepstakes: all of us pay expensive insurance premiums so that a few can win multimillion dollar suits, quit work and retire in comfort. Every year, labor unions and management engage in strenuous negotiations when both sides are probably aware of what the final settlement will be. Every four years, we hold national presidential elections where the issues are in constant struggle for media attention with the adversary aspects of the campaign. And, last but not least, we have internal auditors having bitter disputes with auditees when all are being paid to support the interests of the same employer.

Let not the reader assume that we are against combat—mock or real. Most of us know, or suspect, that life can be very harsh and that a vigorous fighting spirit is needed to cope with adversity. The point is not whether we need to fight. The point is whether we should select more meaningful targets for our fighting energy. The new spirit in the air is suggesting that we have been too busy engaging in mock and/or real

*This shift appears to have been ratified by the results of the 1984 presidential election.

combat amongst ourselves while ignoring the real threat just outside the gates.

ECONOMIC DEMOCRACY

Readers interested mainly in matters of technique may well wonder what all of this has to do with the real world of internal auditing. The answer is that it has everything to do with it. To fail to understand this is to fail to perceive the state of mind of those who decide our fate—those who decide whether there will be an internal audit department, what it will do and what its budget will amount to. These things are decided by policymakers, and if their reasons for doing things sometimes appear mysterious, it's because they often consider things at their level which we, at ours, are only dimly conscious of.

Policymakers have a good feel for the history of economics, management and industrial relations. They understand, at least in a general way, the broad trend toward economic democracy that has taken place since the days of the Industrial Revolution. There was a time when profit and loss information about the firm was known only to its owner and one or two key employees. This was also the time when power, property and economic security were available to the relatively few. Since that time, there has been a progressive downward diffusion of information, power and economic reward. This diffusion first touched the managerial class. It then reached the professional class and quickly went on to include lower-level managers and staff specialists in high demand by expanding corporations.

The foundation for the next stage of this democratization process has already been laid by the labor unions and the law of supply and demand. Even the average employee today possesses wealth and economic security that would have been the envy of more privileged groups just two generations ago. It is not unusual today for the ordinary employee to enjoy the following advantages:

Competitive salary
Medical/dental insurance
Paid vacations and holidays
Company pension plan
Company stock purchase plan (including deferred income plan)
Employee stock ownership plan (ESOP)
Individual retirement account (IRA)

Internal auditors everywhere need to focus on three developments flowing out of the progressive democratization of western economies, including that of the United States: first, there has been a significant increase in the general level of education; second, the ordinary corporate employee is acquiring beneficial ownership of an increasing share of the national stock of economic capital; and, third, the self-esteem of the ordinary corporate employee is on the rise.

RUNNING OUT OF ADVERSARIES

Careful reflection on the three developments cited above help to explain, at least in part, what has been slowly happening to the internal audit function in the typical corporation. The owners of large corporations have, willingly or not, been led to enlarge the privileged groups within the corporation. Corporations are, in a word, becoming a society of "ins" without any "outs." Technology has made everyone important and it has become increasingly necessary to be nice to everyone. The pattern has been developing for years. All it took to make us realize clearly what was happening was the loss of our competitive edge in world markets, the political turnabout in 1980, publication of a book on "Theory Z" and talk about quality circles. Economic democracy and the need to work together has produced industrial democracy right down to the machine operator. Management is still in charge, but it no longer feels it can successfully manage the enterprise without enlisting the cooperative participation of *all* employees. The bad news in all of this for internal auditors is that they are quickly running out of adversaries. The good news is that they have acquired an army of potential allies in a common cause to make their companies more profitable.

SUMMARY

The first priority of most managers is the management of their careers.

Disputes with operating management are almost always damaging to the audit department—even when it "wins." Ironically, auditing's winning a dispute may benefit the corporation in the short term while damaging auditing's own long-term interests.

In certain cases, and with senior management's unqualified support, the auditing department may have to engage in disputes in order to establish its jurisdiction or to reform a delinquent auditee.

The best way to avoid disputes is to devise, and follow, an audit philosophy designed to minimize conflict.

Auditors should be friendly toward all "doers," restrict discussions with them to questions of fact and discuss everything else with supervision and management.

The proper yardstick for the internal auditor is not perfection but adequacy.

The auditor is part of the audit environment.

Many of internal auditing's problems stem from its disclosure practices. Auditing needs to think beyond disclosure and to concentrate on problem solving.

Internal auditing will have to progressively give up its adversary assumptions and style to keep in step with the new spirit of industrial cooperation.

DISCUSSION

The 1980–82 economic recession caused a violent shakeout throughout industrial America. Corporations laid off employees, turned over their management, tightened work rules and bargained hard to arrest wage and salary escalation. The harshness that prevailed during this period is not destined to last. With improvement in world economic conditions, corporations will value their skilled employees more than ever as these employees make the difference between success and failure in the marketplace. The pressures of world competition will make it increasingly imperative that there be more effective cooperation at all levels of the enterprise, from senior management down to organized labor.

If industrial cooperation is to be the pattern of the future, internal auditors must be wary of being styled as mere corporate watchdogs to be let out of their pens only when keen noses are needed to track down fraud and defalcation. A purely adversary internal audit function concerned exclusively with preventive, detective and punitive controls will be an anomaly in an industrial environment marked by positive cooperation among all segments of the enterprise. In order to grow with the enterprise, internal auditing will have to explore ways to make a positive contribution to profits. Since it can only do this with the cooperation of managers and auditees, internal auditing must progressively abandon the adversary role in which it has been typecast and must seek admittance to the mainstream corporate culture.

Viewed in the light of these comments, it is easier to appreciate the wisdom of those internal audit departments which, in recent years, seized upon the opportunity to provide productivity measurement and improvement services to their organizations. Traditionalists reacted to this development with the usual question: what does this have to do with internal auditing? And yet, the venturesome spirits who moved into the productivity measurement area have by now established a new, cooperative relationship with operating management which senior management and board audit committees have not failed to notice. Most likely, internal auditors who have established goodwill for the audit function at the working level will be in a much better position to grow with the enterprise in the new environment of the 1980s and 1990s.

The new internal auditing views its goal as service to the *entire* organization. This ideal will of course never be completely realized since no corporate function can be all things to all people. Nevertheless, internal auditing has greater potential to render beneficial services over a wide range of activities than practically any other corporate function. To realize this potential, however, internal auditing must adopt a suitable philosophy and modus operandi. It will have succeeded in doing so when the great majority of managers and auditees freely admit to having benefited from interaction with the audit department.

Ironically, any move by the audit director to broaden the scope of his department's services will probably be resisted by his own immediate subordinates, who will instinctively resent the intrusion of new people and new disciplines into the audit organization. The audit director can counter this negative reaction simply by pointing out that any expansion of the audit department into new areas will necessarily increase the department's status and broaden the director's span of control. Both of these effects must soon translate into more responsibility and increased compensation for the original leaders of the audit department. In a word, anything which can be done to increase internal auditing's contribution to the corporate welfare benefits all concerned: the corporation, the present internal audit management and those for whom new jobs are created.

CHAPTER 6

Senior Management and the Board

The most sensible people to be met in society are men of business and of the world, who argue from what they see and know . . . .

WILLIAM HAZLITT, "On the Ignorance of the Learned"

NOT A BED OF ROSES

Viewed from the outside, the life of the senior business executive looks entirely attractive and desirable. Power, prestige, glamour, travel, high salaries and stock options are what we see. What we don't see are the crushing responsibilities, the hectic schedules, the pressure on families, the insecurity, the tension, the fear, the anger, the loss of health and the early coronaries.

The game of management is strictly hardball. Winners win and losers lose. The trouble with the game of management is that its rules are so elusive. Only a relatively few senior executives really know where they stand. Most managers are subjected to constant and pitiless appraisal of their performance under standards that change so frequently as to seem almost capricious or arbitrary. And then there is that group of managers in every large corporation who are merely hanging in there as best they can while waiting for the ax to fall.

THE CHIEF EXECUTIVE

The popular perception of the corporate chief executive is badly flawed. He (or she) is seen as having made it to the top mainly because of his expertise. His days are pictured as being taken up in making complex decisions and issuing crisp orders to compliant subordinates. Since the chief executive is viewed as "running the company," it is assumed that his highest priorities are operational in nature and that his decisions are based mainly on operational considerations.

The internal auditor needs a much more realistic understanding of the chief executive, and all senior executives, if he (or she) is to be effective in his work. Let us assume that the internal auditor is in the president's office outlining his arguments in favor of a control proposal involving a number of departments. As he is speaking, the internal auditor imagines that the president is evaluating the merits of his proposal on the basis of operational factors. The president may in fact be doing this, but the important thing for us to note is that the president's mind is actually working along two tracks. On his second track, the president is not following operational logic, but *people* logic. He is judging and assessing the auditor's proposal from the standpoint of its impact on people. Will the proposed controls appear to be warranted in the eyes of the vice-presidents and department heads concerned? Would the facts and arguments advanced by the auditor persuade these people that the risks are as great, and the costs of the proposed controls are as low, as he claims? Are there other control alternatives which might be more attractive to the executive staff? Should the proposal be deferred for a time until conditions are more favorable—for example, upon the retirement in a few months of two key executives known for their aversion to "bureaucratic controls?"

The more one reflects upon the position of the chief executive, the more apparent it becomes that the chief executive does not so much run the company as *run the people* who run the company or otherwise influence its success. The president is principally a coordinator—bringing together stockholders, creditors, major customers and suppliers, and members of his (or her) immediate executive entourage. When things are going relatively well, he is the lubricant smoothing over the rough spots. When things go badly, he is the lightning rod at the center of the storm. When disputes threaten the welfare of the organization as a whole, his is the voice demanding that people pull together—or else!

What are the priorities of the typical chief executive? Perhaps the best way to answer this question is to draw an example from government. In the case of the President of the United States, one would suppose that, apart from ensuring his own re-election, his top priorities would have to do with urgent matters of international relations or domestic policy. In a sense, this is true enough. But there is another sense in which this is not true. Let us imagine that one morning the *Washington Post* brings news of a serious flare-up between the Departments of State and Defense. By ten o'clock, radio and television are announcing fresh developments in what appears to be a growing rift over a major policy matter. The reader can imagine for himself what the President will do. He will cancel as many meetings as he can and use all of his available time to inquire into the interdepartmental squabble which is embarrassing his administration. When he is ready, he will call in his Secretaries, separately or together as appropriate, and issue stern instructions designed to put the matter to rest.

The President has no choice but to do this. If he doesn't act promptly and decisively, whatever his other problems may be, they will quickly become worse if he can't reestablish harmony among the senior members of his administration. So there we have it: a chief executive's first concern is the smooth working of his top executive team. He will do practically anything to satisfy this essential condition of his own success. If routine steps prove inadequate, he will take means that may appear ruthless to those not acquainted with the imperatives of power and top-level leadership. He will allow damage to be inflicted upon the "innocent" in order to placate the feelings of those who are too important to him to permit them to be publicly humiliated. What does this have to do with internal auditing? Everything. Every veteran director of internal auditing understands that unless he handles sensitive audit findings carefully, he could end up being sacrificed upon the altar of boardroom harmony. It has happened before and it will probably happen again.

MANAGEMENT'S NEED TO MAINTAIN THE INITIATIVE

The first law of management is that management must be in charge. Management's insistence on being in charge is not just a question of ego or love of power. Management must be in charge if it is to do its job and be held accountable.

If an executive is to fulfill his responsibilities, he must first assert, protect and maintain his authority. The executive who has lost his authority is no longer an executive. He will have to be replaced. This is why all executives, and especially senior executives, dislike surprises. Surprises pose two problems for the executive: first, they are in and of themselves evidence that he has lost control over events; second, surprises generate movement and forces which operate independently of the executive and which, therefore, threaten further loss of control.

LEADERSHIP COMES FIRST

Life in a well-ordered and well-managed corporation is deceptively calm and serene. Most employees are only dimly aware of the structure and discipline which pervade the organization. This structure and discipline take the form of organization charts, policies, procedures, approved channels and modes of communication, salary schedules, performance evaluation criteria, office standards, codes (or traditions) of acceptable behavior, grooming and dress and so on. All of these things, and more, so shape our attitudes and behavior that we automatically do the right thing in a wide variety of situations without consciously thinking about it. The fact that we do the right thing most of the time is evidence that the system is working. What system, the reader will ask? The answer is simple: the system of leadership.

The best way to explain the point we are attempting to make is to pose a hypothetical question: what if we were given 10,000 people of varied backgrounds, talents and abilities and were required to forge out of them an effective organization able to compete successfully in the development, design, engineering, production, marketing and servicing of a product? How would we go about it? Would we call a mass meeting and solicit ideas from all 10,000 employees at once? Would we ask all 10,000 employees to appear at the corporate site at precisely 8:00 A.M. the next morning, decide by themselves what they wanted to do and choose any office or work station they wished? One hardly needs to go on to be convinced that this approach would produce absolute chaos. Anyone trying to work under such conditions would be frustrated at every turn. He might find it literally impossible to obtain a simple box of paper clips.

The point of all this is that the foremost challenge of management is not technical, but social. That challenge is leadership. Leadership comes first. The conditions of leadership must be met first before any other business can be transacted. Every auditor must fully internalize this idea because it promises to be a central concept of the new style of internal auditing that will emerge in the 1980s and 1990s.

NOT JUST TECHNICIANS

Until now, internal auditors have been viewing themselves mainly as technicians. They have defined their technical turf as including the safeguarding of assets; the reliability and integrity of information; compliance with policies, procedures, laws and regulations; economy, efficiency and effectiveness of operations; and so on. And yet, the truth of the matter is that internal auditors ceased being mere technicians years ago. Originally, when their activities were restricted mainly to the accounting area, they did limit themselves to giving opinions on purely technical matters. But later, they expanded their scope and extended their services to include the offering of recommendations. When they noticed that many of their recommendations were either being ignored or rejected by management, they concluded that they should improve their audit relations and try to *sell* their recommendations. In other words, internal auditors undertook to influence the behavior of management. The pattern of their development as professionals is really quite clear. Internal auditors have remained technical experts to be sure, but they have also become more and more involved in *leadership*. Their difficulty, if one may use the term, has been that they have been doing this unconsciously without benefit of a positive theory to support their actions. It is for this reason that their performance has been uneven and inconsistent. Sometimes they have been truly helpful. At other times, they have ignored the leadership challenge posed by their findings and recommendations. They have, instead, focused on disclosure—telling it like it is—and have been perfectly content to let management pick up the leadership pieces left by their unknowing mischief.

THE MEANING OF HELPFUL AUDITING

Let us assume that someone on a football team finds fault with how a teammate is handling the ball. What does he do? He takes the ball away from his teammate and then just stands there until he is tackled by the opposing team. One could argue that poor disclosure practice is a little bit like that. It amounts to wresting leadership and initiative away from management without having the ability, or willingness, to follow the matter through to a successful conclusion.

Consider the following hypothetical sequence: an internal audit department declares to a manager that she (or he) will be audited; the audit department does not invite the manager to participate in setting the objectives of the audit; it does not communicate with the manager during the audit and withholds information concerning significant findings until the date of the exit conference; auditing communicates its findings to senior management while junior management is still reeling from the shock of the findings; and then, auditing reports its findings to the board audit committee while senior management itself is still in a state of shock. When the board audit committee inquires concerning the full meaning and implications of the findings, no one is prepared to answer—neither auditing nor management.

Although the above sequence is entirely hypothetical and does not reflect usual internal audit practice, it can serve a useful analytical purpose. Note how the initiative has been taken away from management at all levels. Note also how principles of good leadership have been violated. Internal auditing has pursued a course sure to disrupt the morale and working harmony of all concerned. Senior management will have lost confidence in junior management; the board will have lost confidence in senior management; and, when everyone has reflected on what happened, all will have lost confidence in internal auditing.

As was said earlier, management dislikes surprises. Management must be in charge and must feel that it is in charge. Internal auditing must be leadership-conscious in the sense that it must respect management's right to maintain the initiative. Allowing management to maintain the initiative is the very real and profound message in the advice to auditors that they should be there to "help." And, in certain cases, this will take more time than the thirty days traditionally allotted for responses to internal audit findings.

THE AUDITOR'S TIME ORIENTATION

If asked to fill out a questionnaire on their personal traits, most internal auditors would rate themselves fairly high with respect to such qualities as kindliness, helpfulness, patience and consideration for others. And they would be right. Internal auditors as a group are exceptional people with exceptional qualities. It remains, however, that anyone's character self-assessment is usually based on what he considers to be his *fundamental* nature. Fundamental nature translates to one's attitudes and behavior when one is at peace and at rest, when *time* is not a factor.

But consider what too often happens to the best of us when time pressure is applied. How do we react if a traffic jam threatens to make us late for work and miss an important meeting? Are we as kind, helpful, patient and considerate of others when we have been given two days to complete a job which should take two weeks? Of course not. We excuse our thoughtless behavior in such cases by pleading "emergency." Emergencies force us to behave in a manner contrary to our real natures and this is why we don't answer self-assessment questionnaires on the basis of our behavior under stress. Most of us don't even remember how we behave under stress. We choose to forget it.

There is a connection between all of this and the basic time orientation within which most internal auditors do their work. We refer to the fact that audits are "projects" having set beginning and completion dates. There are excellent reasons why audits must have beginning and completion dates. Experience tells us that without them, audits can take forever. Without an adequate sense of urgency, auditors have been known to drag out the planning phase of their audits interminably. Without time-phased, detailed audit programs, we allow ourselves to be distracted and delayed, or we move at a snail's pace or we simply stew in our difficulties and procrastinate. Everyone agrees that audits must be defined as "projects" and must be managed as such.

MANAGEMENT'S TIME ORIENTATION

The necessity of managing our own time on a project basis does not, however, give us the liberty to put senior management on a similar time schedule. In the days when our audits were mainly of the financial or compliance type, it made sense to expect auditees to respond to our findings in a relatively short period of time. The issues were relatively simple and straightforward, and thirty days provided ample time for auditees to verify the audit findings and to decide upon corrective action. But the situation has changed since we have broadened our audit scope to include operational issues requiring the attention of higher levels of management. Trouble is developing at the time interface between the audit function and management. Our project-oriented stopwatch ticks impatiently as management times its own movements by the slower chronometer of leadership.

What happens when an auditor hits upon a major management oriented finding? His excitement mounts as he works furiously to document his case. For him, time started when he initiated his audit and it will stop when the project is closed. The auditor feels that all must be resolved within a few days or weeks since he will soon be reassigned to another project. Nothing in the auditor's past training operates to remind him that he must now begin to conform to management's peculiar sense of time. The schedule he lays out for exit conferences, meetings to review the draft report, final report issuance, date of audit response and audit committee disclosure is incompatible with the pace management usually sets when it ponders a major issue. The result too often is that top management hears about the problem well before the lower levels of management are ready to discuss it systematically. Time pressure breeds psychological pressure which, in turn, breeds anxiety, fear and defensiveness. If sufficient organizational disruption develops, someone at the top inevitably concludes that reestablishing morale has become more important than resolving the audit finding. The finding is tabled and the auditing department is privately condemned as a troublemaker. It might have gone much better had auditing developed a more deliberate approach to the disclosure and resolution of problems.

AN ALTERNATIVE APPROACH TO DISCLOSURE

One alternative way to pace the disclosure of a major audit finding might be as follows. The auditing department segments its finding and focuses initially on a smaller, more manageable portion of the finding. Auditing communicates orally with certain key operating managers and lets it be known that its formal, written finding represents only a small part of a much larger problem. Auditing turns over copies of its documentation of the larger problem and invites operating management to conduct its own investigation. Auditing offers the use of its own resources, if needed, to assist management in its investigation. In effect, auditing transfers the initiative, and control over events, to operating management itself. Operating management feels it must cooperate with auditing in view of the latter's organizational status and access to senior management and the board. If it does cooperate, at least there will be no premature "surprises" causing embarrassment to those concerned.

What happens more often than not, at this point, is that operating management feels a need for auditing's expertise. Auditing is then invited to pursue its analysis of the problem and to make its detailed findings known without delay. Finally, agreement is reached concerning when and how senior management will be informed. When this takes place, operating management is ready and in control. Senior management's questions are readily answered and no one is unduly upset. When the matter has been thoroughly aired, chances are that the auditing department is favorably mentioned as having been "helpful."

By the time the board audit committee is involved, the "problem" has been converted to a management "action" or "improvement" aided by the auditing organization. Instead of concern, recriminations and embarrassment, what we have is warm exchanges of credit and congratulations. There is no doubt that this result is much to be preferred to what would have happened had auditing initiated instant disclosure at the highest levels.

Although the approach described above may appear to be somewhat idealized, its basic premise was inspired by actual internal audit experience. The approach provides food for thought for those of us steeped in the traditions of strict and immediate disclosure at the highest levels. There *may* actually be a better way. When the whole profession sets its mind to it, there is no telling how many successful variations that better way may take.

MANAGEMENT'S DEFINITION OF A "PROBLEM"

We have been commenting on the need for the internal auditor to understand and consider management's peculiar time orientation in developing a disclosure philosophy. Related to this, the auditor may also benefit from an understanding of how management's definition of a "problem" may differ from his own.

Let us assume that an internal auditor has identified what operating management agrees is a fairly serious control weakness. Corrective action was initiated one week prior to the end of the audit and will be completed in three months. Does a problem exist? Some would argue that a problem exists by virtue of the fact that management had not detected and corrected the control weakness on its own. Others would contend that management should not necessarily be faulted in this case, especially if its overall performance was adequate, since the detection of control weaknesses often requires expertise not possessed by the average manager. Still others would assert that a problem will continue to exist until corrective action has been completed.

What would senior management say? Does a problem exist as far as senior management is concerned? Probably the answer would be "no." To senior management, a problem is a defective condition which remains to be analyzed and for which appropriate corrective action has not yet been decided upon. Once the gears have been set in motion to correct a problem, senior management no longer views the matter as a problem. All that can be done has been done, and the matter has no further claim on their time and attention.

Management's view of what constitutes a problem helps to explain why lower-level auditees are often insistent that internal auditors notify them promptly of any major findings. Such auditees understand full well that major findings will have a much less disturbing effect on higher management if the audit report can say that corrective action has already been initiated.

What we have just discussed needs to be considered by internal auditors in the formulation of a sound disclosure philosophy. If internal auditors truly wish to improve operations and to maintain good auditee relations, they must give operating management every possible opportunity to initiate corrective action prior to issuance of the audit report. This will greatly increase operating management's motivation to undertake prompt action. Also, the audit report should disclose the finding in terms designed to minimize the psychological impact of the finding upon readers. This is justified for two reasons. First, by the time the audit report is issued, there is no longer a "problem" requiring action since action has already been taken. And second, the auditor owes it to the auditee, in return for his cooperation, to avoid causing him undue embarrassment. Let no one argue that such an arrangement between the auditor and the auditee is a violation of the auditor's sacred duty to disclose. It is no such thing. There is an old tradition in the auditing profession to the effect that findings should be disclosed at that level of management where effective action on the findings can be taken. This requirement has been fully met in the case under discussion. What is sometimes forgotten is that the requirement can usually be met at fairly low levels of management. The ethical imperative to disclose has been reinterpreted by some to mean that findings should be reported at a level where auditing can get sufficient visiblility* and auditees can get their well-deserved punishment.

CORPORATE DIRECTORS

Boards of directors have long been maligned for their alleged docility, passivity and extreme slowness in responding to new social conditions. Boards of directors may, in fact, exhibit the traits ascribed to them by social critics. However, they are not necessarily as culpable as the critics would imply. Again, it's a question of role.

---

*It is ironic that "ethical" concepts should so often turn out to be little more than precepts for self-advancement.

Under the law, boards of directors are responsible for directing the affairs of a corporation in accordance with its charter. As a practical matter, boards restrict their activities to the review and ratification of major policy proposals and business decisions, the giving of advice, the evaluation of management effectiveness and the appointment and removal of individual officers. The day-to-day operation of the business is given over to the officers of the corporation who are expected to do most of the planning, organizing, directing and controlling to ensure the corporation's success and long-term viability.

There can be no doubt that corporate directors view their first loyalty as being owed to the shareholders of the corporation. Second in their list of priorities is probably ties, commitments and obligations to each other and to certain senior members of management. Third, most boards of directors probably feel real loyalty to employees, certain customers and suppliers, and others who have contributed to the success of the enterprise over an extended period. And finally, directors generally feel an obligation to conform to the widely held expectations of society. With all of that, it remains that boards of directors will generally be very conservative in social and political outlook. This is because the role we have carved out for them is not to change society but to make it work as it is, here and now, while ensuring regular dividends and interest on our hard-earned savings.

Corporate boards of directors can, in fact, be extremely progressive but in a manner which is not generally appreciated. Their principal contribution to the advancement of society is in the economic sphere. They are the ones who promote and support the technological and institutional changes which make possible improvements in the way society extracts wealth from nature, produces goods and services, and distributes these goods and services at diminishing cost (in real terms) to all of us. It is the fantastic wealth generated by modern corporations which fundamentally accounts for our comfortable homes and fashionable clothes, our ample diets, our schools and hospitals, and the dissemination of culture and the arts. This is why boards of directors are politically so conservative. The rest of us feel that our economy will keep on producing all that wealth no matter how we abuse it and take it for granted. Corporate directors know better. They are close to the action and know how things work. They know how fragile the system really is. They understand that the bottom line can go from black to red in the blink of an eye. And if the bottom line stays in the red too long, there go our jobs, our dividends and bond interest, our bank savings, our pension plans, our insurance policies, our tax receipts, our public services, our everything!

NONINTERFERENCE WITH MANAGEMENT

The average employee of a corporation can go for years, perhaps for his entire career, without being aware of his company's board of directors. If, on the other hand, an employee rises to a high-level management or staff position, he becomes very much aware of that group of men and women who converge monthly upon the company from addresses near and far. The company's boardroom may, for lack of conference space, be available to the corporate staff on regular days. But on those special days when a board meeting takes place, access to the boardroom and its immediate surroundings is strictly controlled. Receptionists and guards communicate in hushed whispers as, inside, senior management accounts for its stewardship, answers questions and begs approval of business plans, capital expenditure proposals, and key personnel appointments.

Individuals fascinated by power have every reason to be impressed by the power of boards of directors. The resources commanded by this elite group of people are indeed immense, both in terms of capital and human talent. And yet, the power of corporate directors can be misunderstood by those who are not directly involved with them. The power wielded by corporate boards is largely formal. Boards exercise initiative only on rare occasions. Their normal mode of operation is to review and pass upon the initiatives of others. And by others, we are referring specifically to management.

The principal occasion when a corporate board does assume the initiative is in the selection of the chief executive officer. Good chief executive officers are not easy to find. When a concerned and sometimes frustrated board finally gets the man (or woman) it wants, it seldom can, or wishes to, exercise close control over him. The chief executive officer is usually better qualified to run the company than any other individual on the board.

For the board to closely control the chief executive would be to inhibit and impede the very creative abilities which led to his appointment in the first place. Nor would the chief executive officer himself wish to be closely controlled. Given the heavy responsibility placed upon him, he would insist that he be allowed the freedom and the initiative needed to fulfill that responsibility. This, then, is the commonsense basis for the principle of noninterference by the board in the management of the corporation. The principle may not be universally honored but it prevails more often than not. And the principle almost always holds true when the chairman of the board is also the company's chief executive officer. The full-time chairman is, in a very real sense, both management and the board of directors all wrapped up in one. This individual usually has the sincere admiration and affection of most members of the board. Why do we dwell on this? To understand correctly and realistically the position internal auditors are in when they report to the board. Boards of directors are not management bodies. Boards of directors seldom manage anything. When confronted with a problem, their instinctive reaction is to refer the problem back to management.

BOARD AUDIT COMMITTEES

Audit committees are a special committee of the board whose special responsibility is to oversee matters relating to financial accounting and corporate governance.

The principal functions of board audit committees are to recommend the appointment of an independent accountant, review the accounting policies and financial statements of the corporation, inquire into the adequacy of internal accounting controls and monitor policies and procedures relating to the ethical behavior of the corporation. In carrying out their responsibilities, board audit committees deal mainly with the controller, the independent accountant, the chief counsel and the director of audits. Of all the figures named here, the audit director is usually the most recent "arrival" and the most junior in rank and status.

The Instruments of the Board of Audit Committee

Assuming that a corporation is large, self-confident, and well-managed, the board audit committee will most likely view the controller as its principal instrument. It will have a high regard for the controller's opinion in most matters falling within the committee's jurisdiction, including the selection of an external auditor and the adequacy of internal accounting controls. The committee will then view the independent accountant as its next most important resource. The independent accountant represents the critical element of public acceptance. Keeping the independent accountant happy is serious business since his unqualified opinion of the company's financial statements is a necessary condition for the continued availability of investment capital, both debt and equity, on acceptable terms. Even assuming that a corporation had been held in high esteem for decades by the investment community, one can imagine what would happen to the market price of its stocks and bonds were word to leak out that a qualified accountant's opinion was in the offing.

Third on the board audit committee's list of important instruments will be the company's chief counsel. The chief counsel has special staff responsibility for "corporate governance." Corporate governance has to do with the conduct of the company's affairs in accordance with laws, regulations and generally accepted rules of business ethics. The chief counsel provides advice in these matters to the board, the board audit committee and management.

Fourth on the board audit committee's list of important instruments will be the director of audits. This should not be too surprising in view of the fact that his admission to the councils of the committee probably dates back only to 1980–81. Most audit directors have come to report to the audit committee only as a result of the FCPA. This legislation is very recent, was viewed as unnecessary by most of the business community and, until recently, was expected by many to be significantly diluted by subsequent amendments. In a word, the FCPA has been viewed as "a solution searching for a problem."

As if this were not bad enough, the internal auditor can't even claim exclusive jurisdiction over matters relating to the FCPA. Having a separate jurisdiction would at least provide the internal auditor with room to assert and express himself without affecting the others in attendance at board audit committee meetings. As fate would have it, however, the internal auditor does not have the initiative in either of the two areas with which he is concerned: accounting control and corporate governance. The initiative rests with the controller and the chief counsel.

One might say that at least the internal auditor is *independent* of the controller and the chief counsel. But there is ambiguity even here. Many internal auditors still report administratively to the controller. There is a serious question of how independent one can be of someone who is above him in the command mechanism regulating personnel, facilities, budgets and administrative policies. There is also a question of status. If the status of the internal auditor is significantly inferior to that of the controller, the outside auditor and the chief counsel, there may be severe limitations upon the internal auditor's freedom of expression. Finally, there is the matter of the chief executive officer who may be a regular participant at meetings of the board audit committee. Given the power this individual may have over the fate of the internal auditor, one must presume that his views could significantly influence the auditor's freedom of expression.

Tolerance for Disagreement

There is also a question of the board audit committee's ability to cope with disagreement. Although some research has been done in this area, more is needed.* In any case, every director of internal auditing must assess for himself the psychology and style of his own audit committee. Generally, one would expect audit committees to be at their cheerful best when their proceedings include mainly routine briefings, upbeat reports and favorable answers to ritual questions. Given the role of corporate directors, and their aversion to interference with management, it should come as no surprise that board audit committees should react with hesitation, consternation and even displeasure at the prospect of having to resolve a disagreement.

Should the internal auditor attempt to submit a problem to the board audit committee, the result might very well go as follows:

If the problem was deemed to be nonmaterial, the committee would disclaim interest in the matter and would fault the internal auditor's judgment in having brought it up.

If the problem was considered material, the committee would inquire whether management and the independent accountants were aware of the matter. If not, the committee would fault the internal auditor's judgment in not having discussed the problem with those concerned.

If the problem had been discussed with management and the independent accountants, it would come out that neither management nor the independent accountants agreed with the internal auditor. Privately, the audit committee would probably incline in favor of the position taken by management and the independent accountants. However, the committee would view it as its duty to call for a reconsideration of the matter.

The internal auditor would find himself having to discuss the problem with the same individuals and organizations he had worked with before. By the time agreement was achieved and was reported at the next meeting of the board audit committee, the internal auditor would probably have resolved to do everything possible to avoid a recurrence of this type of incident in the future. He would feel this way whether he won or lost the confrontation.

From the board audit committee's standpoint, the report it would

---

*Readers may be interested in two research projects performed by D. R. Finley, R. L. Grinaker, J. T. McMahon and R. F. Monger of the University of Houston College of Business Administration. One project, titled "Effectiveness of Corporate Audit Committees," was supported by a grant from the Peat, Marwick, Mitchell Foundation and was completed in 1978. The other project, "Conflict Resolution Styles and Audit Committee Effectiveness," was completed in 1979.

most want to receive at its next meeting is that the disagreement stemmed from a misunderstanding and that the matter had now been resolved to the satisfaction of all concerned.

WORKING WITH MANAGEMENT

What is to be concluded from the likely sequence of events discussed above? First, bringing up a problem to the board audit committee represents a failure of management (including the internal auditing function). Second, the board audit committee is not likely to address a problem on its own. It will refer the problem back to management. Third, those with the highest status will attempt to prevail. If they do prevail, they will claim to have been right. If they don't prevail, they will claim that there was a "misunderstanding." Fourth, the board audit committee will, rightly, avoid officially identifying winners and losers in order to maintain morale. Fifth, individual members of the board audit committee may make discrete private inquiries concerning the details of how the problem was resolved. But chances are that these private inquiries will not be addressed to the internal auditor.

The overall conclusion to be drawn by the internal auditor is that board audit committee meetings are an extremely awkward, if not hazardous, mechanism for the solution of problems. Board audit committees were not, in fact, created to solve problems. Their true function is to ensure that problems are solved by management. The wise internal auditor understands this and endeavors to work with management from the beginning, since he knows he will have to work with management in the end.

SERVICE TO THE ORGANIZATION

We have progressed far enough into our thesis that we are now ready to put the question of disclosure in overall perspective.

According to the *Statement of Responsibilities*, internal auditing is an independent appraisal activity established within an organization as a service to the organization. Note the general, even ambiguous, term "organization." The *Statement of Responsibilities* strongly implies that the client of the internal auditing function is, or can be, practically anyone in the organization. The *Statement* most certainly does not point to any official, committee or group as internal auditing's one and only client. Internal auditors may report functionally to the board audit committee, and administratively to the controller, financial vice-president, president or chairman, but these reporting relationships do not define or delimit those for whom the auditor may perform a service.

Internal auditing operates as a service to the entire organization. As a matter of fact, those to whom the auditor does report ask relatively little of him. The board audit committee is interested mainly in his annual assessment of the company's internal accounting controls and , perhaps, in his appraisal of corporate governance. If the auditor reports administratively to the financial vice-president, president or chairman, these officials typically will not ask him to perform a specific service much more often than once or twice a year.

One might say that the auditor performs an ongoing service to the board audit committee and/or to the president or chairman simply by sending them copies of his audit reports. But this is not usually the case. Very few auditors send copies of all their reports to senior management and/or to the board. Any busy senior official with a need to concentrate on his own concerns will soon tire of reading all reports produced by the internal audit department. As a rule, most internal auditors have learned to limit their communications to top management and the board to very brief summaries of things they need to know, or concerning which they need to take action.

DISCLOSURE OF AUDIT FINDINGS

It is interesting, and perhaps very meaningful, that IIA pronouncements appear to eschew the term "disclosure." The term is not to be found in either the *Statement of Responsibilities of Internal Auditing*, the *Standards for the Practice of Internal Auditing**, or the *Internal Auditing Code of Ethics*. Article 430 of the *Standards*, Communicating Results, is silent concerning who should receive reports of audit results. The article simply states that a signed, written report should be issued after the audit examination is completed and that the director of internal auditing, or designee, should review and approve the final audit report before issuance and should decide to whom the report will be distributed. *SIAS No. 2: Communicating Results*, does provide an interpretation of Article 430 but hardly in terms qualifying as hard-line:

> *430.07.2 Audit reports should be distributed to those members of the organization who are able to ensure that audit results are given due considera-*

**SIAS No. 2: Communicating Results*, does use the term twice in paragraph 430.07.3, the last paragraph in the *Statement. SIAS No. 2* is reproduced in its entirety in Appendix E.

tion. This means that the report should go to those who are in a position to take corrective action or ensure that corrective action is taken. The final audit report should be distributed to the head of each audited unit. Higher-level members in the organization may receive only a summary report. Reports may also be distributed to other interested or affected parties such as external auditors and audit committees. (Emphasis added.)

Note how *SIAS No. 2*, in stating that higher management may receive only summary reports, gives the internal auditor ample room to implement a disclosure policy designed to motivate operating management to solve problems and initiate prompt corrective actions.

Article 110 of the *Standards*, Organizational Status, states that the director of internal auditing should submit activity reports to management and to the board annually or more frequently as necessary, and that activity reports should highlight significant audit findings and recommendations. First, it is useful to distinguish between "activity" reports and reports of "audit findings and recommendations." Activity reports have to do with how audit resources were utilized and which areas of the company were covered by the audit program. Activity reports do not, in and of themselves, have to do with audit findings and recommendations. As concerns the actual reporting of audit findings and recommendations, one again has the feeling that the *Standards* are quite flexible. The words "highlight" and "significant" are used in a manner which appears to give the director of audits considerable latitude in reporting audit results. It is safe to say that it would be unwise and counterproductive to alarm senior management and/or the board (and to anger operating management) by reporting audit results in a manner that would resurrect problems that had already been effectively put to rest. Also, audit results can be reported in ways that will not alarm senior management or the board. For example, a problem which was promptly resolved by operating management can be reported not so much as an audit finding but as an operating improvement. This may appear to take credit away from internal auditing but really doesn't. In the long run, management's respect for internal auditing's generosity and good judgment will be worth much more than any short-term credit which may accrue from a dramatic "finding."

In any case, it is relevant to remind ourselves that the IIA *Standards for the Practice of Internal Auditing* are really a guide for the internal auditor and management. The *Standards* are quite general, provide considerable room for interpretation, are not compulsory and are subject to further change and refinement. Board audit committees, senior management, and directors of internal auditing must, ultimately, adopt modes of audit communications that work for their own organizations.

Styles of Disclosure

The style of audit communications adopted by an organization will depend upon the "culture" of the organization and the personalities and management styles of the key individuals concerned. Some organizations are marked by openness, candor, freedom of expression and a high capacity for self-examination. Such organizations are usually small, young, fast-growing, involved in highly competitive markets and relatively insulated from public or governmental interference. They enjoy unity of command at the top and a high degree of creativity at all levels. Such organizations have not yet developed a bureaucracy and therefore are less formal in their communications. There is no insistence that communications be perfect in every detail so long as the communications are found to be useful.

At the other extreme are the large, well-established, institutionalized and highly regulated organizations. These organizations are not permitted, either by the public or by the government, to make mistakes. As a result, there is a need to control communications in every detail. The idea is to maintain an official record that could withstand the most hostile public and regulatory scrutiny. In such organizations, tentative and exploratory communications are handled very informally by a trusted inner circle. After decisions are made, there follows a standardized sequence of formal communications designed to ratify, support and implement the decisions. All of these resulting communications are "perfect" in that they support decisions already agreed upon.

It's easy to see how internal auditors might have to handle "disclosure" very differently in the two types of organizations described above. In the first type, the auditors would work in a relatively forthright manner. They would perform their reviews, write their conclusions and recommendations, and send their reports to the appropriate levels of management. Management would evaluate the findings and accept or reject them as they saw fit. The findings which were accepted would not necessarily prejudice the careers of the auditees concerned. Nor would the findings which were rejected necessarily be held against the auditing department. Providing some good was accomplished, the exercise as a whole would be viewed as having been worthwhile.

In the second type of organization, however, the emphasis would be entirely different. Instead of being straightforward and forthright, the audit process would be more circumspect. Findings would be discussed orally and at some length with various levels of management before issuance of the final audit report. The report itself would be carefully scrutinized by many interests to ensure that the language was "proper." Oral agreements would be made that certain findings would be given immediate attention but that mention of them would be omitted, or considerably diluted, in the final report. The higher levels of management would receive only a summary report containing little that could be viewed as potentially embarrassing to the organization. If mention of the audit were made in the report to the board audit committee, it would be to the effect that the area concerned was reviewed, that it was generally acceptable and that certain suggestions for improvement had been made by the auditors and accepted by management—again, nothing specific to embarrass anyone, but visible evidence that a management review mechanism was in place and working effectively.

That a review mechanism is in fact in place and working effectively cannot be doubted in such cases. When we say that an audit approach is circumspect, we are not saying that it isn't effective. It most certainly is effective and its style is the only truly viable style for a large, established organization with a public and regulatory image to be maintained and lifetime careers to be protected. What counts is that operations and controls are being reviewed, honestly appraised and improved as necessary. The style in which audit results are communicated is of little practical consequence.

Convergence

There is considerable evidence that the second style of auditing described above is the one toward which much of the profession is now converging. Most internal auditors have probably felt subtle pressures to soften their audit communications so as to minimize psychological disturbance to the organization. It will be their challenge as professionals to find ways to do this without diminishing their effectiveness. Interestingly, if they succeed, their effectiveness may actually increase.

The Demand for Disclosure

In Part 1, we established that internal auditing is *internal* and that it is beholden to no one outside the organization. The role of internal auditing is what management and the board of directors want it to be. The duties of internal auditing are arrived at through a process of offer and acceptance as between the director of audits and his clients in the organization. We are now ready to extend the concept of offer and acceptance to the matter of disclosure.

Years ago when internal auditors were mainly financial auditors working exclusively for the controller, their client demanded detailed disclosure and the auditors complied. Detailed disclosure has since become such a long habit for many that they have forgotten how it all began. Disclosure has become a creed without any real relevance to today's reality. Many auditors simply feel that full and prompt disclosure to top management is what their work is all about. They view this as a fundamental ethical principle even though the code of ethics in no way defines the auditor's honesty, integrity and diligence in such narrow and specific terms.

In much the same way that management has the right to define the auditor's role, objectives and scope, management also has the right to define his disclosure responsibilities. How the director of audits handles disclosure depends on what the board and management tell him and what seems to work best for the organization. In other words, the auditor must identify the "demand" for disclosure in his company. What he must not do is to force his own disclosure habits or preferences upon an unwilling clientele. He must keep in mind that his role is changing. If disclosure once appeared to be the ultimate end of internal auditing, this is no longer true today. In a very real sense, internal auditing has joined management in a partnership and now shares responsibility with management in maintaining and improving the organization. Improving the organization is internal auditing's real goal in today's environment. Given this, disclosure must now be relegated to the status of a means, and must not be viewed as an end in itself. Internal auditing must design its disclosure processes to maximize the benefit to the organization.

Realistically, it is too much to expect the board and senior management to develop and promulgate a disclosure philosophy to be followed by the internal auditor. If management were to solve all of the auditor's problems for him this way, he would hardly have a claim to the executive-level salary he now enjoys. Management has a right to expect the internal auditor to develop an audit philosophy for the organization in the light of the organization's needs and preferences. This will not necessarily be an easy matter for the internal auditor, since he will most likely receive mixed signals. However, given sufficient time and trial and error, the auditor should eventually arrive at a formula that works.

Auditors Are Human

Once the auditor develops adequate sensitivity to "demand signals" by the board and management, he may end up being very surprised at what he learns. He may find out, for example, that senior management and the board are not nearly as interested in his detailed findings as he had thought. It will almost certainly be true that their eagerness to know does not match his eagerness to tell. Auditors are, after all, very human.

If they have worked hard and done a good job, they want to tell some-one about it. They want to be recognized and to be appreciated. This is why they want to think that senior management and the board are eager to learn their findings in every detail.

Internal auditors are human in still another way. They want to know that they matter. If they fail to secure prompt agreement from auditees, they feel justified in bringing their unresolved findings up to higher lev-els in the hope of setting off some tail-wringing. When this does happen from time to time, they are filled with elation at the realization that the senior levels do support them and that they do matter. However, it takes just a few such incidents for them to get the message that senior manage-ment fundamentally dislikes receiving appeals for help from the inter-nal auditors unless it is really necessary. This feeling is confirmed sooner or later when senior management goes out of its way to compliment the auditors for having resolved a difficult matter directly with the opera-ting managers concerned.

Auditing Management Performance

As we stated in the chapter on the role of internal auditing, internal au-diting is what internal auditing does. And what internal auditing does can vary widely from one company to another. In some companies, in-ternal audits are used specifically to evaluate the performance of indi-vidual managers and supervisors. This type of auditing of course "de-mands" a very systematic approach to disclosure. The auditor is not free to exercise much judgment in his handling of disclosure since this would affect the objectivity, reliability and completeness of his reports and would be inconsistent with the equal treatment of all managers reviewed. If this type of auditing is required by management, then it should be done. What should also be done, however, is to segregate this form of auditing and to avoid carrying over its strict disclosure conven-tions to other forms where the company stands to benefit from a more flexible and cooperative relationship between auditors and auditees.

Performance auditing makes sense in operating environments requir-ing meticulous observance of set policies and procedures and providing little latitude for creative initiative. It does not make sense in environ-ments characterized by change and the need to innovate. In such envi-ronments, one could almost say that the term "auditee" does not apply. The object of auditing is not so much the performance of people and or-ganizations as the adequacy of systems, processes, policies and proce-dures as these are found to operate across organizational lines. It is in this type of "functional" auditing that mutual cooperation between auditors and auditees is so important and can result in operational improvements of significant value to the company. The term "disclosure" can mean something entirely different in this type of cooperative auditing. Rather than referring to audit exceptions, it can refer to "accomplishments" achieved jointly by auditees and auditors.

Reporting to Senior Management

There is a difference between *working for* senior management and *reporting to* senior management. This is especially true in large organizations.

Years ago, when the internal auditor was part of the controller's organization and was concerned exclusively with accounting matters, he not only reported to the controller but he also worked for him. The auditor's agenda was directly influenced by the controller and it was natural for the controller to want to know the detailed results of the auditor's examinations. The auditor was, in effect, the controller's quality assurance arm, in addition to being an accounting control of last resort in such areas as accounts payable, checking accounts, inventories, ledger reconciliations and balance sheet verifications.

Today, many internal auditors neither report to the controller nor work for him. But they do work *with* him. As a member of the organization, the controller is one of the internal auditor's many clients and it is possible that the controller still wishes to receive copies of all audit reports relating to the accounting function.

Many internal auditors today *report to* the president but *work for* him only infrequently.* The fact that the internal auditor reports to the president does not mean that he should routinely disclose to the president the details of all audits performed in the accounting area. Of course, the president has a right to any information he wants and he need only ask for it. But the point is that it does not serve the president's own best interest for him to receive copies of all audit reports. First, the president should be much too busy with more important matters to concern himself with what should be, at his level, operational details best left to others. Second, any tendency on the president's part to monitor operations through the regular reading of audit reports will undermine the whole psychological structure of delegation of responsibility within the organization. Very few functional executives worth their salt will enjoy having

*This is not to imply that senior management should avoid giving assignments to the internal audit department. On the contrary, senior management often underutilizes the capabilities of the internal auditor. However, senior management should give the auditor considerable latitude in how he approaches his task and reports his findings in order to avoid unnecessary damage to audit relationships.

their boss look over their shoulder in this manner. When the inevitable confrontation occurs, the result may not be simply a change in the distribution of audit reports: it may be a narrowing of the auditor's scope! As we said earlier, if the audits director permits himself to be entrapped by an ill-advised disclosure philopsophy, forces will conspire to ensure that he has little to disclose. He will know this has happened to him when his budget is suddenly constrained and when he begins to receive advice concerning the need to "let up" on precisely those areas where auditing appeared to be making its most useful contribution. When this happens, the internal auditor should not bemoan senior management's lack of courage or lack of fidelity to the internal audit function. He should, instead, blame himself for having treated disclosure as the ultimate goal of internal auditing rather than as a means of achieving operating improvements. The world of business management can be extremely unforgiving. If an individual makes a serious error in judgement, he is seldom permitted to simply change his course and pick up where he left off. What happens more often than not is that doors are slammed shut and opportunities are lost forever.

Reporting to the Board

The ideas discussed in the previous section also apply to auditing's relationship to the board audit committee. There can be no doubt that the audit director should feel obliged to furnish to the audit committee any information it requests. When the committee assigns a specific project to the auditing department, auditing *works for* the audit committee. On the other hand, it's both very interesting and very significant to note the degree of restraint exercised by most audit committees with respect to audit information. Audit committees have, in the audits function, access to a truly impressive concentration of both factual and analytical information. Yet they rarely take advantage of this fact to delve into details of a company's operations. Audit committees are seen to be doing the same thing with respect to senior management that senior management does with respect to operating management: they seek to avoid time-consuming involvement in things best left to others; and they strive to respect the freedom and initiative of those to whom responsibility for managing the corporation has been delegated.

In short, internal auditing *reports to* the board. It does not *work for* the board except in unusual cases. This idea has real implications with respect to the disclosure of audit findings. What the board audit committee needs and wants from the internal auditing function can best be described as bottom-line reporting. It wants to be assured that accounting controls are adequate and performing properly. If they are not, it wants internal auditing to work effectively and constructively with management to bring controls up to par. The committee will not usually welcome an adverse report from internal auditing unless there is a very serious problem which cannot be resolved by working with management. This should happen very rarely, if ever, during the careers of most directors of internal auditing.

BOARD AUDIT COMMITTEE MEETINGS AS RITUAL

Many directors of internal auditing are frustrated by the disinclination of their board audit committees to engage in substantive, decision-oriented discussions. These audit directors may or may not be justified in their frustration. In any case, it is possible to construct a theory explaining why many board audit committee meetings are conducted the way they are. And, if the theory is found to fit the facts, some audit directors may be persuaded to abandon their frustration and to redirect their energies to more productive channels.

In the previous chapter on power it was affirmed that leadership is the most important function in society. The role of leadership is to promote and maintain those conditions necessary for social harmony and cooperation. One of those conditions is popular confidence in basic institutions, including economic institutions.

The 1970s saw a serious deterioration in popular confidence in the integrity of large corporations and the soundness of opinions expressed by certified public accountants. The U. S. Congress was sufficiently alarmed at this deterioration in confidence that it passed the Foreign Corrupt Practices Act in late 1977. One of the fundamental purposes of the act was to provide stronger guarantees that financial statements truly reflect the financial condition of publicly held corporations. The possibility of penalties against corporate officers and directors found guilty of fraud or negligence forced boards of directors to assume greater responsibility for the quality of financial reports and the adequacy of internal accounting controls.

How were board audit committees to discharge this responsibility? Given the fact that committee members were not full-time employees of the corporation, they could hardly be expected to verify financial statements and evaluate accounting controls personally. Their only recourse was to ensure the adequacy of the qualifications of the corporation's independent accountants and internal auditors, and also to ensure that these people were permitted to do their work with the necessary freedom. Once these conditions were firmly in place, many, if not most, audit committees were inhibited from going any further by the following considerations:

Time constraints

Lack of expertise

Reluctance to "interfere" in management

The perceived legal risks attaching to "overinvolvement"

Management's tendency to control the agenda of audit committee meetings, admit to few problems or weaknesses and foreclose discussion of detailed and/or sensitive matters.

These considerations notwithstanding, there was in most cases a real determination on the part of all concerned to comply both with the letter and the spirit of the FCPA. Whatever control weaknesses did exist were to be repaired quietly and without fanfare. Management was given rather firm instructions to protect board members from any possibility of embarrassment or legal penalty under the FCPA. Given this, board audit committee meetings became an important "ritual" symbolizing the board's and management's commitment to sound internal accounting controls. Although little of real significance was to take place at these meetings, the meetings were designed to be a continual reminder to management that significant things were assumed to be taking place inside the corporation. The ultimate beneficiaries of the rituals performed at audit committee meetings were to be the investing public. Board audit committee meetings represent a real form of social leadership whereby highly visible, knowledgeable and responsible figures go on record as testifying that all is well.

If board audit committee meetings are to be viewed in this light, it is clear what directors of internal auditing must do. It is simply this: do all that is necessary to ensure the truth and validity of the ritualistic message being communicated at board audit committee meetings. But do this outside of the committee meetings themselves in cooperation with management, independent accountants, corporate counsel and others concerned. If a problem *must* be brought up to the audit committee, it should first be discussed privately with the chairperson of the committee in a final attempt to avoid an open disruption of the committee's official ritual.

NEEDED: INTERNAL AUDIT EXECUTIVES

The ideas expressed in this chapter on the subject of disclosure may appear to be somewhat unorthodox. They may well be if we define "orthodox" as conforming to generally accepted doctrine reflected in the professional literature. Yet the current literature does not so much describe a disclosure doctrine as assume that one exists—somewhere. There is, in fact, very little on the subject that is detailed and specific. Perhaps this is so because internal auditors everywhere have been led to deviate from what they assume official doctrine to be. The result has been that few authors are inclined to address the subject with any candor.

The ideas in this chapter may not be unorthodox at all if we compare them with *actual* professional practice rather than with an *assumed* doctrine. The ideas may not yet reflect majority practice, but they do represent a valid school of disclosure already existing and thriving in the field today. Partisans of this school have not been very vocal and they need to be encouraged to speak up. It's becoming increasingly clear that senior management and board audit committees will soon be insisting upon having executive-caliber internal audit leaders capable of distinguishing between surface appearances and underlying reality. The profession will have to produce real internal audit executives from within if it is to avoid losing command of its own ranks to general executives from outside the profession. The matter of disclosure is very close to the center of the evolutionary process which the profession is currently undergoing. Internal audit executives devoted to the welfare of their organizations, as well as to the advancement of their profession, must see to it that disclosure practices are shaped to fit the needs of the emerging audit environment.

SUMMARY

The first concern of every chief executive is the smooth working of his top executive team.

Management needs to be in charge in order to fulfill its responsibilities.

Management's foremost challenge is leadership.

Management dislikes surprises because surprises represent a loss of control over events.

Internal auditing has become increasingly involved in corporate leadership without benefit of a positive theory to support its actions.

Helpful auditing consists in allowing management to maintain the initiative.

Internal auditors need to interface with management on the basis of management time—not audit time.

Management has its own peculiar definition of what constitutes a "problem."

Boards of directors are extremely hesitant to interfere in the day-to-day management of the corporation.

Board audit committees are a poor mechanism for solving problems. Their true role is to ensure that problems are solved by management.

There is a difference between working for someone and reporting to someone. Internal auditing reports to senior management and the board but seldom works for them.

The internal auditor is not the ultimate arbiter of what audit disclosure should be in his corporation. He must base his disclosure patterns on the "demand" for disclosure within the organization.

Disclosure is a means—not an end in itself.

Internal audit executives must see to it that disclosure practices fit the needs of the emerging audit environment. The official pronouncements of the IIA give audit directors considerable latitude in this area.

DISCUSSION

This and the previous chapter explore a number of difficulties experienced by internal auditing as it is practiced today. It's as if internal auditing is continually on the verge of being punished for doing what it believes it is being paid to do.

It takes little reflection to realize that many of internal auditing's problems relate directly or indirectly to the matter of disclosure. What is needed is a fresh appraisal of disclosure practices unencumbered by assumptions, slogans and cliches inherited fom the past. One might say that the internal auditing profession should perform an objective operational review of its own disclosure practices.

In our earlier chapter on power, reference was made to the perceived negative forces arrayed against internal auditing and of internal auditor's desire for more power to overcome these forces. An objective appraisal of this condition might well conclude that the negative forces in question are largely generated by the audit process itself.

The reason internal auditing may be generating resistance to its efforts is that its methods are inconsistent with the corporation's existing pattern of leadership. Let us consider the matter of audit disclosure from the standpoint of operating management and the auditee. An audit is declared. Internal auditing is not bound by any obvious materiality standard nor must it include all aspects of an operation in its scope. Many internal auditors reserve the right to report only and all adverse findings to higher management whether or not the findings were resolved and whether or not corrective action was taken. Reports are written in a manner inviting higher management to draw unfavorable conclusions concerning the performance of operating management and auditees. Reports addressed to the board audit committee may invite the committee to draw a similar conclusion concerning senior management. Granted that this description of disclosure practice does not apply equally to all internal audit departments. However, anything approaching this description makes internal auditing a no-win game for too many managers and auditees. Higher management may at first appear to encourage forthright and uninhibited disclosure of the type we have described. But as favored subordinates and even higher management itself begin to feel threatened, the inevitable result is a constraining of internal auditing's scope to only such areas as are specifically targeted by management.

The new internal auditing proposes to make interaction with the audit function a more attractive proposition for operating management and auditees. It proposes to essentially cut off adverse disclosure at the point where assurance of corrective action is provided. Adverse disclosure to higher levels for purely *informational* purposes will be curtailed to the fullest extent permitted by management and the board audit committee.

CHAPTER 7

Independent Accountants

Facts and figures! Put 'em down!

CHARLES DICKENS, *The Chimes*

The public accounting profession has accumulated an enormous amount of prestige since its early origins in Scotland in the mid-nineteenth century. This prestige is entirely deserved given the profession's enviable record for honesty, integrity and diligence in the service of its clients and the preservation of the public trust.

ORIGINS OF A MYTH

It has been estimated that approximately 20%–25% of practicing internal auditors are also certified public accountants. These auditors are aware of the status attaching to the public accounting profession and are therefore inclined to point with pride to their origins in that profession. Somehow the fact that many leading internal auditors come from public accounting has led to the myth that internal auditing itself comes from public accounting. Internal auditing has become accepted by many as being the stepchild of the public accounting profession. It is true that internal auditing owes a great deal to public accounting, but its debt is not that of son to stepfather. Rather, it is that of a brother to his younger sibling who left home and made good.

SOME HISTORY

Both history and common sense tell us that there were large numbers of internal accountants and internal auditors long before the first public accountant was ever chartered. Archeologists have unearthed evidence of accounting and internal auditing activity as far back as ancient Mesopotamia. Public accounting, on the other hand, came into being largely as a result of the Industrial Revolution. When the cottage system of manufacturing gave way to the factory system, there was a need to attract large sums of money from banks and the investing public. Since firms selling stocks and bonds had an interest in presenting themselves in the best possible light, their financial statements were not always an accurate portrayal of their true financial condition. What was needed was an independent appraisal of the financial condition of firms seeking outside capital. The public accounting profession arose in response to this need.

The first unit of the Institute of Chartered Accountants of Scotland was established in 1854. England and Wales established their Institute in 1880 and Ireland followed suit in 1888. The title of Certified Public Accountant (CPA) and requirements for certification were first created in the United States by the state legislature of New York in 1896. It wasn't until 1923 that all states (including the District of Columbia) had enacted legislation providing for the title CPA to be conferred on individuals on the basis of a written examination and acceptable education and work experience.*

Public accounting can rightfully claim that it acquired *professional* status well before internal auditing, since the Institute of Internal Auditors was incorporated only in 1941 and the Certified Internal Auditor (CIA) designation was not established until 1972.† The fact remains, however,

---

Encyclopedia Britannica, 200th anniversary ed., "Accounting," pp. 78–82.
†*Foundations For Unlimited Horizons*, Victor Z. Brink, PhD, CIA, CPA, The Institute of Internal Auditors, Inc., Altamonte Springs, Florida, 1977.

that the private practice of accounting and auditing came well before its public practice, and the earliest public accountants underwent their original apprenticeship under private accountants.

The purpose of this discussion of origins is not to establish the preeminence of private over public accounting or auditing. Rather, it is to remind the internal auditor that he is heir to a history and tradition that has nothing to do with public accounting. Public accounting has, in recent years, been repaying an old educational debt by providing excellent training to thousands of men and women destined to become management accountants and internal auditors. Public accounting has also been responsible, ever since the enactment of the FCPA, for encouraging boards of directors and management to make better use of their own accountants and internal auditors. Fairness, decency and a forgiving spirit require that we show proper appreciation for the support our public accounting brethren have given us in recent years. We say "forgiving spirit" because it's not as if the public accountants were our greatest admirers prior to 1977. Again, our purpose here is not to add fuel to an already excessive rivalry but to encourage internal auditors to be themselves, to think for themselves and to stop looking at their mission, role and scope through the eyes of a separate profession that was created mainly to provide an independent opinion of their employers' financial statements.

COMPARING INTERNAL AUDITORS AND CPAs

It will be a great day for our profession when internal auditors can attend a cocktail party, say that they are internal auditors, and not be asked how their work compares with that of CPAs.

The comparison of internal versus external auditing is unfortunate in that it perpetuates a rivalry between the two professions that is pointless at best and counterproductive at worst. Internal auditors with CPA credentials are particularly sensitive when asked to explain how they differ from public accountants. They too often end up by stressing the similarities rather than the differences between the two professions and go through considerable pain to defend their independence within the organization. Public accountants, on the other hand, steadfastly maintain that internal auditors are not independent and that their work cannot be relied upon unless it has been reviewed and accepted by qualified outside CPAs. The pointless argument goes on and on and is perpetuated by every new generation of internal auditors and public accountants.

Two things will have to take place for the argument to be settled.

First, internal auditors will have to let go of any vestigial regret they may still harbor at not being full-time public accountants. When they succeed in doing this, they will truly see and appreciate the unique opportunities offered by internal auditing and will no longer wish to have internal auditing compared with another profession. Once internal auditors have given up their rivalry with the independent accountants, the latter will have no one to debate with and will abandon the issue. Second, the academic community will hopefully increase its understanding of internal auditing and will recognize it as a distinct field not to be "compared" with public accounting. Whether taught formally in specialized courses, or merely referred to casually in accounting courses, internal auditing needs to be described accurately to college and university students. Internal auditing is not merely external auditing conducted within the firm. And there *is* a vast difference between internal control as addressed by internal auditors and accounting control as addressed by independent accountants.

EMULATING THE INDEPENDENT ACCOUNTANTS

No matter what is said about internal auditors needing to seek their own destiny, a considerable number of internal auditors will still insist upon emulating the independent accountants. If this is done, then let it be done well.

Let us go back to the time of the Industrial Revolution. Tradition tells us that the skilled and experienced internal accountant was regarded with considerable respect by his employer. The accountant typically had above-average intelligence and education. He was thorough and systematic and capable of highly disciplined thinking and analysis. Most important, he had access to the big picture at a time when even basic financial information was kept from everyone else. As a result, many accountants served as advisors to their employers, providing insights and formal studies concerning ways to increase the profitability of their firms. This tradition was maintained by those accountants who left private employment to become public accountants. In the course of plying their principal trade, they could not help but notice that their clients were experiencing many problems outside of the accounting area. In view of the goodwill they had developed over the years, it was logical for public accountants to broaden the range of services offered to their clients. Both sides stood to gain. The CPA firms had an opportunity to increase their revenues and clients would have access to highly professional and reliable consulting services. There is a very simple reason why the management advisory services of CPA firms have been so successful. CPA firms are trusted by their clients. They have continuity and they have a reputation to maintain. They can't afford to tarnish that reputation by selling their clients a bill of goods.

It's quite revealing to consider how the development of internal auditing has paralleled the development of public accounting—if we define the public accounting field as including management advisory services. In the course of performing their audits, internal auditors could not help but become acquainted with numerous problems experienced by their employers outside the accounting area. There were problems in the areas of administration, planning, budgeting, and compliance with policies, procedures, laws and regulations. There were also many problems relating to operational effectiveness and efficiency. Internal auditors had intimate knowledge of their companies' operations. They had a proven capacity for thorough and systematic analysis. And they had acquired a fine reputation for honesty, objectivity and diligence in the performance of their duties. Internal auditors saw an opportunity to increase their contribution to the welfare of their organizations by extending their services beyond the accounting area. Both sides stood to gain. Internal auditors saw their departments increase in size and diversity while employers acquired a knowledgeable and flexible in-house resource with which to address a variety of problems. If this was done in imitation of the CPA firms, it was indeed the sincerest form of flattery.

RELATIONSHIP BETWEEN THE PROFESSIONS

Most CPA firms would willingly concede that they derive considerable reassurance from their clients' support of a well-staffed internal audit function. Such an internal audit function can significantly reduce the risk incurred by the CPA firm in issuing its opinion. Considering the pressure on external audit fees, the attitudes many corporations have toward independent accountants, the increasing incidence of large-scale fraud and the tendency of investors to blame independent accountants for not detecting fraud, CPA firms need all the help they can get. Therefore, there is no reason why independent accountants and internal auditors should not enjoy a cooperative and mutually beneficial relationship. Yet their interaction is too often marked by polite suspicion and even hostility. Why? There are many possible reasons.

Qualifications of the Internal Audit Staff

There was a time, not so long ago, when the chief grievance that independent accountants had against internal auditors was that they weren't "qualified." The complaint arose when corporations encouraged their internal audit departments to displace some of the work being performed by independent accountants in order to reduce external audit fees. The hiring of sizable numbers of CPAs in recent years has effectively neutralized the "qualifications" issue in most cases. Adoption by internal auditors of the independent accountants' working-paper procedures and conventions has also helped to improve the coordination of internal and external audit work.

Competition for Work

There can be little doubt that the desire of board audit committees to reduce external audit fees has had the effect of pitting internal auditors against external auditors. Internal auditors saw an opportunity to expand their staffs while external auditors viewed this as cutting into their business volume and revenues. The matter has been pretty much settled by management's unswerving determination to hold down external audit fees, tempered by the external auditor's own insistence that the overall conditions of his engagement should permit an adequate and independent appraisal of financial records and accounting controls.

Competition for Status

One issue that remains unresolved between external and internal auditors is that of relative status. Still another problem, related to the status issue, is the fear each has that he may be judged adversely by the other in a manner that may influence management and the board audit committee. In a sense, external and internal auditors are vying for the affections of the board audit committee, and each side wishes to avoid being damaged by the other. This is presumably why external auditors are often reluctant to share information concerning their audit programs and working papers with internal auditors. This is also why internal auditors are not attracted to the idea of peer reviews by external auditors.

There is no doubt that internal auditors are currently seeking their place in the sun. There is also little doubt, in the opinion of this author, that they will find that place in the sun. This author also believes that when things have settled into place the independent accountants will be the first to admit that they approve of the result. How can enlightened public accounting firms avoid unnecessary friction with their partners in the internal audit department? The answer is quite simple: avoid projecting a restricted view of the role of internal auditing.

Either on their own initiative, or with the tacit approval of board audit committees, too many external auditors have adopted the attitude that internal auditors are merely an extension of themselves in the client organization. It's true that some internal audit organizations were created, or greatly expanded, primarily at the urging of independent accountants following the enactment of the FCPA. It's true that many internal audit organizations place members of their staff under the supervision of the independent accountants for a number of weeks during the annual external audit. It's also true that many internal audits are undertaken at the specific request of the independent accountants. But none of this supports the conclusion that internal auditors are somehow a less qualified, inferior version of the external auditor. In fact, this view can easily be demonstrated to militate against the best interests of all concerned—the board audit committee, management, independent accountants and internal auditors. For those who may consider these comments to be farfetched, let us cite an actual case of an unfortunate relationship between internal auditors and independent accountants.

A Review of Internal Controls

An Eastern manufacturer of luxury consumer goods suffered millions in losses from hedge transactions undertaken with an investment broker. Although the transactions were profitable on paper, the broker was undercapitalized and had insufficient resources to fulfill his contracts. In the ensuing investigation of the losses, the board audit committee asked the independent accountants why their audits had not detected the fact that a significant item in the company's balance sheet had been of questionable value. The accountants took the position that the transactions involved had been duly authorized and approved by management and that there had been no weakness in accounting control. There had been a weakness in *administrative* control in that there had not been an adequate review of the creditworthiness of the investment broker by the company. However, such administrative controls did not fall within the purview of financial audits performed by independent accountants, or so it was asserted.

The independent accountants made two recommendations to the board audit committee: first, a special group should be created within the controller's organization to review, evaluate and monitor the adequacy of "internal controls"; second, steps should be taken to strengthen the company's internal audit department.

Months later, after the internal audit department was reorganized and strengthened under a new director, the board audit committee requested that the audit department conduct its own review and evaluation of the company's "internal controls." The audit director reviewed the AICPA's and the IIA's pronouncements on the nature of internal control and took special note of the distinction between accounting and administrative controls. He knew that the newly created group in the controller's department had concerned itself almost exclusively with accounting controls, following the method of analysis recommended by the company's independent accountants. The audit director also knew that the company's major loss which had triggered the board's concern over internal controls had been attributed to poor *administrative* control. For these reasons, he elected to interpret the board audit committee's request as relating to internal control as broadly defined in AICPA and IIA pronouncements. Since, in fact, little time had been allotted for his review, he decided to give special emphasis to administrative controls.

The internal auditor completed his assignment and issued a balanced report covering all of the control areas reviewed, including the overall control climate. Although two-thirds of the areas were rated as satisfactory, one-third were rated as requiring improvement. The board audit committee, hoping against hope that its internal control problems were over, was exasperated by the internal auditor's report and asked management and the independent accountants to comment. Both replied in effect that the internal auditor's report was mistaken and asserted that "internal controls" were entirely adequate.

In a later meeting with the company's independent accountants, the internal auditor was roundly criticized on two points: he had not "cleared" his report with the independent accountants, and he had not conformed to the independent accountants' definition of "internal control" as being synonymous with "internal accounting control." By concluding that certain internal controls needed improvement, the internal auditor had made both the independent accountants and management look bad since they had previously, unknown to the new audit director, certified internal controls to be in first-class shape.

The internal auditor attempted to pacify the independent accountants by pointing out that his conclusions concerning certain *administrative* controls did not in fact contradict management's and the CPA's conclusions concerning *accounting* controls, and that the problem appeared to be one of semantics. The scope of internal auditing was much broader than that of external financial auditing. Because of this, internal auditors understood accounting control to constitute only a part of the overall system of control and were in agreement with AICPA pronouncements on this matter. Also, internal auditors were not bound by the same materiality criteria that applied to external audits.

One might think that the disagreement between the internal and external auditors would have been satisfactorily resolved. In fact, it wasn't. It couldn't—because reputations were at stake. Needless to say, the eventual loser was the organization with the least status. Who that was can be inferred from the following facts:

> Management and the independent accountants had held the internal audit function in low regard for years.
>
> The decision to strengthen the audit department was made at the suggestion of the independent accountants. In a sense, internal auditing was a creature of the independent accountants.
>
> The independent accountants regularly employed internal auditors, under their supervision, to perform their annual audit.
>
> It was assumed by all concerned that a planned peer review of the internal audit function would be performed by the independent accountants.
>
> The independent accountants had full access to internal auditing's working papers. On the other hand, internal auditing's occasional requests for information concerning external audit test results were granted with great reluctance.
>
> Meetings of the board audit committee were dominated by the independent accountants.

Not in the Same Business

The case outlined above is a classic illustration of what can happen when internal auditing is viewed as being in the same business as the independent accountants. Such a view sets up internal auditing in a competition it can't win. No matter what the qualifications, skills and experience of the internal audit staff may be, the function is fated to walk in the shadow of its "independent" counterpart whose judgments and opinions have an influence on the outside world and, therefore, are the only ones that count in the eyes of management and the board.

If the board audit committee is seen as internal auditing's only client, much of what internal auditing can and should be will be nipped in the bud. The function will not produce anything of real value if it is restricted to the scope and materiality criteria of the independent accountants. Many thoughtful speakers from the public accounting profession have cautioned their audiences to avoid simplistic dividing lines between accounting controls and other controls. Accounting controls, no matter how well designed, can never provide an adequate defense against all problems. Control problems often start in the "administrative" area only to affect the accounting area later in unexpected ways.

Exclusive preoccupation with accounting controls shows evidence of a Maginot Line mentality. Organizations with this mentality will continue to experience periodic traumas until they learn the advantages of having at least one internal activity in a position to provide early detection of problems before they affect internal accounting control and become "material." This is an important theoretical justification for the unlimited scope of internal auditing.

If public accountants must view internal auditors as an extension of themselves, they should view them not as front-line troops under their command but as advance scouts recruited from the local environs under a loose cooperative agreement. Since there is a psychological barrier imposing limits upon the size of internal audit staffs, the decision to make internal auditors "git and fetch" for the outside accountants should be made reluctantly by management. The opportunity cost of the lost services of the internal auditors will usually be much greater than the savings in external audit fees.

The best way for independent accountants to utilize internal auditors is to review the results of their work for the information it provides about the overall system of control, including internal accounting controls. Also, it would be entirely constructive and economic to occasionally sugest that the internal auditing department perform in-depth reviews of specific areas that the outside auditors are interested in, provided the latter have confidence in internal auditing's objectivity and are free to perform corroborative tests as necessary. Since internal auditors enjoy challenging work, and are always seeking support to perform thorough reviews of significant areas, they will usually be more than willing to honor such requests from their independent accountants.

As often happens, closely allied groups bicker among themselves while the real enemy is forcing the barricades. Independent accountants and internal auditors have vied for prestige and competed for the audit dollar while society has been losing confidence in its economic institutions. The time has come for internal auditing and public accounting to accept each other as distinct professions each with its own mission, role and scope but having a common interest in internal accounting control as well as in administrative controls relating to accounting control.

SUMMARY

Internal accounting and auditing trace their history back thousands of years. Public accounting's history goes back only to the nineteenth century. It is therefore erroneous to view internal auditing as having originated from public accounting.

The mission, role and scope of internal auditing is different from that of public accounting. Internal auditors need a stronger sense of their own identity. Colleges and universities need to do a better job in defining and teaching internal auditing.

The scope of the modern internal audit department can be compared to the scope of the modern public accounting firm *if* the latter's management services department is included.

Internal auditing and public accounting will get along better if they acknowledge and respect each other as distinct professions. To view internal auditing as an inferior extension of public accounting is contrary to the best interests of public accountants, internal auditors, management and boards of directors.

Public accountants should conform to their own AICPA pronouncements and avoid using "internal control" interchangeably with "internal accounting control."

DISCUSSION

The new internal auditing has an interest in seeing an end to the rivalry between internal auditors and independent accountants. Internal auditors and independent accountants meet mainly on the common ground of internal accounting control which comprises only a small fraction of the actual and potential scope of internal auditing.

Internal auditors and independent accountants share two common clients: the board audit committee and the controller. But while the board audit committee and the controller are the only clients of the independent accountants, internal auditing has many more actual and potential clients elsewhere in the organization.

Internal auditors are wrong in comparing their independence with that of external auditors. For this reason, they should be prudent in displacing work formerly performed by the external auditors. If carried too far, the process of displacement could threaten external auditors' ability to render an informed and truly independent opinion concerning the corporation's financial statements. Ultimately, this would damage the interests of all concerned, including the internal auditors.

It is ironic that independent accountants should continue to project a narrow image of internal auditing when this so clearly runs against their own best interests by leaving little room for internal auditing to grow except by competing for the work normally done by the independent accountants themselves. After independent accountants judge that internal auditing has acquired sufficient involvement in matters of internal accounting control, they should encourage board audit committees and management to expand internal auditing's scope to the areas of administrative control, management control and operations. Any improvements achieved in these areas by internal auditors will ultimately bolster and strengthen internal accounting control and will reduce the likelihood that independent accountants will ever have to issue a qualified opinion.

It is interesting to note that systems for the evaluation of internal accounting controls so vigorously promoted by CPA firms after the enactment of the FCPA did little or nothing to prevent the rash of qualified opinions issued on the statements of a number of nuclear electric utilities in the spring of 1984. There is no way of telling whether stronger internal audit programs might have improved matters in these utilities. What is clear, however, is that internal audit scrutiny of nuclear contracts and construction would have been of much greater relevance to emerging problems than general corporate reviews of internal accounting control.

CHAPTER 8

Quality Assurance Reviews

It is much easier to be critical than to be correct.

BENJAMIN DISRAELI, January 24, 1860

A USELESS QUESTION

Few things are as useless as a board audit committee chairperson asking the independent accountant and the internal auditor, sometimes with both of them in the same room, what each thinks of the other's work. Readers collectively will know dozens of cases when a reply might have been made but was not. The writer has heard of only a single case when an adverse comment was offered, by the internal auditor, and it had absolutely no effect that could subsequently be determined.

QUALITY ASSURANCE REVIEWS BY INDEPENDENT ACCOUNTANTS

Internal and external auditors should not be asked to comment on each other's performance for a very simple reason: they work together and are trying to get along as best they can. They may or may not be objective in appraising each other, and they almost certainly lack freedom to express their views. In line with this, independent accountants should not conduct quality assurance reviews of internal audit organizations with whom they have to work. They should be presumed to lack objectivity and freedom. Quality assurance reviews performed by CPA firms can have only two possible results: they will either whitewash any significant opportunities for improvement and deal mainly in trivia, or they will in fact say something significant and earn the undying enmity of their former friends. Perhaps the greatest risk is that something might need to be said to management concerning its use of the internal auditing function but won't be.

QUALITY ASSURANCE REVIEWS BY INTERNAL AUDITORS

This author may be ahead of his time in saying so, but here goes: reviews of internal auditors should be conducted neither by independent accountants nor by other internal auditors. They should be conducted by the management advisory services departments of unrelated CPA firms and, perhaps later, by general business consultants who have developed a suitable capability. Why shouldn't internal auditors perform peer reviews of each other? The question is silly and the answer is obvious. All internal auditors know each other through professional and industry associations, and asking them to comment objectively and freely on each other's performance is like asking doctors to testify against each other in court—an awkward thing at best.

QUALITY ASSURANCE REVIEWS BY THE IIA

Proposals have been put forward in recent months for peer reviews of internal audit departments to be conducted by the IIA itself. Although these proposals have a certain superficial attractiveness, there are disadvantages. First, peer reviews by the IIA will, at least in some cases, tend to pit the IIA against its own members. Second, having its prestige on the line, the IIA will tend to conduct peer reviews in a very safe and conservative manner, focusing mainly on administrative and procedural details and eschewing the substantive judgements that are the hallmark of truly progressive business consulting. Third and most important of all, peer reviews by the IIA will inhibit the evolution of internal auditing by tending to standardize and enforce the status quo. The IIA will have great difficulty in entertaining new ideas while supporting old ones through highly visible involvement in quality assurance reviews.

THE BEST CANDIDATES

To return to our thesis, the best candidates to conduct quality assurance reviews of the internal audit function at this time are the management advisory services departments of public accounting firms having no ongoing audit relationship with the companies concerned. There are a number of reasons why this idea makes the most sense. First, the question of objectivity is neatly resolved. The reviewer is free to do a good job without fear of damaging an important business relationship. Second, the reviewer does have access to financial accounting and auditing expertise from within its own firm. This ensures that the board audit committee's interest in internal accounting control will be fully provided for. Third, the reviewer's broad management orientation provides a greater likelihood that it will properly and correctly address the full scope of the internal auditing function. All that is necessary is that the management advisory services group have acquired credible expertise specifically in internal auditing as correctly defined.* Considering the many excellent people currently entering (and leaving) the field, this should pose no particular problem in the years ahead. This author sincerely hopes that leading management advisory services groups throughout the country will aggressively exploit this promising area of opportunity. The involvement of many advisory services groups in internal audit quality assurance reviews will provide healthy diversity and competition, promote consulting excellence and innovation and afford the internal audit profession leeway to explore new ideas and to grow.

NEED FOR NEW APPROACHES

Consulting organizations desiring to enter the field of internal audit quality assurance reviews will not have the problem of developing basic

---

*The group should be composed largely, though not exclusively, of CIAs.

evaluation criteria from scratch. The Institute of Internal Auditors has already published three manuals on the subject* and may offer still more material in the future. However, there will still be considerable room for the development of new and creative approaches by individual review services. Too many peer reviews conducted thus far by public accountants have used a cookbook approach lacking in depth and insight. Principal emphasis has been on the evaluation of audit working papers: something the CPAs are expert in and can really sink their teeth into. Not that internal auditors don't need to improve their work habits. They do, but the point can be overdone in areas outside of financial auditing. It's a case of not being willing or able to evaluate the bottom line and concentrating instead on the neatness with which the figures in the column have been entered. This is a weakness we internal auditors are quick to spot in others since we are so often guilty of it ourselves.

BALANCED REPORTING

In the matter of balanced reporting the CPAs have really done the internal auditors a favor. Consider the following account: Company X's audit director retired and was replaced by a new director with a clear mandate for change. The auditing staff was soon transformed into a confident, cooperative and effective team. The director personally conducted in-house training programs, supported attendance at IIA chapter meetings and conferences, and organized an in-house CIA review course to be taught by leading members of the staff and selected guest instructors drawn from other departments of the company. The director met formally with each auditing section twice a month for a thorough discussion of audits in progress. Until such time as the staff's report writing skills were sufficiently improved, the director personally participated in the review and final crafting of every audit report. Since the director had considerable experience with other auditing organizations, she was in a good position to judge that her new department was good—and getting better with each passing day.

After about two years, the board audit committee decided it was time for a quality assurance review. The project was given to the company's independent accountants. To assist the accountants in conducting a fair

---

*Alan S. Glazer, PhD and Henry R. Jaenicke, PhD, CPA, *A Framework for Evaluating an Internal Audit Function*, 1980; Urton Anderson, *Quality Assurance for Internal Auditing*, 1983; Professional Standards and Responsibilities Committee, *Quality Assurance Review Manual for Internal Auditing*, 1984. All published by the Institute of Internal Auditors, Altamonte Springs, Florida.

and balanced evaluation, the audit director gathered a wealth of information documenting the audit and administrative achievements of the department. The accountants completed the IIA checklist, conducted a thorough working papers review of a selected sample of audits and interviewed a number of key company executives. At the exit interview, the head of the review team confided to the audit director and one of her supervisors: "You're a good department—very good, in fact. But few people are aware of it yet." There followed a brief discussion of six or so minor exceptions to which the head of the review team appeared to attach little real importance. The audit director was satisfied that the reviewers had a balanced understanding of the strong and weak points of her department and looked forward to receiving the final report.

When the final report did arrive, the audit director and her staff were flabbergasted! The report did not at all convey the impression created in the exit interview. After describing the objectives and scope of the engagement, the report offered a flabby opinion to the effect that the department was adequate overall, made very brief reference to improvements in morale and effectiveness and had nothing to say about the quality of audit results achieved. The bulk of the report was devoted to a lengthy and detailed discussion of the six minor exceptions, making them appear as very serious operational deficiencies. One of the supervisors exclaimed: "Boss, we worked like hell for two years to really improve this department, and as far as I'm concerned we succeeded and it's now one of the best in town. You'd never know that from reading this report." The audit director, who had her own agenda for further improvement in the months ahead, said to her supervisor: "Bill, you've been wondering why I've been after you and your auditors to improve the balance in your reports. You've just been audited, and you've been written up exception style. How do *you* like it?" The supervisor was dumbfounded and slapped his own face. "I'll be damned," he said, "now I know what you've been trying to tell me these past months. I'll never do this to anybody again."

And how did the board audit committee react to the exception report? Just as we would expect. The overall judgment of adequacy and the brief positive statement concerning morale and effectiveness were not noticed. The report did not contain a single reference to the many positive audit achievements of the department. The audit committee chairman was drawn into a detailed discussion of the six exceptions and the audit director was requested to outline her plans for improvement. Nothing in the proceedings provided any basis for the conclusion that the auditing department had, in fact, strived mightily to serve its employer well during the past two years. The company had a long tradition of contempt for the internal audit function and the peer review had done little to upset that tradition.

As was said at the beginning of this narrative, the public accountants have done internal auditors a favor with their exception-style peer reviews by confronting them with the perversity and hardheartedness of their own traditional audit style. But now that internal auditors have learned their lesson and have resolved to reform their attitudes and practices, they are ready to be treated as they propose to treat others —with fairness and due consideration for their achievements and their sensibilities.

IDEAS FOR THE FUTURE

So what advice do we offer to future reviewers of the internal auditing function?

1. Review the internal audit *function*, not just the internal audit department.
2. Review the *entire* audit function, and not just its financial audit aspects.
3. Don't use just the IIA framework as review criteria. Give equal weight to written and unwritten board and management directives relating to the specific audit function under review. The auditing department you are reviewing is not working for the IIA.
4. Evaluate the overall control climate of the corporation. This will tell you a great deal about the challenge facing the auditing department.
5. Don't turn management and auditee interviews into a popularity poll relating to the auditing department. This is too facile an approach. Find out how much interviewees know about the company's internal audit charter and how much they support the charter. Negative attitudes about the internal audit department may reflect a negative attitude about auditing in general. It may also reflect indifferent board and senior management support, or improper use, of the auditing function. Of course, it may also indicate a need for the internal audit department to modify its audit philosophy and/or to improve the qualifications of its staff.
6. By all means review working papers. But adopt realistic guidelines tailored specifically for the internal audit profession and view the whole area in perspective. There is often a creative leap

between basic audit documentation and an auditor's conclusions and recommendations that will never be adequately documented. The best indication of the validity of an auditor's conclusions and recommendations is management's concurrence.

7. Secure a summary of all the accomplishments of the auditing department for the last twelve months. Check it for fairness and accuracy using sample test techniques, and evaluate the department's overall contribution to the organization. *This should be the single most important product of the quality assurance review.*

8. Don't just prepare one report. Things being what they are, no single report will produce the results which your review should achieve. There should be at least three reports:

    A detailed and forthright report addressed to the audit director *only.*

    A summary report addressed to senior management and the board audit committee—with copy to the audit director.

    An oral report to senior management and the board audit committee.

9. If some good would be achieved, there should also be one or more oral reports to key members of management designed to improve the future interaction between the audit function and auditees.

Report to the Audit Director

The detailed report to the audit director, if prepared by an insightful reviewer, could provide an invaluable service to the auditing function. Quality assurance reviewers are in a position to elicit comments, criticisms and suggestions from management as no insider could. They are also in a position to evaluate this information objectively and to pass it on to the audit director in a constructive form. They may also be able to go back to management to correct misunderstandings.

The most difficult challenge facing the quality assurance reviewer is the evaluation of negative comments by interviewees concerning the audit function. Such negative comments must be evaluated in the light of the company's overall management style. Also, negative comments should be accepted as valid only if they are supported by credible, detailed facts and explanations. Reviewers must avoid being manipulated by politically savvy managers seeking to exploit the quality assurance review to damage the auditing function for reasons that have little to do with the support of corporate goals and objectives. Remember: corporate staffs are bureaucracies. Bureaucracies invariably resist change and are almost always oversensitive to the most well-intended suggestions for improvement. To automatically view complaints by a bureaucracy as evidence of defective internal audit practice is the grossest kind of ignorance or, worse still, corruption. Given that even the best-positioned and most powerful line executives can encounter bitter resistance to needed change, can a quality assurance reviewer really demand that a credible internal audit program *never* experience any difficulty?

A good rule for quality assurance reviewers to follow would be this: first, evaluate the *results* of the audit program; then evaluate the psychological pain to auditees, if any. If the reviewer sincerely believes that results can be maintained or even improved with less pain to auditees, then let him tell the audit director how this can be done. If there is merit in the reviewer's suggestions, any audit director in his right mind should be eager to give the suggestions a try.

Audit Philosophy

There will be times when peer reviewers will see an opportunity to suggest a change in audit philosophy to management and the auditing department. To be effective, such suggestions should be well thought out and should reflect the needs and management style of the organization concerned. Reviewers venturing into this delicate area should have actual internal auditing experience and should be thoroughly acquainted with the IIA *Standards for the Practice of Internal Auditing* and other pertinent IIA pronouncements. They should also be acquainted with the works of leading authors in the field of internal auditing.

SUMMARY

Quality assurance reviews should be performed neither by a firm's independent accountants nor by the internal auditors of other firms. Quality assurance reviews should be performed by the management advisory services departments of CPA firms having no ongoing relationship with the client.

Too many reviews conducted thus far have used a cookbook approach lacking in depth and insight.

Quality assurance reviews should include an evaluation of the internal audit department's overall contribution to the organization. This should be the single most important product of a review.

Interviews with management and auditees should be more than a popularity poll. Negative reports should be accepted as valid only if supported by credible facts and explanations.

DISCUSSION

Quality assurance reviews of the internal audit function are too important to be left to public accountants who have a narrow view of the profession and who may have a bone to pick with the particular auditing department under review. Quality assurance reviews should not be contracted for and performed in a perfunctory manner meant simply to comply with an IIA standard for the edification of the board audit committee. Quality assurance reviews need to be viewed as very serious consulting engagements which, if not properly conducted, may not only fail to meet their objectives but may do positive harm to the function reviewed.

Many internal audit departments today still operate in an essentially adversary climate and are expected to follow disclosure practices hardly designed to make friends with operating management and auditees. More often than not, the modus operandi of these departments is mandated by board audit committees and/or senior managements who simply assume that this is the way internal auditing is supposed to work. For peer reviewers to then come in, conduct popularity polls of operating management and simply condemn the internal audit department for poor audit relations is hardly a service worth paying $30,000 for. To fault an internal audit department under these circumstances without prescribing a viable alternative in some detail can only have the result of reducing internal auditing's diligence, self-confidence and effectiveness.

The new internal auditing does in fact believe that the vast majority of internal audits should leave a positive impression of the internal audit function upon management and auditees. However, the achievement of this highly desirable state of affairs will require continued educational effort by the profession, coordinated change in the attitudes of internal audit departments, board audit committees and senior managements, and sympathetic support from reviewers whose knowledge of internal auditing goes beyond superficial familiarity with quality-assurance cookbooks.

Quality assurance reviews of the bottom-line results of the internal audit program will be indispensable given the proposed disclosure practices of the new internal auditing. Under the new internal auditing, much of the good accomplished by the audit program will be hidden from view. Well-directed quality assurance reviews can provide regular assurance to senior management and board audit committees that the audit function is supporting corporate goals and objectives in an effective, efficient and professional manner.

PART 3

The Audit

CHAPTER 9

The Partnership Concept

The idea is now emerging that we may contribute much more to the welfare of our organizations as partners than as critics.

James A. Hooper, IIA North American Conference, 1983

THE CONCEPT

The seeds of the partnership concept of internal auditing were planted by a prior generation of internal audit practitioners. One long-time observer of the profession states that the concept was already evident in the work of Victor Z. Brink at Ford Motor Company back in the 1950s. Dr. Brink certainly makes very specific reference to the concept in *Modern*

*Internal Auditing.** Larry Sawyer gave the concept full-length treatment in his book *The Manager and the Modern Internal Auditor—A Problem-Solving Partnership.*† The concept was later picked up by James A. Hooper in various speeches that he delivered during his 1983–84 term as international chairman of The Institute of Internal Auditors. Various aspects of the concept are being advocated and discussed with increasing frequency by contributors to *The Internal Auditor*, and limited exposure to the *French Internal Audit Review*‡ has convinced this author that the concept is also well established overseas. The partnership concept has been taken by some as no more than a nice-sounding slogan. It is, of course, much more than that since it constitutes a radical redefinition of internal auditing's traditional relationship with management. In fact, the partnership concept establishes the direction in which the internal auditing profession must continue to evolve in order to fulfill the requirements of its new reporting relationship and to cope effectively with the audit environment of the 1980s and beyond.

The partnership concept is so radical that it will probably take many more years for the profession to fully define and assimilate it. Critics will argue that the concept is a denial of audit independence and that it amounts to a sellout to management. Management, on the other hand, may well argue that no one invited internal auditing into a partnership and that it is presumptuous of internal auditors to nominate themselves into a club reserved for their betters.

It is likely that resistance to the partnership concept of internal auditing will eventually be recognized as having been an emotional response—a clinging to the status quo, so to speak. The concept is timely and it fits the realities of the emerging audit environment. It can be shown to make sense both at the rational level and at the emotional level. It is in large part what this book is all about.

What does the partnership concept of internal auditing mean? Fundamentally, it means the abandonment of the adversary philosophy of internal auditing. Internal auditing is no longer an outsider within the corporation, taking pokes at management and feared and mistrusted by practically everyone. It means that the goals pursued by management and internal auditing are the same. It means that internal auditing is independent of the activities it reviews but is in close association with management which sponsors its reviews. In sum, it means that internal au-

---

*4th ed. (New York: John Wiley & Sons, Inc., 1982), 76. See Appendix F.
†(New York: AMACOM, 1979).
‡*Revue Française de l'Audit Interne*, Publiclair, 38, Rue des Mathurins, 75008 Paris; a publication of Institut Francais des Auditeurs et Controleurs Internes.

diting is part of management just as research and development, engineering, production, sales, law and finance are part of management.*

WHAT THE PARTNERSHIP CONCEPT IS NOT

Let us now look at the partnership concept in terms of what it is not. Partnership does not mean being a yes-man. Being a true partner means having the right to one's opinions and the right to be heard as an equal. Nearly everyone reading these pages will understand the vast difference it makes whether one belongs to an organization when offering a dissenting opinion. If one truly belongs, the opinion is at least given a respectful hearing. One's motives are not questioned even if one's judgement might be. If one doesn't belong, the contrary opinion is ridiculed and dismissed out of hand. If the opinion is considered sufficiently offensive, one is apt to be psychologically rejected by the organization such that one's future ability to contribute to the organization is seriously impaired. It follows, therefore, that true partnership with management would enhance internal auditing's freedom of expression and would increase its overall effectiveness.

Abandonment of the adversary principle would not mean an unwillingness to take on tough assignments. Rather, assignments would no longer be as tough. Partnership with management, so long as it is a true partnership, implies greater organizational status. The greater internal auditing's organizational status, the less difficulty it will encounter in the performance of its duties. Audit assignments are sometimes made difficult because auditees consider disputes with auditors as involving little or no risk to themselves. When the auditing department is perceived to be in a close partnership with management, auditees will reassess the risk involved in withholding their cooperation or engaging in hostile behavior. Auditees will be less inclined to indulge in ad hominem attacks against auditors and will feel compelled to address audit findings in a courteous and professional manner.

Recognition by internal auditors of their dependence on management sponsors will not mean the compromise of truth, honesty, integrity or quality of work product. It's a question of competence, character and status. Again, we have to assume a true partnership between internal au-

---

*This is not to deny internal auditing's unique role within the organization. Internal auditing can be different from other management functions and yet still be part of management.

diting and management such that internal audit executives are not personally outclassed by the other managers with whom they come into contact. To think that internal auditors may be compromised by closeness to management is to misunderstand the psychological mechanics of personal corruption. People are not corrupted by others. They first indicate their willingness to engage in fun and games and are then taken up on this by those who would exploit them. Organizations inclined to promote persons of this type to head their internal audit organizations will get what they deserve. Chances are that the result will be the same for those organizations no matter what internal audit philosophy is followed by the profession as a whole. None of this is to deny that internal auditors working closely with management will occasionally be exposed to political pressures by powerful senior executives. This fact does not invalidate the partnership concept, however. It merely defines its attendant risks and limitations. Internal auditors must either accept the problematic aspects of the partnership concept or resign themselves to undemanding careers far removed from the center of corporate action.

The test of any new concept is not that it should be trouble-free. Most things of any consequence involve a trade-off between advantages and disadvantages. Critics of the partnership concept certainly cannot assert that conventional styles of internal auditing do not have their own disadvantages and limitations, the most conspicuous of which is the inability to attract management support for a truly meaningful audit scope.

Let us pursue the partnership concept in greater depth by exploring and examining its application to the types of services provided by the internal auditor. Those services are:

Internal accounting control
Fraud prevention and detection
Financial auditing
Compliance auditing
Operational and management auditing
Contract auditing
EDP auditing
Personnel development
Contacts with outside groups

INTERNAL ACCOUNTING CONTROL

Prior to the enactment of the FCPA in 1977, internal auditors were in the awkward position of being *advocates* of sound internal accounting controls. Being advocates tended to pit internal auditors against the rest of the organization. Auditors were viewed as concerned with trivial matters which no one of any importance cared about. The campaign was especially difficult since auditors were attempting to make their case as a minor division within the controller's organization—itself not a particularly high-ranking organization in many corporations.

The position of internal auditors is now much improved. The Foreign Corrupt Practices Act gave the subject of internal accounting control a certain glamour and prestige it didn't have before. The act caused a raising of the control consciousness of U. S. corporations by infusing senior management and directors with a sense of personal responsibility for accounting control. The act made it possible for internal auditors to shift their position from one of advocacy to one of support to management.

Managers and directors are now persuaded that accounting controls must be adequate and properly documented. Internal auditors are in full partnership with management on this point. The most visible and dramatic proof of this partnership is internal auditing's new reporting relationship. The fact that many internal audit departments report functionally to the board audit committee is directly attributable to the board's interest in internal accounting control as inspired by the FCPA. For internal auditors to continue to act like lonely advocates of internal accounting control is a fundamental error in psychology. It's like a politician continuing to act like a candidate after he's won the office. Senior management and the board rely heavily on internal auditors to protect them from costly and embarrassing breakdowns in accounting control. However, they expect auditors to demonstrate leadership, maturity and professionalism in resolving control issues with the controller, other officers and the independent accountants. What is needed is not a strident fanaticism but a cool and sober persistence.

In the past, internal auditors have had to adopt a whole raft of psychological devices which might be termed intimidatory. The time may not yet have arrived to give these up entirely, but the partnership approach will require a change of style over time. A typical stratagem used by internal auditors is to take a very strong position and to give that position as much visibility as possible with higher management. The implication is made that if junior management fails to act favorably on auditing's recommendation, auditing will refer the matter officially to higher management. This can place higher management in a real bind. Management may, in fact, prefer to accept the risk of not strengthening the control in question. But this can be very awkward if auditing insists on having a confrontation in the official record. If management officially rejects auditing's recommendation, and if luck should go against them, management could be seriously embarrassed and heads might even roll. Unless auditing views a control problem as involving a very material risk, it might be best for all concerned that auditing adopt a more patient attitude. Let the auditing department assess the control problem objectively and without undue emotion and allow management to decide quietly how it wants to react. Give the matter a year or two to percolate until the next review and let all concerned reassess the matter at that time. Chances are that the delay will not cost anything. And if it does, no one will blame the auditing department.

Sometimes it takes an adverse event—an actual control breakdown— to persuade individual managers that controls should be strengthened. Interestingly, it is in such situations that internal auditors can most effectively demonstrate their partnership role. A critic or adversary would exploit a control breakdown to say "I told you so," but a partner behaves differently. He does all he can to minimize the embarrassment to the company, as well as to the specific individuals affected, and offers to help repair the damage that was done.

How does the partnership approach apply in the area of internal accounting control? It consists in assuming that management and the internal auditors are on the same side and that both want adequate accounting controls. Auditing does its technical best to advise management concerning control, but it gives management the latitude it wants in making up its own mind. Partnership boils down to the exercise of patience and the avoidance of an excess of zeal. All of us remember times when we fought too hard over an issue that, in retrospect, did not warrant the heat, emotion and recrimination that was generated. The partnership approach consists in drawing the line of contention closer to the point of true materiality where disagreement is less likely. If such an approach makes it easier to work with management, the resulting expansion of internal auditing's scope will generate so many new opportunities that auditing's increased contribution to the organization will more than make up for any minor issues which were lost or deferred.

FRAUD PREVENTION AND DETECTION

Internal auditors have worked out a convenient position with respect to fraud prevention and detection. On the one hand, internal auditing can't be held responsible when fraud occurs. On the other hand, auditors have a major responsibility for fraud prevention and detection and must be staffed and funded accordingly. This position is not dishonest, nor is it really harmful but it is, as we said, somewhat convenient. Internal auditors claim the right to build individual careers, and even entire staffs, on the basis of an activity for which they cannot be held responsible if it fails. Who is responsible if a fraud occurs? If not the auditors, is it management? And if not management, is it no one?

Internal auditors often have another interesting attitude with respect to fraud prevention and detection. Since cases of fraud involving members of management do happen, management is to be treated as a potential suspect. The habit of viewing management as a suspect is directly tied to certain styles of audit independence which were discussed in Chapter 2. Auditors who consciously or unconsciously assume the position of an outsider, a proxy for the board of directors or an autonomist conduct themselves in such a way as to make managers, both junior and senior, feel that they can't be trusted. Their suspicion of managers as a class is clearly communicated by their facial expressions, tone of voice and lines of inquiry.

There is still a third attitude toward fraud held by some internal auditors which needs to be aired. Fraud may be an embarrassment to a particular department and perhaps to an entire corporation. It may be a tragedy for the guilty party, and a cause for real dismay on the part of his friends and associates. But fraud seldom inspires embarrassment, dismay or a sense of tragedy in internal auditors. To internal auditors, fraud is often viewed as a happy event, an occasion for excitement and perhaps even a source of vindication. Has someone foolishly borrowed $200 from a cash fund until payday and been caught in a surprise audit? Auditing mobilizes into action and generates a level of tension one would expect if it had uncovered a business blunder costing the company millions of dollars. All of the frustration suffered by auditing in the past few years finally comes bearing down on a matter which is clearly black and white. Someone has had the benefit of a free $200 loan for five days. At 15% a year, this works out to forty-two cents. Assuming the guilty party has done this ten times in the past year, which is unlikely, and that the "loans" were for an average of ten days each, the total works out to a whopping $8.33! Some auditors have sternly recommended that veteran employees with otherwise clean records be summarily discharged for such "crimes." Fortunately, in such cases, some manager will recall that the wrongdoer has for years stayed beyond normal quitting time to finish his work, and on more than one occasion performed beyond the call of duty in problem situations where a great deal was at stake.

The above discussion is admittedly infected with a certain hyperbole. But the psychology of fraud prevention and detection is so subtle that some magnification is needed to discern its form and texture. We are not suggesting that internal auditors should be held responsible when fraud occurs. Nor are we denying that internal auditors have a major role to play in fraud prevention and detection. Although thievery and fraud can occur at all levels, it is likely that the larger, more complex frauds will be perpetrated by knowledgeable individuals in positions of responsibility. And finally, there is no denying that fraud prevention and detection work is difficult and challenging and that it will normally be done well only by people able to derive some satisfaction from it. As often happens in professional work, the choice is not between two opposite propositions, since both may be useful in describing complex reality. The real choice is where to position oneself in the working range between the two propositions, and how to shift one's position depending upon the circumstances.

To be in partnership with management in the area of fraud prevention and detection, internal auditors must first disclaim exclusive or even primary responsibility for fraud prevention and detection. The idea is to avoid the impression that fraud is the exclusive business of internal auditors. Managers who are permitted to feel this way will not be as alert as they should be to the threat of fraud, and they may even adopt a position of indifference, if not resistance, to the legitimate efforts of the auditors. They will pander to their own egos and those of their associates by simulating shock and resentment at the very suggestion that someone in their organization might commit fraud. Of course, this is the same mentality which, when a fraud does occur, will excuse its former neglect by saying "Who would ever have thought that good old Joe. . . ."

Internal auditors will do better in the long run by adopting the position that fraud is *management's* business and that auditing's role is to provide expert advice. This is the basic partnership position. Management and internal auditing share a common interest and a common goal, but management carries the ball. Internal auditing will conduct analyses and will offer recommendations, but it will seldom insist that its recommendations be carried out except in cases that pose a clear and present danger or involve compliance with established policy and procedures.

The partnership concept consists in viewing management as the client, not the suspect, in fraud matters. Suspicion of management need never be an issue in the evaluation of controls against fraud. Controls against fraud should be installed as a matter of principle—not as a matter of personalities. The manager who asserts his own honesty owes it to his employer, and to himself, to support controls against fraud. He will avoid all questions concerning his motives or his judgment, and he will ensure against errors or misdeeds by his successors.

Finally, the partnership concept requires that internal auditors stick to the "controls" business and stay out of the "justice" business. Justice, if there be such a thing in the corporate world, is clearly the job of management and the board: it is not the job of the internal auditors. Once internal auditors have proven and quantified a fraud and referred the matter to the appropriate level of management, they should get out of the affair and stay out. Again, overzealous follow-up based on an inappropriate concept of audit independence will do little good and will damage the partnership relationship with management which auditing is seeking to foster.

Let management decide what to do about a fraud. Let it weigh the need to punish and to set an example against considerations of past service, present and future value to the organization, mitigating circumstances and the need to avoid undue embarrassment to the corporation. Chances are that auditing does not know, and will never know, all of the factors bearing on the disposition of a proven fraud or defalcation. More importantly, management may feel that it is not auditing's business to know. Since whatever independence the auditing department enjoys derives exclusively from senior management and the board, auditing should rest content in the knowledge that it did its job well and should not fret over decisions made by its employer.

A final word concerning the disposition of fraud cases. If management decides not to prosecute and to dispose of the matter internally, chances are that it will ask auditing to refrain from discussing the case with other employees. Auditing must be scrupulously respectful of such requests since it is their duty under Article V of the Code of Ethics. Since management seldom feels free to discuss the reasons why it handled a fraud in a particular manner, gossiping about the fraud with other employees can only result in damage to morale. Actually, this thought is offered mainly for the sake of completeness. As was stated earlier in this book, internal auditors have an excellent record with respect to maintaining the confidentiality of information acquired in the course of their duties.

FINANCIAL AUDITING

In the area of internal financial auditing, the partnership concept involves a subtle but very real change of style. Throughout its long existence, the hallmark of financial auditing has been the diligent application of technical expertise. The partnership concept is in no way intended to change this fine tradition. What the concept does suggest, however, is that the diligence of financial auditors be extended and redirected to some degree.

First of all, it will be necessary for financial auditors to participate in internal auditing's overall effort to improve relations with management and auditees. It is becoming increasingly evident that an outsider mentality is not essential for effective internal financial auditing. Let the financial auditor shed his aloofness, relegate the outsider mentality to the independent accountants and pitch in with management in a spirit of partnership to make things work better. Partnership with management will require thinking a little more like management. Financial auditors are and should remain good technicians but the new internal auditing will require that financial auditors adopt a clearer management perspective. Management needs to know more about the materiality and impact of financial audit findings, and financial auditors should strive increasingly to meet that need. Also, management needs to be told not only about problems but also about their causes and the best means of eliminating them.

Making the stylistic adjustments described above will not be easy, and management itself may make it difficult for financial auditors to modify their approach to their work. Of all the internal audit disciplines, financial auditing is the most structured and most tightly controlled. Rigid structure and tight control will be found to be incompatible with the reforms which must be undertaken by financial auditors in the years ahead. It may be possible to find errors and control weaknesses following a ridid audit program and schedule,* but more flexibility will be needed if time is to be taken to assist management in diagnosing problems in detail and identifying appropriate corrective measures.

Rigid audit programs and schedules may be necessary in a public accounting environment. However, financial audit managers and supervisors should bear in mind that an increasing proportion of their subordinates are no longer apprentices but fully certified professionals. Today's financial auditors have a great deal to contribute if given adequate initiative and responsibility. Let audit managers move toward the new direction we have just described, starting with their more experienced financial auditors. The results will surprise them.

COMPLIANCE AUDITING

Compliance auditing seeks to determine whether established policies, procedures, controls, laws and regulations are being observed. Compli-

---

*Too much is made of standard audit programs in financial auditing. Cyclical audits utilizing the same unvarying program end up producing so little of value as to constitute a questionable use of expensive resources. Audit productivity would be increased by modifying the "theory" of a cyclical audit based upon the results of the last audit. As much as 40% of the audit program should be left up to the new auditor.

ance auditing embraces such a wide field that its particulars are practically limitless. In a large corporation, any one organization might be audited for its compliance with standards relating to accounting, personnel administration, planning, budgeting, procurement, payroll, expense accounts, local purchase orders and drafts, cash funds, office standards, security, safety and so forth. The combined procedures manuals of a large corporation, if placed side by side, can take up anywhere from three to ten feet of shelf space. Practically every page of these manuals contains standards by which an auditor could conduct a compliance review, and by which an organization might be found deficient. The infinite forms that compliance audits can take make them similar to musical instruments. One can play practically any tune in any style. It's a question of who calls the tune and sets the tempo.

In the area of compliance auditing, the auditor's effectiveness will depend largely on his attitude: whether he views himself as an adversary or as a partner. If he chooses to be a partner with management, he will find himself doing many things that the critic or adversary would not bother doing. First of all, he will recognize that his compliance audit program does not always address the principal job of the auditee. Rather, it may address administrative matters which are more or less peripheral to the auditee's main mission. Recognition of this fact will give the auditor the right perspective concerning his audit and his findings.

Partnership with management also means that the auditor will involve management in the selection of areas to be audited. Given the practically unlimited scope of compliance audits, the auditor must invite management's views and suggestions concerning where the emphasis should be placed. This does not prevent the auditor from suggesting ideas of his own, and management will usually be more than eager to consider what the auditor has to say in the light of his experience and expertise. The essential point is that management involvement and concurrence are highly desirable in order to give the audit program the legitimacy it will need to be truly effective at the auditee level.

Not only must the management-minded auditor work with management in establishing the overall audit program, he must also consider management's intent in the conduct of the actual audit. The real standard in compliance audits is not the letter of corporate policies and procedures, but their intent. In some cases, management will be glad to describe its intent if asked. In most cases, however, management intent is something to be arrived at through judgment. It is corroborated mainly after the fact—by whether or not management approves of the results of the audit. In any case, the auditor must recognize different degrees of importance, the need for flexibility in unusual cases, the need to balance benefit against cost and the possibility that policies and procedures may have become partly or wholly obsolete. The management-minded auditor is not simply concerned with finding deficiencies. He tries to determine the causes of deficiencies and takes these into account. In tough economic times, few organizations are staffed and funded to do a first-class job in all matters. The main mission takes precedence over administrative details, and it is often those areas covered by compliance audits which are made to suffer.

Management-minded auditors also take the overall control climate into account. Individual auditees normally concentrate on those things which their superiors consider important. If superiors show indifference or open contempt for "bureaucratic rules," one can hardly expect subordinates to be models of administrative correctness. Again, the key is management intent. The auditor audits by management's intent rather than by his own personal standards. If management wants reform now, the auditor adopts suitably high standards. If management prefers to bide its time until key personnel changes have taken place, the auditor concentrates on the essentials and waits for a better day to do a more thorough job.

The management-minded internal auditor is not overly concerned with human errors. Everyone makes mistakes at one time or another and reporting mistakes up the chain of command is not what internal auditing is about. As we have stated many times previously, the auditor's primary purpose is not to disclose, but to promote improvement. There is a vast difference between a repetitive pattern of errors and an isolated mistake. Each should be handled in the best way possible to improve the situation and to make friends for the auditing function. Field-wise internal auditors like to find mistakes but seldom report them. They "forgive" the mistakes as a gesture of goodwill in order to create an audit climate that will be receptive to substantive recommendations that really matter.

With respect to the matter of compliance with laws and regulations, an attitude of partnership with management requires that the internal auditor avoid the role of law enforcer. His responsibility is simply to report his observations to the level of management empowered to take appropriate action.

This discussion hardly exhausts the subject of partnership with management as it relates to compliance auditing. There is no need to go into complete detail if the auditor understands and accepts two basic principles: first, identify management's true intent and audit by that intent; second, conduct the audit and handle disclosure in such a manner as to maximize the benefit to the organization, minimize embarrassment to individuals and promote positive auditee relations. A very common complaint among managers is that auditors are trying to make a name for themselves at managers' expense. This may or may not be true in an individual case, but the complaint tells us a lot about managers' fears and their potential reaction to the audit process. The thing to keep in mind is that we all need to control the natural tendency in each of us to seek exclusive credit for our accomplishments. This tendency is not in keeping with the partnership approach to auditee relations. A wise man once said that one can accomplish practically anything if one doesn't insist on getting credit for it. In the final analysis, the best way for internal auditors to make a name for themselves is for others to say good things about them.

OPERATIONAL AUDITING

We include in operational auditing all auditing having the objective of reviewing, evaluating and improving operational effectiveness and efficiency. Certain internal audit departments even employ auditors with industrial engineering backgrounds to review and evaluate productivity and to assist operating departments in establishing work standards. A partnership approach is particularly important, perhaps even critical, in this type of auditing. The reason lies in the source of support for this activity. Whereas board audit committees may be primary supporters of audits relating to internal accounting control and fraud, they are more likely to be secondary supporters of operational audits. By this we mean that they will support operational audits to the extent that management itself supports them as a useful tool for decision making. Once internal auditors face up to this fact, it is clear that an operational audit program can succeed and grow only if it is conducted in a spirit of partnership with management.

In the area of operational audits, what management wants and deserves is an audit program that helps to solve problems and improves the company's overall effectiveness, efficiency and competitive position. Management wants an auditing approach that promotes the solution of problems at the lowest possible level and avoids overloading senior management. Finally, management wants a reporting style that avoids embarrassment to the management team and causes the least possible disruption to organizational morale. A tall order, the reader will say. True! But perhaps that is why management has moved very slowly into the area of operational auditing. It may be waiting for signs that internal auditors understand and accept the constraints inherent in this type of activity.

Operational auditing is not for beginners, nor is it for crusaders, critics, judges, policemen, inspectors or adversaries. The best single term which describes the successful operational auditor is "internal consultant." The art of consulting, as we all know, involves securing beneficial change through the consent* and cooperation of those affected. Operational auditing requires a high degree of technical knowledge. It also requires well-honed interpersonal skills in order to secure acceptance of audit recommendations.

Report preparation is an extremely important aspect of operational auditing. Reports must properly integrate both the technical and the social aspects of an audit. Not only must reports be technically sound, well-structured, clear and concise, they must also have the right tone. Unless reports reflect a positive and supportive attitude on the part of the auditor, management will react negatively and will not willingly accept the auditor's recommendations.

In summary, operational auditing is best conducted in a spirit of true partnership with management where auditors make a special effort to work in line with management's goals, objectives and operating style. Operational auditing is an activity where the auditor works with management in a joint leadership effort. The objective is not so much to "disclose" as to "fix"; not to "win" but to "help."

MANAGEMENT AUDITING

Management audits are really a special type of operational audit. The ultimate objective of management audits is the same as that of operational audits: operating effectiveness and efficiency. However, the immediate and proximate concern of the management auditor is more one of effectiveness than efficiency. His concern is the effectiveness of the management function.† It is this peculiar emphasis of management auditing that has led to its being given a special name. And it is this same emphasis which gives management auditing its special challenge or, one might

---

*Granted that consent may also require a type of ambient pressure exerted by higher management. Operational auditing works best in a vigorous management climate. It is least effective in environments where mediocrity is the accepted norm.

†Efficiency becomes less and less important as one audits at progressively higher levels of management. Management effectiveness translates into so many efficiencies at the lower levels of the corporation that the efficiency of the management process itself is reduced to a trivial concern.

even say, its special hazards. In a word, management audits are about management. Management audits involve and affect management, often all the way up to the senior level. Management audits are potentially very dangerous to the auditor!

Almost everyone reading this book who has been in auditing several years either has experienced a bad audit or knows someone who has. A "bad audit" can be a hellish experience for the auditor involved. It can cause acute heartache, sleepless nights and a terrible feeling of failure and shame. It can set a promising career back many years and may even require that the auditor pick up the pieces of his life with another employer.

A Fictional Tale of a Bad Audit

Here's how a bad audit might go. Auditor Joe Smith is honest, highly intelligent and very capable. One day, the audit director calls Joe into her office. She tells Joe that he has been selected for a very special assignment. Management has a difficult problem and has asked that an auditor be assigned to look into it. The auditor is to investigate the problem thoroughly and objectively and call it the way he sees it. Joe is to make an appointment with Vice-President "X" who will explain the assignment to him. Joe will be working pretty much on his own so his objectivity won't be affected by anyone. He is to prepare a report of his findings and submit copies of the report to a list of ranking executives to be specified later. No one is to review or edit the report prior to its issuance.*

Joe is flattered at being selected for this high-level assignment and thanks the director for the opportunity to show management what he can do. He is confident that he will do a good job.

So Joe lauches into his project. He interviews the organizations concerned and gathers an impressive amount of facts and figures in the course of his investigation. The managers he comes in contact with are very friendly and cooperative at first. But later, as Joe is induced to discuss his preliminary findings, he notices a sudden coldness in many of the managers who formerly had been so gracious. Wishing to avoid unpleasantness, Joe spends more and more of his time alone in his special office. He ventures out only to get specific additional data necessary to complete his analysis.

Finally, Joe is satisfied he has the answer. He knows what the problem is and can prove it. He can show exactly what went wrong and why. It

---

*It is typical of bad audits that the conditions of the auditor's failure have been set by management itself. Management seldom blames itself for the resulting failure. Blame is fully "delegated" to the auditor.

turns out that serious errors were made by a number of people and organizations. In certain cases, he has it on good word that actions were deliberately taken to thwart senior management's purpose for purely political reasons. In the finest tradition of internal auditing independence and objectivity, Joe lays out his findings and conclusions in a clear, well-written report. He has the report typed, he signs it, shows it to no one and has it distributed. He then returns to the internal audit department ready for his next assignment. In the next few days, he waits anxiously for word from top management. He looks forward to recognition for a job well done.

Joe does hear from management a few days later. He and his supervisor are called in to the audit director's office. "Joe," says the director, "I don't know what you did but I just received a call from Vice-President 'X' and he was really upset. It seems everyone is in an uproar over your report. The matter has reached the President's office and he's the most upset of all. He actually blamed me for putting a 'stupid auditor' on an important assignment. What in hell did you do? What did you write in that report to get people so upset?"

"So help me," Joe replies, "I can't understand this. I did exactly what I was asked to do. I investigated their problem thoroughly and I reported the facts exactly as I found them. I can prove every word that's in my report. What I wrote is the truth. What else could I do? Is it my fault if those people can't handle the truth?"

"Truth" In Management Auditing

Ironically, the first-time management auditor's chief handicap is his past professional training. What has he been taught? That his workpapers are the foundation of his audit report. His carefully prepared documentation is a repository of truth, and he has an ethical duty to pass on this truth in his report. Unfortunately, this attitude can be a prescription for failure.

The management auditor is in fact concerned with truth. But his mandate is different from that of the conventional auditor. He is not expected to report indiscriminately on past truth if the effect will be to seriously disrupt the harmonious working of the management team. An ill-advised report can have the effect of solving a second-order problem for senior management while presenting it with a first-order morale problem. Nine times out of ten, senior management will forgo (for a time) the solution to the second-order problem in order to cure the morale problem created by the auditor's report. The auditor never knows what hit him. Suddenly he is *persona non grata* and everyone associated with management shuns him. All he knows is that he did his best, dug out the truth, reported it faithfully and got no recognition for his pains.

The Injured Woman and the Plastic Surgeon

Imagine a woman in the prime of her life: beautiful, gracious, a joy to all who know her. Suddenly, she has a tragic auto accident. She survives without permanent injury except for one thing: her features are badly disfigured from impact against the dashboard.

After her other injuries have healed, the woman makes her first visit to a plastic surgeon. She sits down before his desk and they begin their conversation. As they talk, the surgeon picks up a large pad and a pencil and begins to draw. He looks intently at the woman's face throughout the interview and draws on his pad. Finally, the surgeon puts his pad face down and indicates that the interview is at an end. He asks the woman to come back for another visit in a week.

The woman rises and almost turns to leave. But she is overcome by worry and curiosity and asks the surgeon, "Before I go, would it be alright for me to see your sketch?" "If you like," the surgeon replies. He picks up the pad, turns it over and shows it to the woman. The woman turns pale, gasps in horror, and dashes out of the office never to return. She thought that the surgeon had studied her bone structure and had begun to create her new face on his pad. But the face on the pad was not beautiful. It was her present face, its distortions clearly delineated by the surgeon's precise artistry.

Does anyone reading these lines doubt that the surgeon was guilty of a gross error in judgment? If we agree that he was, what about his obligation to the truth? Didn't the drawing on the pad truthfully portray the present condition of the woman's face? But, the reader will say, the woman already knew what she looked like in the present. She didn't visit the plastic surgeon to be cruelly reminded of this truth. The woman came to the surgeon seeking a different truth—the truth of what she desperately hoped would be her new-found beauty. Are we to conclude, then, that there is a future truth, distinct from the present truth? Are we to conclude that one can ethically ignore present truth and concentrate on future truth?

Future Truth

In very sensitive matters, the mandate of the management auditor has to do mainly with *future* truth. The auditor will seldom be told this by his supervisor, his director of audits or by management. The auditor must interpret his assignment in this manner in order to be of service to management and to survive. If anything, senior managers are less able to deal with unpleasant truths than most people. Their style of life, carefully built over the years, has led them to expect a pleasant existence. They may accept unpleasantness from those whose power they can't resist, but they will bitterly resent being embarrassed by persons of junior rank. Senior managers and internal auditors can only deal effectively with each other in the arena of future truth. Management seeks a positive, constructive truth around which to rally in the pursuit of a better future. Management auditors are paid to develop acceptable future truths. Audit reports written on this premise come out entirely different from those written along conventional lines. The ugly, embarrassing facts and conclusions developed in the audit are merely a foundation for the recommendations which will be the main stuff of the auditor's report. If such reports do solve management's problems, and if they reduce the chances of auditors becoming casualties, on what theory do we object to them?

Some will say that management will not accept recommendations from the auditor unless he demonstrates in detail how he arrived at them. This is not so, but we will defer our discussion of this matter until a later chapter dealing with the principles of completed staff work.*

Let us make our main point with respect to the partnership approach in management audits. Let no auditor engage in management audits unless he can develop a spirit of kinship with management. The management auditor must be more than a partner. He must be a friend. A person does not treat a friend with the same cold objectivity he metes out to strangers. He wants to help his friend without injuring his feelings in any way. It can be done. Those who say it can't be done have never really tried.†

CONTRACT AUDITING

Contract auditing is probably the least controversial of all the various branches of the internal auditing profession. Contract auditing can produce cash savings for a company that are truly impressive. A capital-intensive company having large cost-plus contracts with outside builders

---

*Chapter 16.

†Management auditors must continually assess their own motives. Are they truly seeking to be helpful or are they consciously or unconsciously trying to embarrass the mighty? An auditor who is confused on this point should simply do what he is being paid to do: in a word, he should be *objective* and *helpful*.

and vendors can make sufficient cash recoveries through its contract audit activity to pay for the company's entire internal audit program many times over.

The mission of the contract auditor is to protect and promote his company's rightful interests in its dealings with outside vendors, contractors and joint-venture participants. Management depends a great deal on the contract auditor and is truly appreciative of his dedicated services. Management's dependence on the contract auditor is particularly evident in the case of joint-venture projects. Here, the internal auditor often acts as his employer's sole representative on the project site, raising and resolving issues that can literally mean millions of dollars to the company.

Contract auditing is hard work requiring a great deal of knowledge, skill and determination. However, contract auditing is similar to fraud auditing in that a mystique can develop around it, resulting in an excess of zeal. Auditing becomes a contest where the objective is to make points: points being dollars recovered from contractors. Here again, the idea of partnership with management can provide some balance. Do auditors conduct their reviews as a private game played by their rules, or do they seek to protect and promote their employer's interest as the employer perceives that interest? If auditors are to be partners with management, the answer should be obvious. The point is that a company's relationship with a contractor is seldom as simple and clear-cut as auditors would like it to be. Entering into a multibillion dollar cost-plus construction contract is almost like getting married. You're in it for better or for worse, and it's going to require some give and take to make it work. Given the history of the company's relationship with a contractor, and given the informal agreements and trade-offs that often occur in large, complex projects, auditors may not be expected to pursue every finding down to the last nickel. It's management's responsibility, not the auditor's, to make final judgments in dealings with contractors. The responsibility of internal auditors is to ensure that management has all the information it needs to make these judgments. If auditors have been given the responsibility of resolving audit findings directly with contractors, they should maintain frequent contact with appropriate levels of management to ensure that they remain in tune with management's intent.

EDP AUDITS

Many companies consider their EDP installations as representing the greatest single concentration of risk to be found in their entire organization. In most large companies, it would be far easier to replace a complete production facility than to recover from the destruction of their information systems. Management is vitally concerned that its computer systems be effective, efficient, fraud-resistant and capable of recovering from disaster. Management and the board rely heavily on internal auditing to provide them with that assurance. As in the case of internal accounting control, there was a time when management and the board were not sufficiently aware of the need for better controls in the EDP area. Internal auditing was a lonely advocate of better EDP controls in those days. Auditing took licks and lumps from management, as all advocates must do in the early stages of a campaign. However, history proved the internal auditor's concerns to be justified and conditions are now ripe for a full-fledged partnership between EDP, EDP auditors, senior management and the board of directors in the area of EDP controls.

Everyone involved in EDP controls is, or should be, on the same side today. If they are not, EDP auditors are in the best position to promote the partnership that should exist. Theirs is the best position because of their independence and mobility within the organization. Internal auditors have more time and freedom to do research and to consult with experts, professional associations and other companies. They have access to all levels of management and can share their research findings with those in a position to influence the EDP control environment. All of this is best done in a manner which avoids confrontation with those responsible for EDP systems and operations.

As we said in earlier chapters, it is becoming increasingly important that internal auditors recognize their leadership role within the corporation. This is especially true of EDP auditors who were hired and promoted mainly on the basis of their technical knowledge. The general environment has reinforced EDP auditors' natural inclination to view themselves as technicians. As a result, they have tended to treat EDP control problems as a technical debate at the working level. To the extent that such an approach has created friction and hard feelings, management has been reluctant to intervene in what it perceives as squabbling among experts over technical matters beyond its comprehension. Management has been afraid to demoralize either of the two groups whose market scarcity has been well publicized. To return to our thesis, this type of situation clearly calls for the EDP auditor to rise above his technical role and to engage the issue of EDP controls at the political level of the corporation. The exercise of leadership at this level will involve researching well-publicized EDP failures, their causes and their cures. If it can be shown that conditions contributing to problems elsewhere are also present in one's own company, management will sooner or later take action to improve the control climate. If the EDP auditor can address EDP control issues in this manner without embarrassing or alienating EDP management and supervision, he will indeed have become a partner with management.

INTERNAL AUDITING'S CONCEPT OF "WORK"

Repeated mention has been made in this book of internal auditing's increasing role in the leadership processes of the corporation. If internal auditing is to live up to its leadership responsibilities it will have to abandon its limited notion of what constitutes audit work.

Current fashion enjoins internal auditors to be as "productive" as possible. This has been translated mainly to mean the development of tight audit schedules and the application of stringent project controls. Even audit supervisors and managers are now getting caught up in the frenetic activity of their subordinates. Senior management and board audit committees have been advised that audit schedules must commit resources to the hilt. All concerned—the IIA, audit committees, senior management and auditors themselves—are together in assuming that the auditing function has only one product: the audit report.

This narrow view of what constitutes audit "work" threatens to crowd out other things which might in fact be much more productive than audit reports whose recommendations are resisted or ignored by auditees and operating management. There is, perhaps, little hope for the immediate future. But in time, as the partnership concept takes hold to a higher degree, senior management and internal auditing will tire of their futile attempts to stamp out symptoms of poor business practice and will take the time to search after root causes and to formulate fundamental remedies. When this happens, there will be somewhat less "auditing" in the traditional sense and more internal consulting. Audit "work" will be more deliberate and reflective in keeping with modes of work associated with leadership. Die-hard audit technicians and project counters will not approve of the result, but insightful observers will view internal auditing as more productive than ever in terms of real benefit to the enterprise.

PERSONNEL DEVELOPMENT

It is not always recognized that the auditing function can be in partnership with management with regard to personnel development. Given that big business thrives on specialization, it has never been easy for young, aspiring managers to obtain a broad understanding of their companies. Today, unless special arrangements are made, access to the big picture is practically unavailable.

In many organizations, management has learned that internal auditing can be a very broadening experience for future managers. A tour of duty in auditing provides practical experience in the application of management principles as well as a unique view of the company as a whole. It gives the individual an opportunity to increase his personal contacts, and it gives the company a chance to observe potential supervisors and managers in action under pressure.

Audit managers and directors can take two views of the concept of auditing as a training ground. They can either resent it because it makes their jobs more difficult and robs them of their best people, or they can welcome it as another way of demonstrating their partnership with management. An auditing department with a high rate of turnover is a much more stimulating place in which to work than one which is static. The majority of the staff can look forward to promotion in the years ahead. First, there is promotion up the auditor grades. Then comes promotion either to supervision within the auditing department or to supervisory or senior staff positions outside of auditing. No one with any ability has to stagnate while waiting for an audit supervisor to retire or resign. Everyone is on good behavior, practices good auditee relations and tries to make friends, never knowing when a sympathetic contact may result in a shining job opportunity.

An auditing department with high turnover is continually enlisting new recruits from inside the company or hiring from the outside. There is a constant infusion of new blood and new ideas, and staff training is a never-ending challenge. Every auditor with a flair for leadership and oral communications is soon drafted to develop and lead in-house seminars. There is, in fact, so much going on and so much incentive to stretch one's abilities that most auditors who leave look back upon their tour in auditing as one of the most valuable experiences of their lives.

In certain organizations, former auditors who accepted promotions or transfers elsewhere sometimes return to auditing. The auditing department can serve as a safe haven for capable employees who, for one reason or another, are not hitting it off in their current situations. Since these former auditors are already well trained, they are put on the most challenging assignments where they can again show their stuff to the operating departments. Such people are usually picked up very quickly by organizations in need of seasoned employees. Auditing has again demonstrated its partnership with management by salvaging people whose careers were in trouble and by redirecting them to fresh opportunities.

There are those who disapprove of high turnover in audit departments on the premise that such a policy will retard the professionalization of internal auditing. The people who believe this may be right. However, the other side of the argument is that internal auditing is, at this stage of its evolution, quite unlike other professions. It is, in fact, so unlike the other professions that it would be unwise to press it too strongly in any direction for fear of damaging the value employers see in it under present circumstances. The best way to lead the profession is the way the IIA is presently doing: by staying a few steps behind, watching where it is currently heading and providing such assistance as it requires to keep on moving ahead.

CONTACTS WITH OUTSIDE ENTITIES

In spite of their low-profile mode of operation, internal auditors do engage in various outside contacts. They meet and work with their companies' independent accountants and they sometimes come into contact with the independent accountants of other companies. It's not unusual for internal auditors to have dealings with Internal Revenue Service (IRS) auditors, regulatory examiners, consultants and third-party management auditors. Internal auditors who perform contract audits are in continual contact with vendors, contractors and joint-venture partners. And some internal auditors even testify in court as expert witnesses in claims litigation.

Partnership with management in the area of outside contacts is based squarely on a proper understanding of the role of internal auditing and the nature of audit independence. As discussed in Part I of this book, internal auditing is employed by management exclusively for the purpose of supporting corporate objectives. Internal auditing is not independent of its employer and has no intelligence-gathering, regulatory or law enforcement responsibility of any kind. Internal auditing owes no loyalty to any entity apart from its employer. Members of the Institute of Internal Auditors are not free to reject these principles since they are bound by the IIA Code of Ethics to exhibit loyalty in all matters pertaining to the affairs of their employers* and to be prudent in the use of audit information.

---

*Except, of course, that members of the Institute may not be a part of any unlawful or improper activity.

Because of the nature of their work, internal auditors possess considerable information of a private, confidential or sensitive nature. In view of this, it would be entirely inappropriate for internal audit departments to consciously seek publicity. In fact, internal auditors should positively shun situations which might involve them in outside contacts best left to others. Whenever such situations arise, audit directors should immediately contact the proper corporate department having jurisdiction over the matter concerned. If auditing cannot avoid a contact, and if the contact poses an element of risk, auditing should obtain the advice of corporate counsel and act accordingly.

The main thing which internal auditors must understand is that their obligation to communicate their audit findings in a forthright manner applies *exclusively* to their employers. Internal auditors have no obligation whatsoever to communicate forthrightly to outside entities. The truth is just the reverse. Internal auditors must *not* communicate to outsiders if this would damage the interests of their employers. The greatest potential for confusion arises when auditors are in contact with others who, like them, are in the business of review and evaluation. The frustration of internal auditors at their inability to secure internal reforms, combined with a feeling of professional kinship with sympathetic outsiders, can lead internal auditors to engage in ill-advised communications with those outsiders. Even when internal auditors are entirely correct in their opinions, gratuitous cooperation with outsiders can lead management to doubt the trustworthiness of their internal audit department.

It all comes back to what was said before about management's insistence on maintaining the initiative. Auditing's role is to help management—when and in the manner it wants to be helped. To help management whether it wants help or not is to deny management the initiative. This is not the way of true partnership.

PARTNERSHIP AND PATIENCE

This concludes our discussion of the types of services provided by the internal auditor and how the partnership concept might apply in each case. There is a danger that veteran internal auditors having read this chapter will dismiss it as Pollyannish. It all sounds too good to be true. An audit department simply decides to adopt the partnership approach, and—abracadabra—everything comes up roses? Not at all. The partnership concept may be likened to a pass through a very steep and rugged mountain range. The pass may be very difficult to negotiate, but it may represent the only hope to cross the mountain range. In much the same way, the partnership concept may take considerable time and effort to implement, but it may offer the internal auditing profession the only way to surmount its present obstacles.

Patience will be an essential element of the partnership concept. Internal auditors should not lose their instinct for the aggressive pursuit of opportunities, since without that instinct they may lose much of their effectiveness. However, partnership with management will require the exercise of patience and restraint in two ways. First, auditors will have to take the time and trouble required to respect management's initiative throughout the audit process. Second, every auditor will have to be conditioned to expect delays and disappointments and to avoid being demoralized by them.

Performance appraisal criteria will have to be adjusted to prevent auditors from trying too hard to sell their conclusions and recommendations when such behavior would jeopardize auditing's partnership relationship with management. As anyone who is involved with management would readily attest, management is a messy business. Management decisions can sometimes fly in the face of all known facts and logic. But one has to go along to get along. To remain productive and to maintain one's career on an even keel, one must accept reality with cheerful and even philosophical patience. To lapse into bitterness and cynicism is to give up, and to give up is to fail.

SUMMARY

The partnership concept is a radical redefinition of internal auditing's relationship with management. It means the abandonment of the adversary philosophy of internal auditing.

True partnership with management will enhance internal auditing's freedom of expression and will increase its overall effectiveness.

Internal auditors must either accept the problematic aspects of the partnership concept or resign themselves to undemanding careers far removed from the center of corporate action.

In matters of internal accounting control, the FCPA has made it possible for internal auditors to shift their position from one of advocacy to one of support to management.

In fraud matters, the partnership concept consists in viewing management as the client, not the suspect. Fraud is management's business and internal auditing's role is to provide expert advice.

Internal auditors should stick to the "controls" business and stay out of the "justice" business.

Financial auditors must become technicians with a management outlook. They need to give more emphasis to evaluations of materiality and impact and to the development of solutions to problems. To do this, they will have to be recognized as certified professionals and freed from the tyranny of rigid audit programs and schedules.

In compliance auditing, partnership means auditing by management's intent.

The best way for internal auditors to make a name for themselves is for others to say good things about them.

Board audit committees will support operational audits to the extent that management itself supports them as a useful tool for decision making. Therefore, it is clear that an operational audit program can succeed and grow only if it is conducted in a spirit of partnership with management. The objective is not so much to "disclose" as to "fix"; not to "win" but to "help."

In very sensitive matters, the mandate of the management auditor has to do mainly with *future* truth. The management auditor must be more than a partner: he must be a friend of management.

It's management's responsibility, not the contract auditor's, to make final judgments in dealings with contractors. Contract auditors must protect and promote their company's interest as the company perceives that interest.

EDP auditors must rise above their purely technical role and engage the issue of EDP controls at the political level of the corporation.

Internal auditing must progressively give up its narrow definition of audit work and must be prepared to engage in more deliberate and less structured activities involving the leadership processes of the corporation. Greater involvement in internal consulting will enhance the productivity of the internal auditing function.

Internal auditing can demonstrate its spirit of partnership with management by cheerfully giving up its best people for transfers and promotions elsewhere in the organization.

The obligation of internal auditors to communicate their audit findings in a forthright manner applies exclusively to their employers. Internal auditors have no obligation whatsoever to communicate forthrightly to outsiders unless so instructed.

Partnership with management is patience!

DISCUSSION

During his tenure as IIA Chairman of the Board in 1983–84, James A. Hooper attended numerous chapter meetings in various parts of the country and gave a speech entitled "Management and the Internal Audit Function—A Vital Partnership." The speech was invariably well received, and many of those in attendance would step forward to engage Jim in private discussions after the meeting. On one such occasion, an auditor asked him how he had come to conceive of the speech. His reply was that too many internal auditors thought of their profession as still struggling for recognition and acceptance. It was Jim's own feeling that the profession had achieved this objective. All auditors had to do was to operate on the premise that they were in fact in partnership with management and their relationship with management would begin to improve almost immediately.

The new internal auditing represents an abandonment of obsolete concepts and attitudes tending to prolong an adversary relationship with auditees, operating management and even senior management. The new internal auditing does not wish to be associated exclusively with preventive, detective and punitive controls. It embraces the concept of management control as including all positive measures tending to promote the achievement of corporate objectives. By cooperating in the development of such control measures, through internal consulting at all levels, the new internal auditing seeks to make a positive contribution to the success of the enterprise in a spirit of partnership with management.

CHAPTER 10

Audit Relations

To business that we love we rise betime.
And go to 't with delight

WILLIAM SHAKESPEARE, *Anthony and Cleopatra*

THE NEW INTERNAL AUDITOR

Every internal audit department has at least one auditor with an unusual ability to make useful findings *and* to cultivate the warm support of auditees at the same time. Until recently, such auditors were viewed as rare finds, persons possessing a special gift. However, the fact that the relative proportion of such auditors has noticeably increased in recent years leads us to suspect that we may be witnessing the emergence of a new type of internal auditor destined to dominate the profession in the years ahead. To use a Darwinian metaphor, changes in the internal audit environment have led to the evolution of a new species: the new internal auditing has brought forth the new internal auditor. The new internal auditor may in fact be a young person, but he may just as easily be someone in his fifties. The main distinguishing characteristic of the new internal auditor is not age but attitude.

THE BASIC PSYCHOLOGICAL POSITION OF THE NEW INTERNAL AUDITOR

Whereas the old breed of internal auditor was formal, aloof and mildly menacing to the auditee, the new breed of internal auditor is professional, friendly and supportive. The difference between these two psychological positions is more significant than might appear on the surface.

The formality and aloofness of the old-style internal auditor was a valid reflection of his personal role definition. The old-style auditor saw his role mainly in terms of making adverse findings and disclosing these findings to higher levels of management. The old-style auditor saw himself as an inflictor of pain. Given this, his formal and aloof attitude toward the auditee made sense. It was an honest psychological position. One doesn't try to get on a friendly basis with an auditee when it's one's intention or expectation to cause him pain.

The friendly and supportive attitude of the new internal auditor is not merely a matter of personality. The basis of his attitude goes deeper than that. It reflects an entirely different personal definition of the auditor's role. That role is not to make adverse findings and to disclose them. Rather, it is to help the auditee find ways to do a better job and to be more successful. Given this, the friendly and supportive attitude of the new internal auditor makes sense. It too is an honest psychological position. If one is seeking to help someone else be more successful, what is more natural than to offer him the hand of friendship?

A CHARACTERISTIC THAT HASN'T CHANGED

In order to properly describe the new internal auditor, it is necessary to point out that he possesses at least one characteristic in common with the old-style auditor: a burning dedication to effectiveness and efficiency. Unless a person is possessed of this passion, he cannot be a true internal auditor. Whether one audits in the old way or the new, one cannot do a good job and produce results unless one's heart and mind are driven by a strong preference for truth, correctness, accuracy, logic, consistency, economy, efficiency and effectiveness over their opposites. Fortunately, a predictable percentage of the population possess this characteristic. When this characteristic is combined with the right kind of background, education and experience, we have a candidate for the internal audit profession. Audit committees and senior management personnel should not be concerned if such individuals choose to practice their profession in a friendly and helpful way. Results will not be compromised. If audit committees and senior managers doubt this, let them fail to promote an environment permitting internal auditors to achieve results. Internal auditors' instinct for achievement is so strong that they will be driven to employment elsewhere.

THE NEW MANAGER

It would be misleading to suggest that the new internal auditor can succeed on his own merely by exhibiting the attitudes and traits we have just described. It would also be misleading to imply that the old-style internal auditor was entirely wrong in maintaining an attitude of formality, aloofness and adversariness. An objective discussion of audit styles must take management culture into consideration.

The typical old-style manager was a hard-bitten individual with highly developed territorial instincts. He lived in a world of inviolable organizational boundaries. His slow rise from within his organization and his insulation from outside contacts made him view the world as consisting either of friends or enemies. Internal auditors were outsiders and therefore enemies. One never admitted a weakness or an error to outsiders. "Stonewalling" was the invariable response to external criticism. Given this attitude among typical old-style managers, it was entirely appropriate for internal auditors to be formal, aloof and adversarial. Internal auditing was combat, and anyone attempting to be friendly and helpful in such an environment would have been viewed as a weakling and would have been ineffectual.

The new manager is quite different from the old. He has considerably more formal education, became a manager since the advent of the computer age, and properly understands his company as a system comprised of many complex and interrelated subsystems. Being systems-minded, the new manager probably has a better appreciation of staff functions and may even have performed staff duties earlier in his career. The new manager is more sophisticated, better informed, more in tune with modern business practice and is probably acquainted with the concepts of management control and internal review. Given these and other things, the new manager is less likely to resist the internal audit process *provided* it appears to have legitimacy and senior management support.* Also, the new manager is more apt to accept the internal auditor's express or implied invitation to engage in a mutually supportive relationship and to view such a relationship as preferable to an adversarial one. His choice of an actual position will depend largely upon whether he has confidence in the internal auditor.

MANAGEMENT CONFIDENCE

The concept of management confidence deserves more attention from the internal auditing profession than it has received until now. The importance of the concept lies in the fact that it constitutes one of the two keys to successful audit relations. The second key, likability, will be discussed at a later point.

What is management confidence and why is it so important in audit relations? Management confidence breaks down into two separate elements: (1) respect for the auditor's competence; and (2) trust in the auditor's intentions.

Competence

Competence is a basic and necessary quality which every successful internal auditor must have. The world of business is tough and competitive and has little patience with incompetence. Let anyone point to an auditor with a proven record of successful audit relations and almost certainly that auditor is respected for his competence. There are, of course, degrees of competence and internal audit supervisors and managers must take great care that individual auditors are not placed in positions

---

*This point cannot be emphasized enough. A friendly and supportive attitude on the part of internal auditors will not eliminate the need for management support of the audits function. For the new internal auditing to work, management must first institutionalize the concepts of management control and internal review within the firm. Once he senses the corporation's unalterable commitment to these two concepts, the individual manager will have every incentive to cooperate with the new internal auditing and may even solicit its assistance in solving problems.

where their competence will be found wanting. Too many mistakes in this area will almost always cause damage to audit relations.

Trust

Competence alone is not sufficient for success in audit relations. It is, in fact, insufficient for successful human relations generally. What good is it that a person be competent if he can't be *trusted*.

Trust has always been an important value to the internal audit profession. However, the profession has traditionally viewed trust mainly in terms of its relationship with the employer. Trust has been seen as flowing from loyalty, honesty, integrity, objectivity and the like. Unfortunately, experience amply demonstrates that trust so defined has not necessarily endeared internal auditors to auditees and operating management. It too often has meant an adversary audit style and career-threatening disclosure practices.

Perhaps the most significant thing that can be said about the new internal auditor is that he has made the bold decision to actively enlist the personal trust of operating managers and auditees. It's as if the auditor is saying: "I will do my job, and I will do it well. But, if you cooperate with me, I will do it without causing you any harm." It is precisely this attitude on the part of the new internal auditor which accounts for his genius in audit relations. The new internal auditor fully acknowledges his primary loyalty to the owners of the enterprise, the board of directors and senior management. He also acknowledges his special obligation to his "client"—the specific manager who requested the audit or who is the implicit sponsor of the audit. Notwithstanding these loyalties and obligations, however, the new internal auditor sees himself as able to enter into a helpful and supportive relationship with the auditee and his immediate superiors. How does he manage it without compromising his code of ethics or the quality of his work product?

THE SECRET TO GOOD AUDIT RELATIONS

First, the new internal auditor starts out with an enormous amount of goodwill for everyone. He sees himself as ultimately training for management. He knows that making waves and getting people upset is not usually the way to attract an offer of a management position. His intention is to take people and things as they are and to go from there. His mind is bent on finding problems but his motive is not disclosure. His motive is problem solving. Nor is it his intention to play the hero and to solve problems for the auditee. Rather, he plans to work closely with the auditee and to yield the initiative to him the moment he is ready and willing to accept it.

The new internal auditor does not view auditing as a secretive process culminating in a dramatic audit report. He believes that the truly important things in an audit take place *during* the audit and not after the audit report is issued. The real product of an audit is beneficial change in the mind of the auditee. The audit report is not the product: it is a report of the product.

The new internal auditor is not a loner. He doesn't believe in keeping the auditee guessing concerning how the audit is coming along. He spends considerable time with the auditee, telling him what he has found, and enlisting his thoughts and comments. When a significant problem is uncovered, he and the auditee exchange information and ideas about it. More often than not, the auditee is able to suggest a solution or can confirm the feasibility of a solution suggested by the auditor. If all goes well, the audit's principal conclusions and recommendations are as much a contribution of the auditee as of the auditor. The auditee's concurrence with the audit findings is assured and much of the needed corrective action is either planned or underway by the time the audit report is issued.

WHAT ABOUT DISCLOSURE?

The new internal auditor is keenly aware of the need to exercise judgment in the reporting of audit results. He knows that ill-advised disclosure practices can severely damage the long-term effectiveness of the auditing function. His guiding principles with respect to disclosure are:

Concentrate on the achievement of operational improvements by providing detailed disclosure mainly to auditees and others directly concerned with corrective action.

Base assurances to higher levels of management mainly upon the expected condition of the area reviewed after corrective actions have been implemented. Assuming the likelihood that corrective action will be taken, avoid disclosure of adverse audit findings to higher management.

If senior management support of the audit function is dependent upon acceptance at the lower levels, avoid involvement in the evaluation of managerial performance since this usually presses auditees into a defensive posture.

Limit disclosure at the senior management and board audit committee levels to a description of the audit program and the general results achieved.

Never disclose detailed audit findings to secure credit for the auditing organization at the expense of auditees and operating management. When disclosure cannot be avoided, try to present audit results as joint achievements by management and the auditing group.

Generally manage disclosure in such a way as to promote acceptance of the internal auditing function at all levels of the organization. *Maintain the personal trust of auditees and operating managers.*

DISCLOSING AUDITEE MISCONDUCT

But, the reader may ask, what if an audit uncovers gross incompetence, dereliction of duty, abuse of authority or fraud? What does the new internal auditor do then? How does the new internal auditor honor his express or implied commitment to avoid harming the auditee? The answer, of course, is that he can't. His sincere intentions to perform a helpful audit are invalidated by circumstances beyond his control. The auditee cannot blame the auditor for the harm which may befall him. He must blame himself. The auditor is a professional and is not free to violate his ethical duty to report highly adverse findings to appropriate levels of management. His duty must prevail over his goodwill toward the auditee.

Even in such a case, however, there are ways in which the auditor can remain faithful, at least in part, to whatever personal commitment he might have made to the auditee. The auditor can avoid fanning the flames of the auditee's predicament and can ensure that management is apprised of any extenuating facts and circumstances which rightfully bear upon the adverse findings. It should be emphasized, however, that cases of auditee misconduct are relatively rare. Our main point concerning the new internal auditor is that he does not withhold his goodwill from an auditee on the one-in-three-hundred chance that his audit may uncover misconduct. The new internal auditor is content to presume his auditees to be innocent until proven guilty since the presumption is borne out in the vast majority of cases and promotes a vastly more productive audit environment.

LIKABILITY

We said earlier that management confidence was the first key to successful audit relations and that this included respect for the auditor's competence and trust in his intentions. We now come to the second key: likability.

Likability is just what the word implies: the quality of being liked. A good test of likability is what happens when the auditee first meets the auditor in the morning. Does his smile indicate that he is genuinely happy to see the auditor? Does he initiate banter and small talk, showing that he enjoys the auditor's company? Some readers may scoff at this, thinking that it is a pipe dream to expect auditees to like auditors. Yet everyone knows at least one auditor who is living proof that the notion of auditor likability is not absurd.

The problem with too many auditors is that they have been taught that they are not supposed to be liked. They were taught this a long time ago and they have never gotten over it. They go through great pains to mask their personal qualities in order to appear "professional" and to inspire "respect" and even fear. It does not occur to them that the traditional injunction against being liked may be incompatible with more recent urgings to be helpful and to "sell" their audit recommendations.

Granted that not everyone is equally likable and that some individuals have superior talents in this area than others, the fact remains that likability can be developed—just as competence and trust can be developed. For those of us who are less gifted in being likable, it is important that we work at it every day. We literally can't afford to waste the 3 to 5 years we will be in auditing before we resume the cultivation of this critical quality. Developing our likability at parties and other social functions is not enough. We have to master its techniques as applied to the workplace.

If there remain any skeptics at this point of our exhortation concerning likability, let them consider Ronald Reagan. Are they to deny the tremendous asset that likability has been in the career of this man? Will they insist that likability must always result in the compromise of one's objectives when Reagan has so obviously used his likability in the pursuit of his? Perhaps some of us are too far gone and are destined to go into retirement aloof, unsmiling and unbending in our determination to be "independent," feared and isolated from the social community of the corporation. In any event, the time has come for the new internal auditing and the new internal auditor. The way of the future is clearly shown by those who consistently produce better audit results through the use of their "people skills."

A FRENCH VIEW

The internal auditing profession's current effort to develop a new approach to audit relations is by no means restricted to the North American continent. The environmental forces pushing the profession toward a fresh definition of its role and modus operandi are apparently active in other parts of the world as well. Common elements in the industrial culture of highly developed countries are producing similar problems which, in turn, are eliciting remarkably similar proposals for corrective action. The following is the author's translation of excerpts from an article by D. Baulon, Director of Internal Auditing at PECHINEY, in the September-October, 1983 issue of the *French Internal Audit Review*:*

> *Reasoning on the basis of priorities, the auditor must ultimately focus on two principal objectives: to inform, and to persuade. . . .*
>
> *Too often, internal auditing's sole product is a cold-blooded report describing operational and control exceptions and weaknesses without any thought to the probable consequences of the report. . . .*
>
> *The problem of audit report writing must be viewed in the larger perspective of a political collaboration between auditors and auditees whereby conclusions and recommendations are arrived at through joint effort. The problem of auditee agreement with the audit report will practically disappear since the auditee will have the impression of having developed his own solutions to his problems. . . .*
>
> *Internal auditing must develop a politics of communication which will ultimately reduce the relative importance of the final audit report. . . .*
>
> *Internal control is the responsibility of management—not of internal auditors. The role of internal auditors with respect to internal control is to provide expert advice and consultation. Emphasizing the idea that auditors are not themselves controllers, but merely staff experts in control, may help to integrate internal auditing into the organization and reduce its disturbing character. . . .*
>
> *The role of the internal auditor is not to find mistakes. Everyone makes mistakes and the auditor most of all. Neither is fraud detection the primary role of internal au-*

*Revue Française de l'Audit Interne, PUBLICLAIR, 38, Rue des Mathurins, 75008 Paris, France.

diting. Misguided emphasis on mistakes and fraud poisons the well of auditor-auditee relations and impedes the search for opportunities to enhance the profitability of the enterprise. . . .

The internal auditor must therefore become integrated into the society of the corporation and must live in it as a fish in water. He must meld into the human and technical landscape of the firm and gain the confidence of its personnel. . . .

THE NEW INTERNAL AUDITING

So here we have it. The new internal auditing is seen as a human relations concept uniting the new internal auditor, the new manager and the auditee in a new relationship marked by *respect* for each other's competence, *trust* in each other's intentions and a *liking* of each other's humanity. If the old internal auditing is in fact reaching a dead end, and if a new internal auditing is sorely needed, what better definition of it could we have?

THE INFLUENCE OF SENIOR MANAGEMENT

This book has, on a number of occasions, referred to the fear which is often inspired by the internal audit function. Let us inquire into this matter of fear a little more deeply. Why should members of the organization fear the internal audit function? After all, internal auditing is only a staff activity having no power to fire, demote or otherwise punish anyone. Clearly, if internal auditing is feared, it is because it has the mandate to evaluate operations and the privilege of communicating its findings to the highest levels of the organization. Auditees and managers do not fear the internal audit function in itself. They fear it because it may cause the wrath of senior management to come crashing down on them.

No discussion of audit relations can be complete unless it acknowledges the critical role played by senior management. Audit relations can be viewed as a communication/action loop involving the auditee, the auditor and management: Willingly or unwillingly, the auditee provides information to the auditor who, in turn, provides information to management. Management may, in reaction to the audit findings, communicate information to, or initiate action against, the auditee.

Management by Fear

All experienced leaders consider fear to be a necessary factor in respect for authority. However, fear alone may produce discipline but it can-

COMMUNICATION/ACTION LOOP

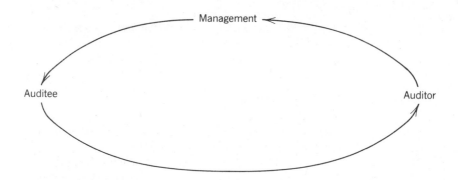

not produce excellence. This is why most enlightened organizations de-emphasize fear in their leadership styles in favor of more positive motivators.

It is unlikely that the new internal auditing can ever be successfully introduced in organizations managed largely through fear. Such organizations are apt to stack the deck against harmonious audit relations by imposing performance criteria and incentives upon the internal audit function which perpetuate an adversary mode of operation. Even if internal auditing attempted to change its style, it could not succeed unless management changed its ways of using the internal audit function.

Management Uninvolvement

Another way that senior management can influence relations between auditors and auditees is by failing to exert any conscious, consistent influence one way or the other. There is a particularly damaging style of management uninvolvement which goes like this: Both management and internal auditing strongly support the myth of audit's independence from management. As a result, senior management and internal auditing consider it an ethical imperative never to communicate with each other except in a very formal way. There are no private informal meetings to review recent events and to discuss possible ways to make things go better. Internal auditing is viewed as a specialty—almost a science —with the director of internal auditing being the resident expert. There is no recognition of internal auditing as having a social dimension where senior management itself is the real expert. As a result, senior management and internal auditing go their own separate ways, neither sure of what the other is up to. Sooner or later, stress develops to the point where senior management intervenes explosively in the audit process. The result of such intervention is usually to drastically diminish internal auditing's perceived organizational status and, therefore, its ability to build a productive relationship with auditees.

Management Meddling

The wrong kind of management involvement can greatly complicate internal auditing's efforts to build a sound rapport with auditees. Certain managements show a cynical disinterest in the long-term growth and development of the auditing function. Auditing is to be used and manipulated on an ad hoc basis as senior management sees fit. If auditing attempts to apply a consistent audit relations philosophy, it is strenuously faulted one day for being too soft and on another for being too harsh. The only thread of logic which appears to run through these episodes has to do with whether an auditee is "in" or "out" with the top. If an auditee is "in," he will easily convince senior management that auditing has been unreasonable when in fact it has not. If an auditee is "out," no amount of documentary evidence can persuade senior management that the auditee has ever done anything right. This type of senior management meddling in internal auditing thoroughly politicizes the function and destroys its credibility as a profession. It reduces internal auditing to just another staff function under the direct command of a management which is feared and mistrusted.

Management Can Play a Positive Role

The foregoing discussions of management by fear, management uninvolvement and management meddling clearly demonstrate that management can exert an adverse influence on the internal audit function. It must be quickly pointed out, on the other hand, that management's influence can also be very positive. Not only can management support constructive relationships between auditors and auditees, it can even cause an adversary audit function to change its ways. It can do this by consistently declining to punish auditees for routine shortcomings uncovered by the audit process and insisting only that deficiencies be corrected. If it also takes every opportunity to chide internal auditing for its inflammatory reporting style, internal auditing will soon realize that the time has come for a change.

SUMMARY

The new internal auditing places emphasis on human relations. It represents the interaction between the new internal auditor, the new manager and the new audit environment.

The new internal auditor is respected for his competence, trusted for his intentions and liked for his personal qualities.

The new internal auditing is conducted in the open and involves regular contact with operating managers and auditees. Audit results are a joint product of auditors and auditees such that the contents of audit reports are known and agreed to prior to issuance of the reports. The relative importance of the audit report is diminished by the new internal auditing.

The success of any activity within the enterprise must ultimately be credited to senior management. Internal auditing is no exception in this respect. The new internal auditing can take hold only when senior management has created conditions permitting auditors, operating management and auditees to cooperate in a mutually supportive relationship for the advancement of the enterprise.

DISCUSSION

In our Introduction, we described the main characteristic of the new internal auditing as a reaching out to the entire organization as potential clients. This chapter views the new internal auditing as uniting the new internal auditor, the new manager and the auditee in a new relationship marked by respect for each other's competence, trust in each other's intentions and a liking of each other's humanity.

The new internal auditing has emerged spontaneously in organizations which have tested the limits of an internal auditing supported mainly at the top. These limits have been found to be very real and to fall far short of the "unlimited scope" which the profession has been pursuing these many decades. Senior management has been quite forthright in explaining why it cannot support internal auditing much more than it already has: there is too much resistance at the lower levels. What is needed is more acceptance at those levels.

Operating managers and auditees have also been very forthright in explaining why they resist the audit function: there is too much disclosure.

Referring again to our Introduction, this book set out to examine the audit environment and to let it speak for itself. We have done this, and the environment has spoken. It now remains to be seen whether the internal auditing profession has heard the message and whether it can do something about it. Those who have embraced the new internal auditing think they have an answer: modify conventional attitudes toward audit independence, audit relations and audit disclosure, and cultivate support of the audit function *below the level of senior management.*

CHAPTER 11

Management Support

By their votes ye shall know them.

PRESIDENT HARRY S. TRUMAN, September 23, 1948

TWO ENDS OF A POLE

Of all the aspects of internal auditing, the two which historically have been of greatest concern to the internal auditor are management support and audit independence. While the auditor has been seeking greater support from management, he has also been asserting his independence from that same management. The internal auditor has, in a sense, been attempting to take possession of the two separate ends of a ten-foot pole. The closer he comes to one end, the further he gets from the other. Only lately has the internal auditor begun to suspect that his two most important objectives may in some way be incompatible. Can he really assert his independence from a management on which he is so obviously dependent for support?

For a while, it seemed that enactment of the FCPA and his new relationship with the board audit committee might rescue the auditor from his dilemma. By and large, however, the auditor's new reporting relationship has only complicated his life even further. If anything, management support has become more complex, more subtle and perhaps even more elusive than ever.

AN INADEQUATE MODEL

The professional literature has treated the subject of management support rather superficially. Even the expression itself can mislead the auditor into thinking that he is dealing with a relatively simple and uncomplicated reality. The word "management" connotes the president, the chairman, the board audit committee or some such highly focused origin of support. Management, however defined, either supports the audit function or it doesn't. If it does, the function grows and prospers. If it doesn't, the function suffers from neglect and stagnates.

The prevalent management support model might be said to reflect conditions found in a typical small bank or savings and loan institution:

Internal auditing reports functionally to the board audit committee and administratively to the president.

Audit activities relate mainly to internal accounting control.

Audit programming and staffing are closely reviewed by the board audit committee.

Auditing enjoys a high degree of "independence."

Audit reports are reviewed in detail by the board audit committee and the president.

In this model, the board audit committee is a very active sponsor of the internal audit function. Management support means the support of the audit committee. By extension, management support may also mean the support of the president. There may be some ambiguity concerning auditing's independence from the president but there is little or no ambiguity below the level of the president. The "auditee" is essentially everyone below the president. As a practical matter, day-to-day audit independence applies to all activities below the president.

To the extent that the simple model described above fits the facts in many small organizations, the model serves a useful purpose. However, it is limited to a relatively simple and straightforward version of internal auditing which is not all that difficult to manage. The model is not an adequate reflection of reality as it is found in larger firms. It does not do justice to the complex and dynamic nature of management support in medium to large audit departments having a broad scope going well beyond financial audits and reviews of internal accounting control.

SUPPORT BELOW THE PRESIDENT

It is a common occurrence at professional conferences to meet internal auditors who are frustrated by their inability to secure management support for new activities they consider to be highly desirable. These auditors need to be told how the larger audit organizations with truly broad scopes got to where they are. But they are not likely to get this information at conference general sessions. If they are determined enough, however, they may get the education they are looking for by socializing with veterans of large audit organizations. The first thing they will learn is that recommendations to broaden the scope of the audit function are much more effective when supported by forces outside the audit organization itself. In fact, if senior management receives the same advice from its internal auditor *and* operating management, it finds such advice almost irresistible.

Imagine, for example, that an internal auditor is strongly convinced that a major construction project should be subjected to audit. She suggests this to the president. The president will most likely hesitate to approve such a move on his own. He will probably discuss the matter with the vice-president in charge of engineering and construction. Chances are at least sixty to forty that the vice-president will view the proposal as an attempt to check up on him and his people. If he can, he will try to block the proposal by saying that since the project is going as well as can be expected, an audit would not be worth the time and expense and would cause trouble with the project team. Failing to find a consensus on the internal auditor's proposal, the president will probably turn it down. Imagine, on the other hand, that the internal auditor has managed to secure support for her proposal from the vice-presidents of both engineering and construction and procurement. Given the inherent merit of the audit director's proposal, and the support of the two vice-presidents most involved in the project, the proposal now stands an excellent chance of obtaining senior management approval.

WHO IS MANAGEMENT?

In large corporations, the idea of "management" is really a convenient myth. In the real world of large corporations, there is no one person or group one can go to for the final word in all matters. Corporations may try to speak with one voice to the outside world, but they seldom offer this convenience to those on the inside. Inside the corporation, management is a diffuse and complex entity comprising the board, the chairman, the president, vice-presidents, a large number of department heads and various key staff individuals. These people are not necessarily of the same mind on any particular issue and many are in open conflict.

The single most important distinguishing characteristic of large corporations is the extent to which major responsibility is delegated downward to highly powerful, highly competent and highly paid executives. There is no way that the chairman and/or president of a large corporation can keep abreast of details in the way the head of a small company can. Innumerable major decisions are made every year at levels below senior management. The really big decisions may be reviewed by senior management and the board, but this review amounts to little more than ratification. Senior management and the board would not long tolerate subordinates whose recommendations had to be repeatedly rejected. In effect, therefore, most decision making takes place below the level of the chairman and the president. Decisions are effectively made by highly responsible executive, senior and junior vice-presidents. In certain cases, important decisions may be made by key department heads or senior staff personnel. The reality which we are describing may be termed "delegated authority" and it is this reality which the new internal auditor must reconcile himself to.

The internal auditor must give up his exclusive fixation on senior management and/or the board audit committee. In fact, the behavior of senior executives and audit committee members is a constant reminder to the internal auditor that he must deal effectively with delegated authority in most matters. Audit committees and senior management are seldom jealous of the loyalty of the internal auditor in the sense that they want him to avoid contact with the rest of management. They want him to resolve problems below their level whenever possible, and they have been around long enough to know what this entails.

The Corporate Mind

Let us adopt a metaphor and view management as the "mind" of the corporation. Let us specify our metaphor even further by dividing the corporate mind into a limited conscious component and a vast subconscious component. Conscious thinking and volition take place at the level of the board, the chairman and the president. Conscious thinking and deciding is, at any moment in time, reserved for relatively few matters of immediate concern to the corporate organism. All else is relegated to subordinate regions of the corporate mind which are expected to perform their functions with minimal intrusion upon conscious thinking. How, then, does management support for the internal audit function fit into our metaphor?

Management Support

Let us imagine that a corporation is about to set up an internal audit function for the first time. Working with the independent accountants and other groups, the chief corporate counsel drafts a charter for an internal auditing department. He (or she) presents his draft for review and approval at the next meeting of the board of directors. The board and senior management review the draft together and decide to approve it. The conscious element of the corporate mind has acted. Later, the director of audits prepares an operational plan as well as personnel and expenditure budgets for the coming year. These are reviewed and approved by senior management and the board audit committee. The conscious element of the corporate mind has acted again. It will act once more when it reviews the audit director's mid-year report to the board audit committee. Estimates might vary, but let us say that the corporate mind has devoted all of five conscious hours to the internal audit function during the first year of its existence.

The cycle repeats itself in the following year but with two differences. Internal auditing's charter is no longer an issue and therefore does not come up for official discussion. However, considerably more attention is devoted to the results of the internal audit program. Specific audits may come to the attention of the chairman and/or the president from time to time. The views of the vice-presidents concerned may be solicited. Their views concerning internal auditing's contribution to the organization may also be solicited at the time senior management reviews internal auditing's next annual plan and budget. These views may then be passed on in private discussions with members of the board audit committee. A consensus will be quickly reached concerning the degree of support and the amount of resources to be allotted to the internal audit function. During this second year, not much more than five to seven hours of conscious attention will have been given to the internal audit function. During the same period, the internal auditor may have spent little more than one hour in private conference with senior management, and another hour or two in discussions with the audit committee in full view of the controller, the independent accountants and senior management.*

*The internal audit function comprises only a part of the agenda of typical board audit committee meetings.

Chances are that the internal auditor did not have the opportunity for any significant *private* discussion with the board audit committee during the *entire* year.

There is nothing wrong about the process we've just described, but it does have its peculiarities. Of all the activities reporting to senior management and/or the board, internal auditing probably spends the least amount of time in direct and substantive interaction with these two groups. Internal auditing may actually have the distinction of being discussed much more often in its absence than in its presence. The situation strongly suggests that management support of the internal audit function is dependent to a significant degree upon the workings of the corporation's "subconscious mind."

Senior management and the board audit committee may read internal auditing's budget requests and activity reports, but they engage in surprisingly little *meaningful personal* communication with the auditing department. In making decisions about the degree of support and the amount of resources to be given to auditing, they rely very heavily upon information and opinions offered by key officers and executives who in turn are influenced by attitudes emanating from the deepest recesses of the corporation's subconscious mind. The inevitable conclusion to be drawn from this by internal auditors is that support of the audit function must be cultivated not only at the senior management and board levels but also at the levels of delegated authority where the corporation's day-to-day attitude toward internal auditing is determined.

NEED FOR DISTINCTIONS

As was stated in Chapter 4 on power, it is a myth that internal auditing is uninvolved in corporate politics. Its involvement may have its own distinctive character but it is still involvement. We have also established that "management" in a large corporation is a convenient myth representing what is in fact a diffuse and amorphous entity which few individuals, if any, totally understand. How, then, can an audit organization analyze and describe its political relationships and interactions with management? Obviously, to speak of internal auditing as having either good, bad or indifferent management support is not very helpful as a basis for action. Clearly, an internal audit organization proposing to manage its political relationships must know more than this. It must distinguish between different sources, types and degrees of management support.

Sources of Support

Sources of support for the internal auditing function can be *primary* or *secondary*. Some members of the organization support internal auditing because they themselves derive direct benefit from it. These are *primary* supporters. Others support internal auditing mainly because some primary user supports it. These are *secondary* supporters.

Types of Support

Certain individuals support all aspects of the internal audit function. These are *general* supporters. Other individuals support only certain specific aspects of the audit function. These are *specific* supporters.

Some individuals support one or more audit *activities* but do not support the specific managers, supervisors or auditors engaged in those activities. These are *functional* supporters. Other individuals not only support certain audit activities but also support the people engaged in these activities. These might be termed *personal* supporters.

Degrees of Support

For the sake of completeness, it is necessary to distinguish between *positive* support, *negative* support (opposition), and *neutral* support (indifference). Positive and negative support may, in turn, be described as *strong* or *weak*.

An Illustration

Let us assume that a new corporate president has been elected with a mandate to reform and modernize management practices on a broad front. The president feels that many, if not most, organizations within the company need to be stimulated to rethink their operations. He (or she) then selects the internal auditing department as one of the means to provide that stimulation. He encourages the director of internal auditing to develop a very broad capability including financial, EDP and especially operational and management audits. The president will of course expect most audit recommendations to be well founded, but he will not be unduly concerned if mistakes are occasionally made. Auditees will be allowed to reject recommendations which they strongly consider to be ill-advised, but they will not be free to reject the audit process. Such a president can be described as a *strong primary general* supporter of the audit function. Since the president's use of the audit function is far more extensive than would normally be envisioned by the audit committee or the chairman of the board, the latter might be described mainly as *secondary general* supporters of the audit function. Their support is largely dependent upon the president's continued primary support.*

A Second Illustration

Let us now assume another company where the controller historically has used her (or his) own internal audit division to perform quality assurance tasks relating to the accounting function. The controller in this case is a *primary general* supporter of the internal audit function. The president is a *secondary general* supporter of internal auditing, relying mainly upon the judgment of the controller in matters relating to the mission, size and composition of the audit group.

At some point, the company's board audit committee becomes persuaded that internal auditing should no longer report to the controller but should report to the committee itself. Given the committee's strong commitment to sound internal accounting controls, the committee becomes a *primary general* supporter of the audit function. Since internal auditing's new independence of the controller appears to be a concern to her, the controller decides to follow the audit committee's lead in her support of internal auditing. She has shifted her position to one of *secondary general* support.

Multiple Sponsorship of the Audit Function

Let us further assume, with respect to the same company, that the sales vice-president has had some serious problems relating to inventory control and customer order processing. He (or she) feels that he requires an ongoing compliance audit program to maintain necessary performance standards in his regional sales offices. He negotiates with the president and the director of internal auditing for the creation of a new, specialized audit group comprising seven auditors. The board audit committee is advised of the vice-president's request and agrees. Now we have a spe-

---

*The point being made here is of crucial importance to internal audit theorists and strategists. Except perhaps in the financial services industry, too much is being made of board audit committee support of the audit function. Even the IIA itself comes close to promoting the idea that the audit committee is, or should be, the primary sponsor of the full range of internal audit activities. For a long time to come, it will be much more realistic to view audit committees as primary supporters mainly of audit activities relating to internal accounting control. The support of audit committees with respect to the rest of the audit program will be secondary at best.

cialized activity within the audit organization which derives *primary specific* support from the sales vice-president and *secondary specific* support from the president and the board audit committee. The committee's and the president's support in the future will be more or less contingent upon the sales vice-president's assurance that the new audit group is effectively meeting its objectives.

Note that the addition of the new compliance audit group has changed the character of the internal audit function. Auditing no longer enjoys *primary general* support from anyone. It must look to the board audit committee for primary support of its financial audit activities and to the sales vice-president for primary support of its sales office compliance coverage. In a very real sense, auditing now has two bosses (sponsors) and must worry continuously about keeping them both happy.

An Increasingly Complex Pattern of Support

Again with respect to the same company, let us assume the creation of another specialized audit activity. The company is becoming increasingly aware of problems in the EDP area. Systems development projects are a hotbed of interdepartmental squabbling, are resulting in the resignation of valuable personnel, are overrunning cost and schedule estimates and sometimes fail together. Increasing attention is being given in the media to massive computer errors and fraud. Sensing an opportunity, the director of audits proposes the creation of an EDP audit function. The proposal is discussed by the president, the chairman, the controller and the board audit committee. All agree that the idea is timely, and the proposal is approved. The director of audits is instructed to "ride herd" on the data processing (DP) department and all other organizations involved in computer systems development.

Initially, the primary specific supporters of EDP audits include the board, senior management and the controller. The DP manager and his staff are hostile to the new audit function and may be classified as *primary specific opponents*. In a few months, however, the EDP auditors make so many adverse findings concerning the controller's role in systems development that he turns from being a *primary specific supporter* of EDP audits to a *primary specific opponent*. In time, both the DP manager and the controller are replaced with executives of much higher caliber and with proven ability and experience in computer systems development. Both executives begin by being *secondary specific supporters* of EDP auditing.

Somewhat later, EDP auditing begins to show signs of errors in judgment. It fails to react appropriately to the new audit environment and continues to operate in a strongly adversary mode. Morale at the working level both in data processing and in the controller's area becomes progressively worse. Both the controller and the DP manager find that audit reports are exacerbating a difficult management and leadership problem. They feel threatened. They discuss the matter with the president and he shows signs of sympathy toward their case. Perhaps EDP auditing is getting a little out of hand and becoming part of the problem.

Discrete conversations are held with the director of audits who, in turn, talks with his EDP auditing manager. Unfortunately, this has no effect and the situation worsens. In just a few months, the president has changed his position. He may still be a primary supporter of the EDP audit function, but he now distinguishes between his support of the *function* and his support of the *leadership*. This is a cue to the DP manager and the controller that they must maintain their secondary support of EDP auditing but are free to attack its leadership. Eventually, the political tide shifts in their favor. The result? An EDP audit manager and two supervisors circulating fresh resumes around the local business community and still wondering what happened to them. Didn't auditing report directly to the board audit committee? How could managers lower on the organization chart upset the applecart that way? In time, and perhaps after reading this book, they'll figure it out and be the better for it. The profession will have acquired three new adherents to the new internal auditing and the partnership concept.

Fortunately for the director of audits, he survives the shake-up of his EDP audits division. As he mulls over the implications of his trying experience, his private conclusions about himself are mixed. He was not disloyal to his EDP audit manager. He did caution him that the environment had changed and that he should go easy for a while. Unfortunately, the EDP audit manager did not react quickly enough and had to be let go. On the other hand, the director of audits did not recognize the true seriousness of the situation. And even if he had, it isn't at all clear that he could have succeeded in turning his EDP audit manager around in time. To do so would have required management support concepts that he is only now beginning to develop.

Another Activity—Another Sponsor

A few months later, a situation comes up which offers the director an opportunity to try out some of the new ideas he has formulated. A chance discussion with the production vice-president discloses that the vice-president is wrestling with a difficult problem. He has been trying for months to persuade his managers that they should be more aggressive in identifying opportunities to improve productivity. The only response he's received is that opportunities for improvement are very limited and that time and resources are lacking to pursue them. The vice-president has thought of setting up a methods group within his organization but isn't sure it would get him the results he wants. His predecessor tried this years before and found that the group became politically polarized within a year and lost much of its effectiveness. What he needs is help from outside his organization. However, the company has no resources matching his needs, and outside consultants are too expensive and usually lack a feel for the company.

A few days following this conversation, the director of audits hits upon an idea. What if *he* acquired the capability to help the production vice-president with his problem? He already has a good operational auditor with an engineering degree and proven ability to relate to the technically oriented departments of the company. The auditor is ready for supervision and could be made the head of a special group specializing in productivity reviews and industrial engineering. If the group proved successful in the production department, it might expand its services companywide.

Multiple Disclosure Patterns

The audit director asks the production vice-president to lunch and explains his proposal. The vice-president is intrigued by the idea of a corporate-level staff of industrial engineers backed up by the status of the internal audit department and led by people with company savvy. But he sees one problem. Doesn't the audit director report all of his findings to senior management and the board? That kind of visibility is not what he had in mind. It could result in off-the-wall instructions from the top on how to do his job and that could be a disaster for him and his department. The audit director has anticipated this objection and offers the following solution. The productivity-improvement support activity will be managed separately from the regular audit program. There will be no "findings" relating to internal accounting control, which is the board audit committee's real area of concern. Detailed reports will go no higher than the vice-president of production. All that will be reported at the senior management and board levels is how audit resources are being utilized and what general results are being obtained. Auditing will be presented as working in a support role with respect to production management. If the program occasionally produces dramatic results, these will be presented as accomplishments of the production department with the support of auditing. But there will have to be reporting of some kind. Internal auditing is staff, and management has always insisted on a full accounting of the use made of staff personnel.

Service to the Organization

The vice-president of production agrees to the audit director's proposal and states that he will put the matter to the president when he meets with him in a couple of days. Soon, everything is settled and the audit department acquires a new area of responsibility with growth potential. The audit director has learned his lesson. There is more to management support than senior management and the board audit committee. As stated in the IIA's *Statement of Responsibilities of Internal Auditing*, internal auditing is an independent appraisal activity established within an *organization* as a service to the *organization*. This broad concept of service permits internal auditing to provide assistance anywhere it is needed in the organization. For this concept to work, internal auditing must cultivate the support of *all* of management consistent, of course, with the proper observance of priorities.

MANAGEMENT AND AUDITEES

Under the new internal auditing, the terms "management" and "auditee" assume a dynamic character such that the same individual can one day be management and on the next, the auditee. As a practical matter, whoever is the explicit or implicit sponsor of an audit becomes "management" for purposes of that audit. The term "auditee" then applies to whatever activity or organization is subject to review in a particular audit.

If, therefore, a relatively low-level manager were to request an audit of a clerical activity under his jurisdiction, he would be viewed by internal auditing as "management" and the clerical activity would be the "auditee." If significant findings were made, and if the manager proposed to take corrective action, auditing would presumably handle disclosure in such a way as to avoid undue embarrassment to the manager who requested the audit. Such an approach to disclosure works to the benefit of the overall organization by encouraging managers to seek the assistance of the auditing organization. It results in problems being solved which might otherwise remain undetected at considerable cost to the organization.

IMPORTANCE OF SCOPE

Most internal auditors find it necessary for good audit relations not to report "wildcat" findings which are clearly outside the stated scope of an audit. This time-proven courtesy to managers and auditees will be especially important in the context of the partnership concept and the new internal auditing. When a manager requests a service from the auditing department, and the auditing department enters into a client relationship with that manager, it would be a culturally unacceptable form of role switching for auditing to seize upon an extraneous finding, declare its obligation to a higher sponsor and turn the client into an auditee. This sort of thing may be necessary in extremely unusual cases, but any abuse would be bound to damage internal auditing's effectiveness in the long run. Fearing that internal auditing can't be trusted, managers at all levels would avoid calling upon auditing for assistance. The result would be a decline in the demand for audit services and severe damage to auditing's ability to contribute to the welfare of the organization.

MANAGEMENT SUPPORT AS DEMAND

It is likely that the very idea of "management support" has handicapped audit organizations in their efforts to expand the scope of their services. The term "management support" acts as a defective compass pointing in the wrong direction as internal auditors struggle to find their way out of their predicament. Auditors ready to acknowledge the futility of their present course need only discard their compass marked "management support" and reach for the other marked "demand for audit services." This compass will serve them much better in their search for the open valley and green fields of the new internal auditing.

GROWTH CYCLE OF INTERNAL AUDIT ORGANIZATIONS

Experience and reflection strongly suggest that the growth cycle of internal audit organizations can be broken down into three phases:

    Birth and infancy
    Adolescence
    Maturity

Birth and Infancy

Initial demand for audit services invariably springs from a strongly felt need by someone at a fairly high level in the organization. Most internal audit organizations in existence today trace their early beginnings to the controller's need for a quality assurance activity within the accounting function. Audit organizations established in recent years probably trace their origins to their board audit committees' need for assurance concerning the adequacy of internal accounting controls. In either case, it is interesting to note that the initial demand for internal auditing was sufficiently strong that it was not dependent on urgings by internal auditing itself. Internal auditing didn't exist. It was created and nurtured by someone who wanted it.

Adolescence

As internal auditing grew in various organizations, it became increasingly aware of its strength and abilities. It began to chafe at the boundaries placed around it and to yearn for greater freedom. Being a typical adolescent, internal auditing asserted its independence from its creators and insisted upon its "right" to an unlimited field of play. Senior management was not unsympathetic toward internal auditing's desire for a larger role and did, from time to time, allow it to explore new territory. Predictably, internal auditing got scratched and bruised and came racing back to seek management's "support." Internal auditing invented the idea of management support as a means of being allowed to do what it wished whether others liked it or not. Management did, in fact, provide support when it suited its purpose. This usually happened when management was already unhappy with an auditee and did not mind (or even welcomed) the disturbance which an audit would create. But management could not support internal auditing's demand for unlimited freedom since this would produce effects at variance with management's need to maintain a positive leadership climate.

This is where many internal audit organizations find themselves today. Bolstered by obsolete or ambiguous internal audit doctrines, they remain self-centered, self-righteous, assertive of their independence and insistent upon support. Internal auditing is like the businessman's son: eager, ambitious and insistent upon a greater role in the family business. The businessman, on the other hand, knows from years of experience that business "ownership" involves many constraints and that one cannot always impose one's will on employees, vendors, banks and others upon whom the business depends for survival.

Maturity

A number of internal audit organizations have already passed into maturity and a growing number of others appear ready to take the leap.

The clearest sign of incipient maturity in audit organizations is a progressive abandonment of the idea of independence from management and the realization that the support of senior management and the audit committee cannot make up for lack of acceptance on the part of the rest of the organization.

The mature audit organization seldom talks about independence. Its operative concepts are usefulness, integrity and quality of work product. Nor does the mature audit organization waste its psychic energy on futile hopes of enlisting more top management support. Instead, it seeks to stimulate a greater *demand* for its services. It does this not by cultivating senior management and the audit committee alone, but by cultivating all potential clients throughout the organization.

The key to achieving greater support from the audit committee and senior management is to secure positive acceptance of the internal audit function at the lower levels. An unfortunate aspect of internal auditing today is that it is largely an *imposed* service to the organization. The new internal auditing will seek to stimulate demand for audit services below the level of senior management. This will require new attitudes concerning audit independence and audit disclosure, and the forging of a new relationship with operating management. Aloof and critical attitudes toward operating management (and auditees) must be replaced by a willingness to work in a helpful mode with all levels of the organization.

STRATEGY OF THE NEW INTERNAL AUDITING

The new internal auditing will use its mandate to conduct regular financial, EDP and compliance audits as a means of maintaining contact with the organization. Every auditor, audit supervisor and audit manager will be a salesperson, continually on the lookout for situations where operating management may need assistance in solving problems and identifying positive measures to improve operations. Drawing from the strength provided by its organizational status and separation (audit independence), internal auditing will selectively enter into consultant-client relationships with operating management. We say *selectively* because such relationships will be deemed acceptable only when they clearly promote corporate objectives, conform to senior management's wishes, assure quality of work product, and respect the code of ethics of internal auditing. Auditing will use its independence and will plead inadequate resources in order to avoid engagements which seek to exploit its status to promote sectarian objectives of doubtful merit best left to established political processes. Where sectarian conflicts threaten the welfare of the organization as a whole, auditing may use its independence to initiate inquiries which, although objective in nature, will tend to support the "right" side in the conflicts.

It is through a strategy such as we have just described that the new internal auditing will promote greater acceptance of the audit function at the level of operating management. Once senior management begins to hear good things about the audit function, it will acquire a new and broader appreciation of its potential and will once again permit it to grow.

AUDIT SCHEDULING

Current fashion has it that internal audit departments should develop set audit schedules for the coming year, secure senior management and audit committee approval of these schedules and invite judgments concerning their effectiveness on the basis of conformance to the schedules. Internal auditing may be setting a trap for itself in promoting such an approach to audit management.

Military commanders have always preferred to communicate with civilian authorities in terms of objectives and general strategy—not in terms of detailed plans. In this manner, military commanders reserve the initiative and flexibility they require to seize opportunities and react to unforeseen emergencies. In like manner, directors of internal auditing should not request approval of detailed plans and schedules from senior management and the board. Instead, they should seek agreement concerning general audit objectives and retain the freedom and initiative to operate not as a bureaucracy but as a true management function.

In most medium to large corporations, internal auditing finds itself pursuing a variety of moving targets, reacting to changing priorities and developing new approaches, tools and techniques. Any attempt to formulate and enforce rigid plans and schedules in such an environment can only result in ineffectiveness and waste of resources. If the new internal auditing is to truly serve the whole organization, it will have to maintain the ability to respond to unforeseen management requests on a timely basis. There will have to be planning—but planning must never be permitted to stand in the way of the best interests of the enterprise.

SUMMARY

Internal auditing can't assert its independence from management while being so obviously dependent on it for support.

Prevailing models of management support are often based on simple stereotypes which do not reflect the complex realities of most medium to large corporations.

The single most important distinguishing characteristic of large corporations is delegated authority. Internal auditors must give up their exclusive fixation on senior management and/or the board audit committee. The behavior of senior executives and audit committees is a constant reminder that internal auditors must deal effectively with delegated authority in most matters.

Internal audit organizations proposing to manage their political relationships will need to distinguish between different sources, types and degrees of support. Management support can be primary or secondary; general or specific; functional or personal; positive, negative or neutral; strong or weak.

Management support patterns are dynamic and subject to change. They require continuous monitoring and evaluation.

The ultimate key to achieving greater support from the audit committee and senior management is to secure acceptance and support at the lower levels of the organization.

The term "management support" was better suited to earlier periods of internal auditing's development. In attaining professional maturity, auditing will do better to think in terms of demand for audit services.

Internal auditing serves the entire organization. Practically any level of management can be a client of the internal audit department. Internal auditors must treat clients as clients and must support their legitimate interests consistent with proper observance of the order of loyalties within the organization.

Under the new internal auditing, every auditor, audit supervisor and audit manager will act as a salesperson.

Flexible planning will be required so that the new internal auditing may seize opportunities and react effectively to unforeseen management requests.

DISCUSSION

All of the previous discussions concerning the role of internal auditing, audit independence, ethics, power and the attitudes of board audit committees, management and auditees have been a prelude to this chapter on management support. In this chapter, we have constructed an alternative to the simplistic management support model described or assumed in much of the professional literature. Our model attempts to describe the vastly more complex environment to be found in medium to large firms where internal auditing operates well beyond the traditional boundaries of internal accounting control. In such firms, we see internal auditing as having to manage a variety of activities with reference to a complex and subtle pattern of management support.

Our model of the internal auditing function within a medium to large corporation will have a disturbing quality for some of our readers. This should come as no surprise. After all, large corporations are a relatively new institution whose culture is alien to most Americans even today. One might wish that support of the internal audit function in large American corporations were simpler and more forthright—but wishing will not make it so. In fact, reports concerning modes of consensus building and decision making in Japanese corporations lead us to believe that American corporations have by no means exhausted the viable limits of social subtlety and complexity.

Readers may ask how the management support model described in this chapter was arrived at. The model does not reflect observed reality in any one organization. Rather, it is a logical composite of actual conditions and *tendencies* existing in various organizations. Its value will depend upon whether it rings true to other experienced professionals and helps to bring the profession closer to its long-time goal of "unlimited scope."

PART 4

The Audit Report

CHAPTER 12

A Question of Professionalism

Write makes might.

ANONYMOUS

THE REPORT-WRITING PROBLEM

In 1982, a survey of directors of internal auditing disclosed that report writing ranked very high among the problems being experienced by the profession. More recently, a corporate chief executive told his audience at an internal audit management conference that few if any auditors knew how to write. Although the chief executive may have been engaging in rhetorical overstatement, report writing does present a persistent problem to many auditors. To be fair, however, it must be acknowledged that writing an audit report is a considerably more difficult task than writing an ordinary business report.

The internal audit profession has striven mightily to respond to the report-writing challenge. Audit departments have availed themselves of in-house corporate training programs as well as formal courses and seminars offered by various outside organizations. Many approaches have been used. Some programs have emphasized basic English grammar and usage. Others have concentrated on business English and the writing of business correspondence and reports. Although all of these programs have done some good, their results have not been dramatic. There are probably two reasons for this. First, writing is a skill which takes considerable time and effort to develop. It is unreasonable to expect overnight results. Second, the programs didn't go far enough. General courses on remedial English or business writing did not address the unique aspects of audit report writing.

COURSES ON AUDIT REPORT WRITING

Some organizations and individual entrepreneurs did finally recognize the unique nature of the audit report-writing problem and began to offer programs tailor-made for the internal auditor. Chances are, however, that even these latest programs will produce disappointing results. Even though many internal auditors have asked to be shown specifically, and in detail, how to write their reports, there is a danger in yielding to this request. Any course which attempts to make financial, operational and other types of auditors from different industries and companies write reports in the same way is probably doomed to failure. The results will be rejected by the very managers and supervisors who sent the auditors to the course in the first place. Every auditor who attends a report-writing course must ultimately contend with the format and style preferences of his own organization. If what he has been taught is too specific, he won't be able to use it.

There is still another difficulty in teaching audit report writing which must be recognized. What needs to be taught goes beyond "writing." Or, to put it differently, the idea of writing must be broadened to include a host of things which have little to do with stringing one grammatically correct sentence after another. Consider this: what is the difference between a first-class novelist and a hack journalist? Obviously, both know how to "write." Both are capable of spelling words correctly, composing grammatical sentences and building coherent paragraphs. What distinguishes the novelist from the ordinary writer is that he possesses a special kind of *knowledge* and *feeling* about his subject. That special knowledge and feeling causes him to express himself in a special way. The same is true of internal auditors. Writers of effective audit reports must have mastered certain technical aspects of report writing; but they must also possess a special kind of knowledge and feeling about internal auditing in general and about their own management and auditees.

AUDITING AND REPORT WRITING

In order to really do the job, courses on report writing must ultimately teach auditing. We do not mean that *everything* about auditing must be taught in a course on report writing. But there are a number of things about auditing which must be explained and referred to in order to deal adequately with the problem of report writing. In fact, one might say that teaching report writing forces one to consider many important aspects of internal auditing which are seldom addressed on their own. This is why this book on the new internal auditing includes five chapters on the subject of report writing. Many aspects of internal auditing in general, and of the new internal auditing in particular, will be specified and clarified as we discuss audit report writing.

MANAGERS AND SUPERVISORS

Most supervisors, managers and audits directors have risen to their present rank partly because of their superior communication ability. Interestingly, it is precisely those who are already skilled at audit report writing who may find these chapters most useful. Why? Because it is one thing to write effectively and quite another to show someone else how to do it.

Most good writers are "instinctive" writers. They can write well but they can't explain how they do it. This is why the review of audit report drafts can be such a frustrating experience for supervisors and managers. Their instincts can emit powerful signals when something about a report is all wrong, but they can't articulate a clear explanation of it. Auditors are told to go back and try again. They do, but they fail more often than not. Or they are given instructions that take considerable time to implement but which still fail to satisfy the reviewer. Given sufficient incentive and sufficient time, reviewers of audit reports might be able to reflect upon their inner mental processes and work out a systematic exposition of how they put a good audit report together. Chances are, however, that they will never have the occasion to do this. It takes too much time and effort. This is unfortunate, because an up-front explanation of what it takes to write a good audit report is badly needed by the inexperienced internal auditor.

THE AUDITOR'S PERSPECTIVE

Frustrating as the report-writing problem may be for the manager and supervisor, it is doubly so for the auditor himself. The auditor likes his work, but he would like it much more if he didn't have to struggle with report writing.

The whole process of getting his report approved by his supervisor is unpleasant for the auditor. He knows before he starts that whatever he does will be poorly received. His initial draft will be severely criticized, but not in a way which provides a clear idea of what should be done. Three or four drafts later, the auditor will be convinced that the supervisor won't be satisfied until he has written the report himself.

As if this were not bad enough, there is no guarantee that a report which has made it through the supervisor will be approved by the manager. Typically the manager will have objections or insights of his own that will require further modification of the report. This is why the auditor dislikes report writing. It's nothing but a hassle from beginning to end. Everyone knows what he doesn't like, but no one can tell him beforehand what he does like. It's as if rules are being invented on the spot just to find fault with his work. The report is too long or too short, too general or too detailed, too vague or too blunt. If there are any consistent rules governing the writing of audit reports, why can't someone spell them out ahead of time?

REPORT-WRITING GUIDELINES

Frustrated writers of audit reports have a legitimate complaint. Why can't managers and supervisors outline their criteria for acceptable audit reports? Auditors would then have some idea of what they are striving for. What is needed is an overall theory of audit report writing that can be referred to by all those involved in the report writing and review process. The process would still have its rough spots, but progress would come more easily. Auditors would learn more quickly how to meet the requirements imposed by their superiors.

The following chapters represent an attempt to build a general theory of audit report writing. The theory has been used with considerable success in actual internal audit practice. Also, it has been well received by a significant number of experienced internal auditors at seminars conducted in Southern California. All of this notwithstanding, the material in these chapters is offered with considerable hesitancy and reservation. The material may not be entirely suitable to the purposes and preferences of every audit organization. In certain cases, the specifics discussed may not be acceptable but the *principles* underlying the specifics may have general applicability. Or, the chapters as a whole may provide sufficient insight into the report-writing problem to facilitate readers' efforts to formulate their own guidelines.

PROFESSIONALISM AND REPORT WRITING

Surprising as it may seem, many internal auditors are not motivated to improve their report-writing skills. Simply put, they seriously doubt that report writing is as important as some people say. These auditors much prefer the field-work aspects of internal auditing and find report writing a bore. The truly important part of internal auditing takes place in the field, they say. Report writing is just so much window dressing.

One cannot refute this point of view by minimizing the importance of field work. Field work *is* extremely important and many audits fail because of technical or human relations errors committed by auditors in the field. If auditors who minimize the importance of report writing are in fact good in the field, they must be given full credit for that. No audit director would want an auditor who is only skilled in report writing but can't perform field work effectively. In fact, if an audit director were confronted with an either/or choice, he would have to choose the auditor who is good in the field and leave it to supervisors to improve the auditor's reports. Insofar as the final product is concerned, however, the audit director has no viable choice between good field work and good report writing. He must have both. It's a question of professionalism, and the true professional seeks excellence in all that he does. In a competitive world, he has no choice but to do this.

Two Aspects of Professionalism

It's interesting to note that practically any profession one can think of has two basic types of tasks: back-room tasks and tasks involving interface with the client. Consider a doctor, for example. First, she (or he) meets with the patient (client). She does everything possible to put the patient at ease and to gain his confidence. She inquires about the patient's complaint and symptoms. She conducts an examination and performs or orders various tests. These are client-interface tasks, and the doctor must do them well if she wants to develop a prosperous practice. After the patient leaves, the doctor must analyze test results, look up information in her medical library and perhaps consult with associates. These are "back-room" tasks and it is essential that the doctor perform these tasks correctly in order to diagnose her patient's illness and prescribe the proper treatment. Then the doctor must once again meet with the patient. It is at this critical point of client interface that value passes from the doctor to the patient. The doctor must persuade the patient that she has correctly identified his illness. She must also motivate the patient to submit faithfully to the prescribed course of treatment. Unless the doctor is competent in all aspects of her work, she will lose her patient—either to the illness or to another doctor. It is clear in any case that the doctor does not have the luxury of choosing whether she will excel at her back-room tasks or in her relations with her patients. She must excel at both.

Excellence in All Things

The same is true of all other professions. The truly successful must excel in all that they do. Attorneys must excel both in the law library and in front of the jury. Musicians must excel not only in the practice room but also on the concert stage. Professional soldiers must not only excel in war games, they must also win battles. And internal auditors must not only produce sound conclusions and recommendations, they must also be able to convince and persuade management through the excellence of their communications and human relations. Audit reports may not represent the *only* point of interface where value is passed from the auditor to management. As was pointed out in Chapter 10, the new internal auditing may have the effect of reducing the relative importance of the audit report in the overall scheme of things. However, diminished relative importance is a far cry from little or no importance. Internal auditing has no choice but to exploit to the fullest every opportunity to inform and persuade management and auditees. Audit reports will continue to provide such an opportunity, and auditors must make the best of it.

IMPORTANCE OF THE AUDIT

In certain cases, auditors who complain about their inability to write good audit reports are complaining about the wrong thing. The trouble may not be with their writing skills but with their audit skills. Lest any of us become too absorbed in the fun and challenge of report writing, it is well to remember that any good audit report must first start with a good audit.

Nothing so effectively points out errors and omissions made during an audit as trying to make sense of the results on paper. Let's face it: some audit reports are poor because the underlying audit was poorly executed. Some reports appear badly organized and lacking in coherence and authority because the audit itself had no clear purpose or plan.

Importance of the Audit Plan

There is a secret to good report writing which all experienced auditors, analysts and consultants understand: the writing of a good report begins when a project is being planned. Truly professional auditors do not distinguish between planning an audit, performing it and writing about it. It all takes place together in their minds. An audit plan is satisfactory when the auditor can clearly see himself performing the audit successfully and writing a clear and persuasive report on the result. There is a direct causal relationship between audit planning, auditing and audit report writing. One can't have a good audit report without a good audit. And one can't have a good audit without a good audit plan. The plan need not be in writing, but it must exist in some form—perhaps only in the auditor's mind. For those who are not convinced, consider the following true case in point.

An EDP auditor once told his manager that he was coming to the end of a particular audit and was worried about his report. When asked why, the auditor replied that he had no findings and wouldn't have much to say in his report. The manager said that that shouldn't pose any problem; no one ever said that "findings" had to be unfavorable. All the auditor had to do was to state his objectives and scope, specify his criteria for each area reviewed and certify that controls and operations were adequate. This elicited a sheepish look from the auditor. He couldn't do as the manager suggested. He couldn't certify any of the areas he had reviewed. He hadn't approached the audit that way. He literally had nothing to say in his report. He hadn't come upon any adverse findings, but neither did he have a documented basis for pronouncing any area satisfactory.

Bill of Health

Our story, which actually happened, provides a particularly pertinent illustration of the relationship between the audit plan and the audit report. The auditor in the story had done no planning whatsoever. He had not identified specific objectives or established any evaluation criteria. He had simply jumped into his audit and thrashed about for five weeks expecting to stumble over some obvious deficiencies. Unfortunately for him, he had not found any. There might have been a time, in some organizations, when auditing could be done this way. Controls were so few, and problems so prevalent, that practically anyone, no matter how ill-trained, could go into an area without any plan whatsoever and come out with an armful of findings a short while later. There was no need for professionalism. Unfortunately for those of us who dislike structure and planning, things have changed since the early days of internal auditing. Operations and controls have become much more sophisticated, and so has internal auditing.

We can reinforce our point by again referring to the medical profession. Imagine that someone bursts into a doctor's office saying, "Doctor, help me. I'm dying." The patient is bleeding profusely from an injured right arm. The diagnosis takes only thirty seconds: dislocated shoulder, fractured upper arm and severed artery. No trick to it. Any first-year medical student could have done it. Imagine, on the other hand, that the doctor's next patient is an applicant for a $10 million insurance policy. The insurance company wants a complete medical examination before it issues a policy. Now that will require professionalism. Diagnosing a broken arm is one thing. But certifying a person who looks hale and hearty to be in perfect health is quite another. To do the latter, a doctor must know precisely what she (or he) is seeking to determine and must conduct systematic tests. Unless the doctor approaches her task in this manner, she will be unable to issue a credible bill of health. Similarly, unless an internal auditor knows his objectives, identifies appropriate evaluation criteria and conducts all necessary audit tests, he will be unable to write an audit report that is truly effective and professional.

SUMMARY

Report writing ranks very high among the problems acknowledged by the internal audit profession.

Efforts to improve auditors' report-writing skills have not always been successful.

Good report writing is a question of professionalism. It deserves to be done well for its own sake.

Although the relative importance of the audit report may diminish under the new internal auditing, the audit report will continue to provide an important means of informing and persuading auditees and management.

Report writing cannot be separated from auditing: one is an extension of the other.

There is a direct, causal relationship between audit planning, auditing and audit report writing. Many difficulties in audit report writing are traceable to poor audit planning.

DISCUSSION

Although audit reports may play a less critical role under the new internal auditing, there is a way in which they may present a greater challenge than before. Today, much of internal auditing is conducted on its own terms. Internal auditors establish the overall audit program as well as the objectives and scope of individual audits. Auditees and managers have little to say about the audit process and have been conditioned to accept audit reports as reflecting the standards of an alien profession which they are not qualified to judge or criticize.

Under the new internal auditing, operating management will play a much greater role in defining the objectives and scope of auditing and internal consulting engagements. Internal auditing will be conducted less on its own terms and more on the terms of operating managers. Operating managers may, as involved clients, entertain higher expectations with respect to audit reports than they did formerly as passive auditees.

The new internal auditing will depend less on top-level management support and more on acceptance by operating management. The new internal auditor will in a sense be in business for himself. If he is to succeed, he must master the art of report writing as must any professional management consultant.

CHAPTER 13

Audit Report Fundamentals

Nature is always hinting at us.
It hints over and over again.
And suddenly we take the hint.

ROBERT FROST, Comment

THE FOUR FUNDAMENTALS

Internal auditors who are new to the profession or who have not had any training in report writing will be relieved to learn that a good audit report need only satisfy four fundamental criteria:

1. Objectivity.
2. Authoritativeness.

3.   Balance.
4.   Professional styling.

Basically, that's all there is to it. The auditor has only four things to keep in mind as he plans, writes and polishes his report. If he satisfies these four criteria, he is guaranteed to have an above-average report. He is also guaranteed that his supervisor and manager will like the report. They may not be able to explain exactly why, but they'll like it. They may ask the auditor to make minor changes here and there, but they will go out of their way to tell him he did a fine job. This chapter discusses each of the four criteria. Let us begin with the first: objectivity.

OBJECTIVITY

Objectivity Is Not Self-Preoccupied

An objective audit report addresses the subject matter of the audit, not the procedural or housekeeping details of the audit process. Many clues tell the reader whether a report was written by a seasoned professional or by a relative amateur. The clue most often dropped by the amateur is self-preoccupation. The amateur doesn't write about the topic: he writes about *himself* and about *his* audit. Let us say that an auditor with a tendency toward self-preoccupation has performed an audit of accounts payable. She (or he) writes a story describing how she went about auditing accounts payable. There are details concerning how she planned, initiated and accomplished the audit. More space is devoted to a description of the audit tests than to the test results themselves. We are not told that 12% of payments reviewed were not supported by receiving reports. Instead, we read that "one of the tests performed by the auditor was to examine the completed payments file in room 213 to determine whether . . . ." This language focuses on the auditor and what she did rather than on operations and controls, which should be the real subject matter of her report. A little of this in an audit report may not be all that bad, but some reports are full of irrelevant details about the auditor: what he did, how hard he worked, how long something took, how he was treated and so forth. It's as if one had paid good money for a set of family portraits only to find that the photographer had somehow managed to include himself in every picture.

When an auditor decides to get out of the subjective mode of writing, he at first experiences considerable difficulty. Once he surmounts that difficulty, however, the result can be a complete transformation of his writing style. Suddenly his reports come to life. Auditees and management can't help but find the reports interesting because the reports are about their world, and not the world of the auditor.

Objectivity Deals with the World of the Auditee

Objective audit reports do not attempt to make readers conform to the auditor's way of thinking by making continual references to auditing concepts, categories and terminology. If these are truly relevant to the area reviewed, there is a way of translating them into the concepts and vocabulary of the auditee. For example, operational auditors often find it useful to view operations in terms of planning, organizing, directing and controlling. These concepts are extremely powerful tools for the evaluation of operations. It does not follow, however, that audit reports should necessarily be organized and written on the basis of these abstract concepts. If the concepts are relevant, there is a way to address them in terms reflecting the real world of the auditee.

Let us assume that an auditor has correctly diagnosed an area as deficient with respect to planning. He (or she) has two ways to make his case. The less desirable way is to describe what good planning should be and then show that certain necessary elements of good planning are lacking. This is a less desirable way because it is subjective. It consists in judging the auditee's operations by standards understood mainly by the auditor. The auditor's standards may be valid, and his evaluation may be entirely correct, but the tone of the report will seem foreign to the auditee. A far better way for the auditor to make his case, if it can be done, is to cite specific evidence of ineffectiveness and/or inefficiency in the auditee's operations which are traceable to poor planning. Having made his point in the auditee's own terms, the auditor can then suggest specific corrective actions of a planning nature which would eliminate the ineffectiveness and/or inefficiency. Reports written in this style have an entirely different tone. Their credibility to management is much higher since they deal with the concrete, objective world of operations rather than the abstract, subjective world of management theory and internal auditing.

Note well, in this case, the relationship between report writing and auditing itself. The auditor's resolve to write a report reflecting the world of the auditee may actually require a different kind of field work. The auditor would devote more time to identifying and measuring the *impact* of poor planning before attempting to persuade management to take corrective action. *Impact* is an extremely important internal auditing concept in that it translates easily into something management understands and takes seriously. Impact is objective.

Objectivity Is Not Self-Serving

There is still another way in which true professionals differ from amateurs in their writing style. Professionals are self-confident and assume that the value of their work is recognized by others. Amateurs, on the other hand, are unsure of themselves. They are especially unsure of being properly understood and appreciated. As a result, the writing of amateurs is sprinkled with self-serving comments designed to impress the reader with the wonderful contribution made by themselves or by their organizations.

There is a time and a place for auditing to report on its achievements, but that should seldom be the audit report—whose chief purpose is to enlist the concurrence of auditees and managers. Let's face it: most auditees and operating managers prefer to be the heroes in matters falling within their own territory.

Self-serving comments by auditors do nothing but alienate the reader. Note again the connection between audit report writing and auditing generally. Report writing is not an isolated, technical skill. It involves the same human relations principles which must be followed throughout the audit process.

Objectivity Is Impersonal

We all bemoan the fact that modern life is becoming increasingly impersonal. At one time or another, we all have the impulse to contribute to a return to a warmer and more personal style of business communications. It's a nice thought, but it usually doesn't work in the area of audit report writing. There is much to be said in favor of a depersonalized approach to writing audit reports.

In order to be effective, audit reports need to separate audit considerations from personal considerations. The idea is to focus the reader's attention on the proper subject matter of the audit report, which is operations and controls, and to avoid interjecting personalities into findings, conclusions and recommendations. In other words, the writer should let the facts speak for themselves. There is an interesting paradox in effective audit report writing. The writer must be extremely sensitive to people while seldom if ever actually mentioning people in his report. It's as if the auditor demonstrates his human relations skills in the things he *doesn't* say.

How does the auditor go about depersonalizing the language of his report? First of all, he avoids writing in the first person—singular or plural. An audit report is not an "I" or a "we" document. It's not a report about the auditor, *his* findings, conclusions or recommendations. A well-written audit report reads as though it has nothing to do with the auditor. To the extent that the contents of the report may be unwelcome by the auditee, the report at least does not invite undue attention to its author.

Another way by which the auditor can depersonalize his report is to avoid all unnecessary references to the auditee. Proper names should almost never be mentioned in an audit report. It is better to use titles because titles have less personal impact. In very sensitive matters, organization titles are better than personal titles, and functional titles are even better than organization titles. Note the increasing personal impact conveyed by the following alternative ways of referring to the auditee:

Reference to the Auditee	Impact
Accounts payable (function)	Low
Accounts Payable Division (organization title)	Moderate
Manager of Accounts Payable (personal title)	High
Mr. Jones (proper name)	Very high

Objectivity Does Not Arouse or Offend

When auditors say they are "objective," they usually refer to their freedom from bias. Most auditors are very proud of their objectivity and view themselves as having a special claim to this admirable quality. Yet auditors may not have as much to be proud of as they believe. It's not difficult to be objective when one knows little or nothing about an area. The real trick is to maintain one's objectivity to the end—right through to the completion of an audit and the writing of the audit report.

If the truth be admitted, too many auditors have completely lost their objectivity by the time they finish their audits. Their objectivity has in fact diminished with every adverse finding so that by the time their reports are written the auditors have developed a clear bias against the auditee. The proof of this is in the language used by the auditors in their reports. Consciously or unconsciously, the auditors have selected words and phrases designed to arouse the disapproval of higher levels of management and bound to offend the sensibilities of the auditee. Probably half of all changes requested by reviewers of audit reports have to do with the elimination of objectionable language. Again, it's a question of letting the facts speak for themselves. The truly professional writer of audit reports describes his findings with meticulous objectivity and eschews all modes of expression that tend to project his personal feelings or to manipulate the emotions of his readers. Audit reports should read like a news item in the *Christian Science Monitor* and not like an opinion piece in a Hollywood scandal sheet.

AUTHORITATIVENESS

"Authoritative" may seem like a strange word for describing what an audit report should be. Note, however, that we said *authoritative*, not authoritarian.

What do we mean when we say that audit reports should be authoritative? Simply, that they should be believable, or credible. Authoritativeness is that quality in a truly effective audit report which compels the reader to agree with the substance of the report. The reader may not necessarily welcome the findings, conclusions and recommendations but he is not inclined to disagree with them. He believes the auditor and he believes the audit report. Viewed in this way, authoritativeness is at the very heart of effective auditing and audit report writing.

Authoritativeness starts with a clear, relevant and timely statement of objectives and scope. The reader may well ask "what else is new?" In fact, a really good statement of objectives and scope is so rare as to be a cause for celebration when one is actually found in a report. Too many auditors lose their authoritativeness at the very beginning of their reports by writing statements of objectives and scope that are weak, ambiguous, unclear, wordy and downright irritating. The auditor has attempted to tell his reader what his audit was all about and has failed at this simple task. From this point on, regaining his credibility will be strictly an uphill struggle.

The mistake most often made in the statement of objectives and scope is to conceive of it in terms that are too complicated. The writer should think through what it is he set out to do and say so in the simplest, shortest and most direct way possible. If the scope of his audit is implicit in his objectives statement, then he should omit mention of scope altogether. The whole statement of objectives and scope should seldom take more than one-quarter to one-third of a page. If an auditor begins with a very effective statement of objectives and scope, he has taken the first basic step toward authoritativeness in audit report writing.

Solid Facts and Observations

Nothing is more impressive to the reader of an audit report than solid facts and observations that ring true because of the way they were gathered, organized and presented relative to a valid audit objective. Assume that an auditor's objective was to determine whether discounts were being taken on invoice payments. Her (or his) report states that a stratified scientific sample was taken of all June payments. Of the 200 invoices in the sample which offered discounts, discounts were taken in 92% of the cases. The average error on discount calculations was $18.16 (against the company). Estimated cost to the company of lost and erroneous discounts was $17,572 for the month of June and $210,864 for the year. Such facts, properly presented and supported, constitute a highly authoritative statement of the results of the audit. The reader may regret these results, but he will not be inclined to doubt them.

Sound Evaluation Criteria

Audit conclusions are not based on facts alone. An auditor may have correctly calculated an organization's personnel turnover at 20%. But this fact alone does not of itself suggest any particular conclusion. The turnover rate must be judged relative to what *it should be* as determined by historical comparison, comparison with similar firms in the industry, local labor conditions and so forth. To be fully authoritative, audit reports must have more than solid facts and observations. They must also utilize evaluation criteria which the reader knows to be sound. Many auditors experience difficulty in selling their conclusions simply because the criteria used in their evaluations are unstated, highly questionable or entirely subjective.

Note again that we are not viewing report writing as an isolated technical skill separate from the audit. The identification of appropriate evaluation criteria is actually a part of audit field work and does not relate strictly to report writing as such. But the audit report is where all the aspects of an audit—be they good or bad—come together. For this reason, the audit report provides a convenient locus for the discussion of what is merely good *audit practice*.

Relevance, Materiality and Impact

There is a type of objectivity which every auditor needs to have if he is to write effective audit reports. He must be objective about his own audit. The time to do this is when he writes his report. The auditor must get out of himself, so to speak, and look over his own shoulder. Quite apart from his personal commitment to the audit, his involvement with it, what he did and why he did it, and the time and effort that it took, the auditor must evaluate how the report will look on paper to the reader.

This is the crucial moment of truth for the auditor. Will he exercise cold-blooded objectivity and strike out what is irrelevant, immaterial or lacking in real impact?

If the auditor leaves weak material in his report, he risks diluting the effectiveness of his entire effort—especially if he is dealing with an auditee who is hostile, potentially hostile, or merely unpredictable. Better to throw away the soft stuff or pass it on orally to the right parties. If the auditor has the judgment and common sense to do this, he will be left with a report that is *authoritative*, one that commands management's respect and agreement. The auditor will have shown that he is a professional, someone who doesn't relate everything he has done simply because he did it, someone capable of making choices in order to win his objective. It's very much like being stranded in the wilderness with a long and dangerous journey ahead. If a person in such a predicament insists on carrying all of his belongings, he may very well fail to reach safety. On the other hand, if he makes the right choices and carries only the things he will really need, his chances of survival will be greatly improved.

Reasonable Recommendations

There is one last idea with respect to authoritativeness: recommendations must be reasonable, practical and cost-effective. Young CPAs recently out of public practice must be particularly careful on this point. Since they have experience mainly in material problems of accounting control which had to be corrected no matter what the cost, they have not often had to make close benefit-cost judgments concerning their recommendations. Their attitude tends toward the blithe and simplistic: "There's a problem—so fix it. We recommend such and such." CPAs in public practice are not encouraged to spend any amount of time researching alternate ways to correct a problem and selecting the best approach. Traditionally, it's up to the client to do as the CPAs suggest or to perform the analysis required to develop a better alternative. This has worked well enough in public accounting but it no longer works satisfactorily in internal auditing. Busy and hard-pressed managers expect more from their internal auditors. Internal auditors are supposed to be experts in their companies' systems and procedures. They have the freedom and mobility to talk to anyone, anywhere, at any time. Their failure to make benefit-cost judgments indicates that they don't care about helping the auditee. They feel content to walk away from the auditee, leaving him with a problem that he is less qualified to investigate and resolve.

If an auditor truly wishes to write authoritative audit reports, let him take the time and trouble to research his recommendations. He shouldn't present the results of his work as the last word on the matter since most auditees prefer to retain some degree of latitude in making decisions. However, the auditee will usually end up accepting the auditor's recommendations and giving him credit for a job well done if the auditor has maintained adequate contact with the auditee during the audit, and if the tone of the auditor's report is correct.

BALANCE

Balance has to do with creating a fair and realistic picture of the organization or activity under review. Balance is fairness. Balance is treating the auditee as the auditor would want to be treated if their roles were reversed. Balance is, or should be, the golden rule of internal auditing. However, the rule is honored much more in the breach than in the observance.

As mentioned before, internal auditors are usually very nice people. Most of them think of themselves as fair in their treatment of auditees. However, it remains that old doctrines, old habits, the need to conserve audit resources and various circumstances surrounding a project can conspire against true balance in the reporting of audit results.

Need for Empathy

Working exclusively on the audit side of the fence can eventually dull the auditor's awareness of the auditee's feelings of vulnerability. If the reader feels he may be slipping into this trap, he need only reflect upon his own likely reaction in two situations where he would be the object of another's scrutiny and evaluation: performance appraisals and audit peer reviews.

An Imbalanced Performance Appraisal

Let the reader imagine that he (or she) has successfully completed eight audits during the year. Two were routine and identified no significant opportunities for improvement. Five audits produced a combined total of over $400,000 in audit savings. The eighth audit, however, was one the auditor would just as soon forget. The audit was requested by management and the auditor was given rather stern and specific instructions on how the audit should be carried out. Feeling that his instructions were not consistent with good professional practice, the auditor purposely deviated from instructions in order to give the auditee a fair break. No matter. The auditee got wind that something was up and came on like a cornered bear. By the time the audit was over, it was decided that the auditor's performance had been less than optimal and that he had somehow been guilty of poor auditee relations.

Now comes annual performance evaluation time. How does the "system" perceive and record the auditor's accomplishments during the appraisal period? How does it express its gratitude for the auditor's diligence, hard work, voluntary overtime without pay and solid audit results? First, the system views it as a waste of time and paper to dwell on the auditor's positive achievements. Second, it fears that praise will only lead the auditor to entertain unrealistic expectations concerning promotion. The result is an exception-style performance appraisal. The appraisal does state that the auditor's performance was "generally satisfactory" but its main emphasis is on three deficiencies: (1) failure to meet man-hour and schedule targets in four out of eight projects; (2) weaknesses in report-writing skills; and (3) serious shortcomings in human relations. The general picture of the auditor created by the performance appraisal is that he is slow, that he can't write and that he can't get along with people.

How would the reader react if this were his performance appraisal? Predictably, he would say that the appraisal was unfair. If told that the appraisal was entirely based on facts, the reader's only recourse would be to assert that the appraisal lacked balance—that its unfairness was due to the biased selectivity of the facts it contained.

An Imbalanced Peer Review

Chapter 8 relates an actual case of a peer review of an audit department. The case clearly demonstrates how the time-honored exception principle can distort reality to the point of actually perpetrating a falsehood. Junior auditors may not be able to relate to the threat posed by such peer reviews, but audit supervisors, managers and directors should have no difficulty in imagining the harm they could do to a hard-striving audit organization.

The point of all this should be eminently clear. Internal auditors are a highly ethical breed of men and women. Surely they acknowledge an obligation to treat auditees as fairly as they themselves would insist upon being treated in performance appraisals and peer reviews. If they do acknowledge such an obligation, then let them honor it not just in words but in their *actions*.

Ways to Improve Balance

Time being the scarce resource it is, it is unlikely that management will ever sanction giving as much space and emphasis to favorable findings as to opportunities for improvement. Nonetheless, internal auditors truly insistent upon writing balanced reports can devise a variety of acceptable ways to do so. The following are only a few examples which come to mind.

1.   Word the objectives and scope statement in such a way as to *clearly* convey the highly selective nature of the audit.

2.   If a preliminary survey was performed, list all major areas covered by the survey and those excluded from detailed review for lack of any evidence of significant problems.

3.   Include a discussion, however brief, of all significant auditee achievements noted during the audit.

4.   Avoid exaggeration or overstatement in discussions of discrepancies and deficiencies.

5.   Avoid giving the impression that the auditee is solely responsible for problems when this is not the case. Point out extenuating circumstances, shared responsibility, budgetary and other constraints, lack of training, inadequate policies, guidelines, procedures and so forth.

6.   Say and emphasize the right things in oral reports to auditees and to higher levels of management.

In a full-blown operational audit of an organization, internal auditors should not restrict themselves to half-way measures. Their report should be fully balanced—period! Everything which was included in the original audit plan should be fully covered in the final report. In the vast majority of cases, this will produce a result reflecting credit to all concerned. Since most organizations do a good job in most things, auditees will be highly gratified that their positive achievements were recognized by the auditors.* The opportunities for improvement identified in the audit, if properly presented in the light of the overall findings, will not appear to pose a threat to reputations and careers. Managers will be inclined to agree to all reasonable recommendations, and the auditors will

---

*By "positive achievements" we are not referring only to the unusual or the heroic. The tendency toward mediocrity is so compelling in some organizations that even the maintenance of satisfactory performance can be a positive achievement.

receive credit for having stimulated valuable improvements in operations and controls. In the long run, internal auditing will be building a reputation for true professionalism and partnership with management.

Balance! It's a major factor in effective report writing and a key concept for the new internal auditing of the future.

PROFESSIONAL STYLING

In addition to being objective, authoritative and balanced, effective audit reports must also be properly styled. All professions—in fact, all human activity—tends to conform to certain stylistic patterns in order to meet the expectations of society. The elements of style in audit report writing are:

Structure
Clarity
Conciseness
Tone
Editing

The following discussion will address each of these in turn.

Structure

Structure in report writing has to do with the relationship of the parts of a report to the whole. Structure presents the single greatest challenge in effective audit report writing. Quality in any audit report starts with structure. If the structure of an audit report is wrong, nothing can be done to improve the report until the structural problem is corrected.

The single best test of good structure is whether a report leaves a clear overall impression with the reader. A reader should be able to read the report only once and be able to discuss it effectively from memory.

Another test of good structure is whether a report lends itself to easy speed-reading. Readers who have taken a course in speed-reading need not be reminded that success in this skill is highly dependent on the manner in which a text is organized. A well-organized text can be read very rapidly with excellent comprehension and retention. A poorly organized text produces nothing but a blur—even when read slowly and deliberately.

Audit report structure is a highly technical subject to which we will devote the next two chapters. We will therefore complete our discussion of audit report styling and return to the subject of structure at a later point.

Clarity

Clarity in an audit report is the quality of being easily understood.

Clarity must of course start in the mind of the writer. There is no way that an auditor can write clearly about his subject matter unless he understands it clearly in the first place. To understand his subject matter, the auditor must possess the necessary intellectual qualifications, must have planned his audit properly and must have done his field work diligently and thoroughly. Again, we see that audit report writing is not an isolated technical skill but an extension of competent audit planning and execution.

Clarity may start in the mind of the writer, but it doesn't end there. "The proof of the puddin' is in the eatin'," as they say. If clarity is the quality of being easily understood, the test of audit report clarity is not the auditor's own assessment of his report but the reader's reaction to it. No matter what the auditor may think, if the reader says that something is not clear, then it's not clear! The auditor should set aside his pride of authorship as completely irrelevant in the matter of clarity. He has not achieved clarity until the reader's reaction proves that he has. Here again we see the difference between the amateur and the professional. The amateur is concerned largely with his own reaction to his work product. The professional, on the other hand, understands that his mission is to meet the needs of others. For the professional internal auditor, the only acceptable definition of report clarity is the quality of being easily understood *by the reader*.

Some Technical Considerations

Clarity requires a sound report structure. A text may be clear in its details yet unclear as a whole. Such a text is like a maze. One can clearly discern every path and every turn and yet have no idea how the paths and turns relate to the all-important entrance and exit. On the other hand, a text may have a perfectly sound overall structure but be irritatingly unclear in its specifics. Clarity at the detail level requires coherent paragraphs, logical sentences and use of the correct words.

This last consideration, use of the correct words, merits emphasis. Nothing undermines the writer's intent more effectively than carelessness in the choice of words and word combinations. The worst crime against clarity is to use words and expressions out of habit rather than to project actual thought. Writers who do this sort of thing to their readers don't realize the harm they may cause to their careers. The world being as competitive as it is, writers of gobbledygook don't stand a chance. They won't be taken seriously by anyone, least of all by those who make promotion decisions.

Who Is the Reader?

The greatest challenge to clarity in audit report writing is that audit reports are usually distributed to many readers. Clarity was described earlier as the quality of being easily understood by the reader. Clarity, then, is very much reader-related. What may be clear to one reader may not be clear to another since readers can vary widely in education, experience and knowledge of the subject.

The phenomenon of multiple readership often explains why auditors, supervisors and managers have difficulty in agreeing on report language. Each person is looking at the same report differently and evaluating the appropriateness of its language with respect to the reader he considers most important. On the one hand, the auditor wishes to be understood by the people he worked with during the audit: specialists, supervisors and functional managers. The audit supervisor, on the other hand, may consider one or more decision makers at the department-head level to be the true audience of the audit report. Finally, the audit manager may be concerned with the impression the report will make on certain vice-presidents who are also on the distribution list. Reconciling all of these readership interests can be very difficult. In fact, the solution often is to issue more than one version of the same report: a detailed and technical version to the lower levels, and a "management summary" to the higher levels, with certain readers at the intermediate level receiving both versions. It is true that the usual motive for issuing a management summary is to reduce higher management's reading time. However, a management summary can also be used to make things *clearer* for higher management.

Solving the Problem

How does an auditor write a report which will be distributed to many readers? By whose criteria does he evaluate the clarity of his writing? Who is his reader? The moment one poses this question forthrightly one realizes there can be only one answer: the principal decision maker on the list of addressees—the manager whose overt or covert concurrence will be required to secure acceptance of the audit recommendations.

This individual may not be the direct addressee of the report, but he is the one the report must convince. If the report is convincing to him, everyone else concerned with the audit will adopt a compliant attitude toward the findings. This is the way of the corporate world. Opinions of subordinates can go either way depending upon the position taken by the decision maker, and the seasoned writer of audit reports understands this. The writer may appear to be addressing his report to the nominal recipient, but everything about the report is carefully crafted to appeal to the real decision maker on the distribution list. Such an approach to the writing of multiple-reader reports seldom involves any compromise of clarity for lower-level readers. Anything which is clear to a higher-level reader will almost always be equally clear to lower-level subordinates. If lower-level readers require detailed information which would be distracting to the higher-level reader, such information can be provided in exhibits or appendices located at the back of the report, or it can be provided separately.

Clarity for Senior Managers

How does one make things clear for the senior manager? Larry Sawyer made the point very effectively a number of years ago in one of his early books. He assumed that a senior management reader might not understand the implications of the audit finding that invoices were not always matched to receipt documents prior to payment. His solution: to write that management had no assurance that goods and services paid for had actually been received.

Sawyer's point is a classic of management psychology that is as relevant today as the day it was written. Managers think mainly in terms of impact. Their initial reaction with respect to many audit findings is "so what?" Unless managers understand the "so what" of a finding, they understand nothing. Management readers are interested not so much in facts as in what the facts *mean* to their companies and to their organizations.

Clarity Is Not Harshness

A common error among many auditors is to confuse clarity with harshness. This is the "calling a spade a spade" syndrome which afflicts even the most experienced auditors in times of emotional stress.

Clarity and harshness are in fact two different things altogether. Clarity relates to the communication of *information* whereas harshness has to do with the communication of *attitudes* and *feelings*. The writer of harsh audit reports is wrong in complaining that his readers can't handle the truth. What they really can't accept is the insensitivity, or even hostility, reflected in the auditor's choice of words.

Most successful audit report writers have a touch of the diplomat in them. They have an instinctive or acquired ability to express themselves clearly while respecting the sensibilities of their readers. Auditors struggling to eliminate harshness from their writing style should read the work of such writers and look for aproaches and techniques that work well for them.

Conciseness

Conciseness in audit report writing is the quality of being complete without being lengthy. What are the characteristics of a concise audit report?

A concise audit report avoids unnecessary discussion of the audit process. It wastes no time in getting into its subject and it sticks to the subject.

A concise audit report tells the reader what he needs to know and nothing else. It does not go on and on in a counterproductive effort to impress the reader with the extent of the writer's knowledge.

Conciseness requires good structure. The writer should make each point and then move on to the next without anticipating or recalling other parts of the report. Circular writing is poor writing. It results in redundancy and frustrates all efforts at conciseness. Any audit report, if properly sequenced, can be written in linear fashion without any need to peer ahead or to look back. A good rule for concise audit report writing is: don't mention a topic until you mean to cover it; when you do cover it, do so completely; after you've covered it, drop it.

There are times when a clever writer can make a report both long and short at the same time. The trick is to use exhibits and appendices at the back of the report. As long as the primary points are summarized briefly in the main body of the report, busy readers who are not interested in detail can ignore the exhibits and appendices and cut down their reading time by half.

Tone

An audit report should read like an audit report and have the tone of an audit report. The trouble with some writers of audit reports is that they project their long-term career aspirations in their manner of writing. In trying to prove that they could do other things besides auditing, they merely end up demonstrating that they can't even handle their present job well.

An audit report should be low-keyed, impersonal and unemotional. The focus should be on findings, conclusions and recommendations. The interjection of personality and emotion in audit reports is extremely dangerous. At the very least, it will distract readers from the business at hand and will damage the auditor's credibility as a professional. At worst, it will inspire an "us versus them" attitude in the minds of auditees that will make agreement on the findings practically impossible.

An audit report should not emulate the style and tone of management. Auditors are staff and they should behave and write like staff. A staff person does not command, order, instruct, request, reject, accept, deny, approve, disapprove, advocate, urge, encourage, discourage, criticize or praise. Such action words are appropriate only for people who are in charge. Auditors may legitimately use such words within the audit department, but when they are in the field the action word which best fits their role is "recommend."

Neither Criticism nor Praise

It's interesting how internal auditors disagree over the use of criticism and praise in audit reports. Roughly one-third of all auditors assert their right to criticize auditees when they deserve it but view it as unprofessional to praise anyone. Another third admit to both criticizing and praising auditees depending upon the circumstances. The last third would view criticism as unnecessary, counterproductive or both, but would see nothing wrong with occasional praise. Almost no one thinks that auditors should neither criticize nor praise, yet this is precisely what the position of internal auditors should be in most situations. Why is this? Because criticism and praise are equally unnecessary and pose needless risks to the auditor.

Criticism poses a risk because it may backfire. Criticism may turn a potentially cooperative auditee into a highly defensive adversary, and it may provide the auditee with an excuse to enlist the sympathy and support of powerful allies. Praise can also backfire on the auditor. It may cause the auditor's objectivity to be questioned. Or, if a pattern of praise is established in a series of audit reports, expectations by future auditees that they too should be praised may hamper the auditor's freedom of expression. Finally, since the scope of most audits seldom reflects the full range of an auditee's responsibilities, praise will be based on incomplete knowledge of the auditee's overall performance and may conflict with the better-informed opinions of senior managers. Consider the effect upon the credibility of an audit department if it had written glowing praise about a manager just a few days before he was fired for dishonesty or incompetence. It could happen.

The main thing to keep in mind about criticism and praise in audit reports is that both are essentially inappropriate and unnecessary. According to tradition, internal auditing is concerned in part with "evaluating the quality of performance in carrying assigned responsibilities." This may have an appealing ring to it, but a growing number of thoughtful internal auditors are currently striving to get away from the performance evaluation business. Performance evaluation stands in the way of the new relationship which the profession is seeking to promote with management and auditees. Performance evaluation is, and should remain, strictly a management function. The proper role of internal auditing should be the evaluation of operations, processes, controls and results, without any explicit or implicit reference to personalities. If the results of internal audit evaluations cast discredit upon specific managers, let this be an inference drawn by management rather than a conclusion drawn by the internal auditor. If it is agreed that auditing should generally restrict itself to the evaluation of operations, processes, controls and results, it becomes clear why we say that criticism and praise are unnecessary. If an auditor produces an adverse evaluation of something, the element of personal criticism is entirely gratuitous. Conversely, if the auditor evaluates something favorably, surely management knows to whom credit should go. Praise by the auditor is again entirely gratuitous.

If there be an auditor who doesn't believe our thesis concerning criticism and praise, let him experiment just once. Our prediction? He will instantly feel greater freedom to do a good and thorough job and will experience a significant reduction in his level of anxiety. If he is the kind of auditor who usually comes up with numerous findings, he will also experience a marked improvement in his auditee relations. Who knows, if he masters the art of securing operating improvements without ever criticizing people, he may even be viewed as a candidate for promotion to management.

Editing

The point was made earlier that perfection is seldom an appropriate standard by which to conduct an audit. Nor is perfection an appropriate standard by which to evaluate an internal auditor. An auditor can be far from perfect and yet be very, very effective. And an audit report can be less than perfect and be entirely acceptable except in one respect: editing. Editing is the one aspect of audit report writing where perfection is the only applicable standard.

Perfect editing means:

No spelling, punctuation or grammatical errors.

No incorrect use of words.

No awkward phrases.

No unclear or overlong sentences.

Perfect editing is important because it shows that the auditor cares about his work product. A fair-minded manager will usually be inclined to forgive an occasional error of fact, a conclusion that isn't quite right or a recommendation that may be less than optimal. But on what grounds do we ask a management reader to forgive sloppy editing? There are none. An auditor who didn't care enough about his work product to edit it properly has accused himself of a lack of professionalism. He has only himself to blame if management finds him guilty.

SUMMARY

The fundamentals of audit report writing are objectivity, authoritativeness, balance and professional styling.

The elements of professional styling are structure, clarity, conciseness, tone and editing.

Audit reports should not deal with the auditor, the audit process or audit concepts. They should deal with the world of the auditee. Audit reports should be impersonal; they should not be self-serving nor should they arouse or offend.

Authoritativeness comes from a clear statement of objectives and scope, solid facts and observations, sound evaluation criteria, relevance, materiality and impact, and reasonable recommendations.

Internal auditors need to work harder at providing balance in their reports. Balance needs to be given more than lip service if the new internal auditing is to succeed.

Structure represents the single greatest challenge in effective audit report writing.

Reports distributed to multiple readers must be clear to the decision maker most likely to influence the response to the audit findings. That decision maker is the real addressee of the report no matter who the nominal addressee may be.

Clarity and harshness are two different things: clarity appeals to the mind while harshness appeals to the emotions.

Conciseness requires good structure. A concise report tells the reader all he needs to know — and nothing else. A writer shouldn't mention a topic until he means to cover it. When he does cover it, he should do so completely. After he has covered it, he should drop it.

Audit reports should have the tone of an audit report. They should be low-keyed, impersonal and unemotional. Audit reports should neither praise nor criticize, but should report favorably or adversely on operations, controls, processes and results. Praise and criticism are risky and unnecessary.

The only applicable standard in the area of editing is *perfection*. Poor editing shows that an auditor doesn't care about his work product.

DISCUSSION

The strategy of the new internal auditing will involve placing less reliance on senior management support and cultivating greater acceptance on the part of operating managers and auditees. This strategy will exert a strong influence on the manner in which audit reports are written. The new style of audit reports will continue to be professional in quality but will adopt a friendlier and more helpful tone. Criticism will be avoided, as will exclusive focus on adverse findings. Objectivity, balance and supportiveness will be the hallmarks of report writing under the new internal auditing.

Under the new internal auditing, final audit reports will seldom be used as instruments of confrontation with operating management. Disagreements will be negotiated largely through informal processes taking place *during* the audit. If auditors consider that their positions have the support of upper management, they will utilize all available means to demonstrate this fact prior to issue of their final reports. If management support is not forthcoming, auditors will feel less of a need to register their disagreement "on the record" in final audit reports, except in cases where the welfare of the organization is *materially* affected.

The concept of partnership with management, and of helpful auditing, requires that management's prerogative to reject an audit recommendation be fully respected — even in cases where the auditing department strongly disagrees. One possible strategy for the handling of disagreements is to transfer the unresolved findings to a holding file for later reference. Special research can be conducted at leisure to more fully support the findings. Follow-up reviews can be performed to determine whether adverse conditions may have deteriorated even further. If a condition is sufficiently adverse, management itself will finally come to realize that it has a problem and will probably ask auditing for help.

CHAPTER 14

Macrostructure

Order and simplification are the first steps toward the mastery of a subject.

THOMAS MANN, *Buddenbrooks*, Pt.XI, Ch. 5

As was pointed out in the previous chapter, structure represents the single greatest challenge facing the writer of audit reports. It is probably safe to say that the vast majority of the readers of this book have experienced significant problems relating to audit report structure—either as auditors, audit supervisors or both. What are the symptoms of structural problems in an audit report? A typical case would run something like the following:

SYMPTOMS OF DEFECTIVE REPORT STRUCTURE

An auditor has just completed a difficult project and presents his report to his supervisor for preliminary review. The auditor feels justifiably

235

proud of his work on this audit. He had to wrestle with very difficult technical and managerial issues and was finally successful in producing sound and credible conclusions and recommendations. He is looking forward eagerly to obtaining his supervisor's reaction to his report. He is so eager, in fact, that he chooses a moment to submit his report when his supervisor is not busy. He sits down, an unmistakable hint that the supervisor should read the report immediately.

After two or three minutes, the supervisor asks a question. The auditor's reply is that this subject is covered at a later point in the report. After another minute or two, the supervisor winces and says: "Mr. Peerless is never going to buy this." "He has no choice." the auditor replies. "You'll see later on." "Where?" asks the supervisor. "On page thirteen, I show that the problem is much more serious than he thinks and that he must take corrective action soon to avoid a really embarrassing situation." The supervisor skips over to page thirteen, reads, and says: "I see—that bad, huh? Tell you what, Charlie. Why don't you leave me alone with this report and I'll get back to you first thing in the morning."

After Charlie has gone, the supervisor goes back to the beginning of the report and reads it through quickly. She goes back to the beginning again and this time she reviews mainly the topic headings and subheadings. Her main impression is that things don't flow well. The report is hard to follow. She runs through the report one more time and comes to a conclusion. The report cannot be released in its present condition. In fact, the condition of the report is such that it can't even be critiqued. The supervisor wouldn't know where to start. Somewhat tired, the supervisor looks at her watch and finds that it's time to call it a day.

The next morning, Charlie walks into the supervisor's office and says: "Well, boss, what do you think of my report? Do you want to talk about it now? I think we ought to release it as soon as possible." "I agree," says the supervisor diplomatically, "but I need a little more time with the report before I can talk to you about it. Please come back after lunch. I should be ready by then."

Fortunately for Charlie, his supervisor has had considerable experience in audit report writing. She knows that she must not allow Charlie to pressure her into a premature discussion of his audit report. Anything she might say at this stage would only confuse matters. She decides to spend the entire morning analyzing Charlie's report and preparing for their meeting after lunch. What she must do is read through the report slowly and identify each of its findings. Then, she will place the findings in logical groups and will attempt to order the findings in the most effective manner. After she has done this, the supervisor will devise major and minor topic headings and build a report outline for Charlie to follow.

Promptly after lunch, Charlie appears at the door of his supervisor's office and says cheerfully: "Well, boss, are you ready for me?" "Come on in," says the supervisor. "Yes I am ready. I think we have a very good audit here, and I want us to do the best possible job in selling our findings to management. To do that, I think we'll have to change our report structure a bit. But it shouldn't be too difficult . . . ."

DEFINITION OF AN AUDIT REPORT

An audit report can be defined simply as a collection of audit findings. This may seem like a simplistic statement but it is, in fact, an extremely useful insight for any writer of audit reports. The definition underlies all that will be said about audit report structure in the next two chapters.

TWO ASPECTS OF AUDIT REPORT STRUCTURE

All audit reports may be said to have a macrostructure and a microstructure. Macrostructure has to do with how report findings are grouped and sequenced. Microstructure has to do with how each finding is organized and presented. To use an architectural analogy, macrostructure has to do with the type, number and location of areas in a house, whereas microstructure has to to with the design and layout of each of the areas. The principles of audit report macrostructure are discussed in this chapter. The subject of audit report microstructure will be addressed in Chapter 15.

A NEED FOR ORDER AND SIMPLICITY

Readers familiar with the history of computer programming will remember the time when programs were too complex to be revised by anyone but the original programmers. Core memory limitations forced programmers to pack as much code in as little space as they could. As a result, program logic was so twisted and convoluted as to be unintelligible to anyone but the author of the program.

Later on, as systems became larger and computers more powerful, there arose a need to organize and manage teams of programmers to work together on a single project. Two requirements became apparent: first, a way had to be found to apportion programming tasks in a distinct and logical manner; second, the resulting overall system had to be maintainable by others who might replace the original programming team.

These two requirements led to the development of "structured design," an idea that can be borrowed to explain the characteristics of good audit report macrostructure.

STRUCTURED DESIGN

The essential idea of structured design is that any complex problem or task can be viewed and defined from the top down in such a way that each level of instructions completely defines all instructions below that level. This can be illustrated with a simple example, the standard payroll application.

The task of a payroll system might be defined as computing the payroll. As every auditor knows, computing the payroll in a typical corporation is an extremely complex operation taking into account executive, professional and union personnel; different pay grades; straight time and overtime; shift differentials; various deductions; federal, state and local taxes, and so forth. Assuming that one wished to apportion the programming of such a payroll system among four different programmers, how would he do it? How would he stake out distinct programming territories while ensuring that each programmer covered his task completely without overlapping with the tasks of the others? And how would he ensure that the completed work of each programmer dovetailed neatly into that of the others? The concept of structured, top-down design provides a very convenient solution to this problem. Consider the following structured definition of the payroll application.

STRUCTURED DEFINITION OF
PAYROLL APPLICATION

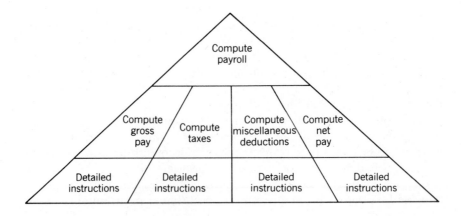

Note how such a view of the payroll application permits a clear and distinct breakdown of the payroll problem into manageable parts. The reader can select any one of the four major components of the problem and can easily imagine himself analyzing, designing and programming his part of the problem without requiring complex coordination with the other members of the project team.

Application to Audit Report Writing

The concept of structured design illustrated above provides an excellent basis for a philosophy of audit report macrostructure. Any audit report can be viewed as a logical pyramid constructed as follows.

LOGICAL PYRAMID OF THE AUDIT REPORT

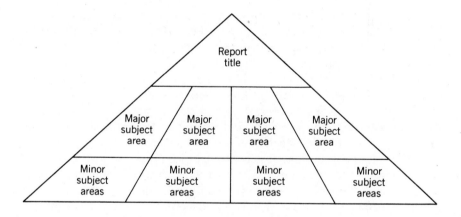

The title of an audit report, if properly conceived, clearly defines the scope of the entire report. The report is divided into no more than four to six major subject areas which are clearly differentiated, have a clear and logical relationship to each other and together cover the entire subject matter of the report. Clarity is immediately achieved if a reader can grasp the scope of, say, an entire twenty-five page report by assimilating only four to six major section titles.

Each major subject area is itself broken down into distinct but logically related subareas.

The result of such a structured approach to writing is an audit report which the reader can "navigate" without getting lost or confused. The reader always knows where he is within the overall structure of the report.

PRINCIPLES OF MACROSTRUCTURE

Macrostructure in audit report writing is governed by five basic principles:

1. Grouping
2. Sequence
3. Convenience
4. Attractiveness
5. Flexibility

We will discuss each of these principles in turn.

The Grouping Principle

Of the five principles listed above, the grouping principle is the most critical and the most difficult to apply. Good structure in an audit report requires that related things be grouped together.

The human mind is made extremely uncomfortable by anything resembling chaos or infinity. The mind craves order, categories and limits. When the mind became aware of life on earth, it set to work and divided life into animal and vegetable. It then took the animals and divided them into fishes, birds, reptiles, insects and mammals. Scientists succeeded in identifying some 800,000 species of insects by 1962 and has been discovering thousands of new species each year since then.* So insistent is the human mind on reducing everything to categories and limits that it will not rest until the very last one of the many millions of insect species on earth has been discovered and assigned to its proper entomological category. Society so values the ability to put things in categories that it defines a good part of intelligence in terms of this ability, measures it in intelligence quotient (IQ) tests, and opens or closes career doors to students accordingly.

Application to Report Writing

The best way to demonstrate the importance of the grouping principle is to imagine a major audit involving 25 findings. Imagine further that the auditor's report addressed these findings in random order and eschewed the use of any titles, subtitles or paragraph breaks. The read-

---

*Peter Farb, *The Insects* (New York: Time Inc., 1962), p.11.

ers of the report would be confronted by page after page of unorganized and undifferentiated text. Can there be any doubt as to their probable reaction? Most certainly, their reaction will be a persuasive lesson concerning how the human mind craves order, categories and limits.

As stated earlier, and will be repeated again, an audit report can be viewed simply as a collection of audit findings. The grouping principle requires that the auditor start his report-writing task by first identifying each of his findings and then grouping them in a manner that will facilitate his writing of the report and the reader's understanding of it.

The process of properly grouping a collection of findings can at times be simple and at other times very subtle and complex. The best solution is usually a reflection of the inherent logic of the subject matter and of the intellectual/emotional orientation of the reader. The auditor should not simply assume that his findings should be grouped according to the breakdowns contained in his audit program. Let the auditor imagine that he is a prospector for precious and semiprecious stones. Although his prospecting plan may have been based on geographical divisions, it doesn't follow that he should present his findings to potential buyers according to the locations where the stones were found. His buyers would probably prefer to examine his findings according to diamonds, rubies, emeralds, sapphires, opals and so forth.

The Sequence Principle

The sequence principle is the second most important principle of audit report macrostructure. Sequence determines the order in which groups of findings are arranged, as well as the order in which individual findings within each group are addressed. A good audit report leads the reader through a carefully conceived logical sequence. The sequence should be linear. It should not anticipate future points nor repeat points already made.

Emotional Sequence

Although the audit report writer will normally be concerned only with logical sequence, there will be times when he will have to consider *emotional* sequence as well. In the case of sensitive findings pointing to the need for significant change, the report writer must anticipate and "manage" the reader's emotional as well as intellectual response to the report narrative. Complex reports can therefore have two sequence vectors built into the narrative flow as follows:

TWO SEQUENCE VECTORS OF NARRATIVE FLOW

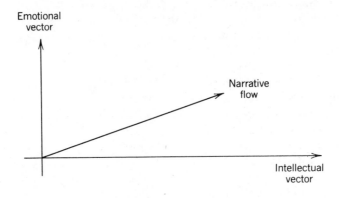

The narrative flow is seen to proceed steadily upward along two gradients: the intellectual gradient (credibility) and the emotional gradient (acceptability). In this scheme, the auditor's objective is to maintain the narrative flow in a *positive* direction with respect to both vectors at all times. At no point in the narrative should credibility and/or acceptability be permitted to reverse their direction.

Tapping the Subconscious

Although this discussion of the sequence principle may seem abstract, it should be kept in mind that audit reports cannot be written according to simple sets of instructions. The truth is that audit report writing is ultimately an art form, just as everything is an art form as soon as one ventures beyond routine, repetitive processes. Audit report writing provides an opportunity for the new internal auditor born in the age of Aquarius to demonstrate that he or she is at one with the times. The new internal auditor is, or can become, adept at the manipulation of his subconscious mind as a means of solving problems.

The notions of logical and emotional sequence are best used not as explicit instructions but as *objectives* and *criteria*. The objectives are tossed into the recesses of the subconscious mind with the command to produce a solution meeting the objectives. When the subconscious mind does suggest a solution, the conscious mind judges and evaluates the solution according to the objectives which are now used as criteria. If the solution is less than optimal, the conscious and subconscious minds continue to interact until a satisfactory result is achieved.*

*Readers not familiar with this process may consult publications on the psychology of creativity and problem solving which should be available at any good library.

A True Case

Dave was a brilliant auditor with a rare gift for detailed research and analysis. One day he was asked to perform a comprehensive review of a certain department's administrative practices. Dave produced a long list of findings showing serious deficiencies in such areas as typing, filing, telephone, budgeting, project control, stationary and supplies and so forth. The findings were supported by an impressive array of statistics proving that the auditee organization was not utilizing its labor, equipment, space and other resources in an efficient manner. Dave's supervisor reviewed his findings in detail, agreed that they were solid and suggested that Dave proceed to the writing of his report. The first draft was ready in about a week's time.

Dave was very disappointed when told by his supervisor that his first report draft would require more work. He challenged his supervisor to explain what was wrong with the report. The answer was that although the report was essentially correct in its technical conclusions, it would almost certainly elicit an adverse reaction from the vice-president who had requested the study. "Please be more specific," Dave demanded. "What did I do wrong?" "Wrong is not the point," replied the supervisor. "You are an outstanding auditor and your recommendations in this audit deserve to be fully accepted and implemented. It's a question of how best to accomplish this."

Again, Dave insisted that the supervisor be more specific and that he cite just one thing which should have been handled differently. The supervisor turned to the first section of the report, paused to reflect, and said: "For one thing, we say some extremely unkind things about the department's organization right in the beginning of the report. Do we have to start the report this way? Mr. Jones is bound to be offended by what we have to say about his organization. He'll be so upset, he won't be able to get beyond the first two pages." Dave replied: "I was taught that the most important findings should be located at the front of a report. My most important finding is that Mr. Jones' worst problem is his organization. It underlies all of his other problems in the area of administration." "That may be," the supervisor replied, "but our present approach presents two problems: first, our criticism of his organization this early in the report is mainly an assertion. We provide little or no support for our conclusion, second, we are being very critical of someone who actually came to us for help. Surely, there has to be a better way to communicate the results of your study. We have to sequence your findings in such a way that Mr. Jones will be prepared to accept your drastic conclusions about his organization." "Well, I give up," said Dave in a challenging tone. "You tell me what I should do. I just don't know." The supervisor, knowing that he was being tested, declined to be provoked. "Fair enough. I'll give it a try. Let me sleep on it and we'll talk about it again tomorrow."

The supervisor was not a trained psychologist and could not have explained what he was about to do. All he knew was that every time he'd had a problem like this in the past, it only took a few hours of rest after thrashing out the problem for a solution to pop into his head. He was confident this would happen again. And it did!

The next day, the supervisor called Dave into his office. "Dave," he said, "I think I know how you should build your report. You don't have to criticize Mr. Jones' organization. In fact, you don't have to criticize anything. Mr. Jones deserves a lot of credit for asking us to review his department's administrative routines. He sensed an opportunity to make some improvements and he was right. Our job is simply to prove that he was right.

"In your report, address the specific administrative areas first: typing, filing, telephone, budgeting and the rest. Do what you've already done with these areas except don't write in terms of deficiencies. Instead, point up the opportunities to improve effectiveness and efficiency. In every case, you'll be recommending some sort of centralization combined with the adoption of new equipment and/or techniques. When you're all through with the specific areas, then address the subject of organization. In order to implement the centralization of his administrative routines, Mr. Jones will need to establish a centralized administrative support staff. There's nothing actually 'wrong' with Mr. Jones' organization today and it would be entirely inappropriate to criticize it. But if he wants to implement your recommendations for improvement in specific areas, an organizational change will be necessary. I believe that if you sequence your findings and recommendations as I've just described, you will have a fine report. What do you think?"

"I think it'll work," said Dave. "But I do have one question: How did you come up with this idea?" "Actually, the idea just popped into my head this morning while I was shaving," replied the supervisor.

And there we have it. We need not ask anyone how to implement the report-writing guidelines in this chapter. We should simply ask our own subconscious. It knows.

Convenience

Good architectural design builds *convenience* into a structure. This is also true of good audit report structure: it must have convenience built in.

Building convenience into an audit report requires special effort on the part of the auditor. By taking that effort, the auditor shows that he has high professional standards and that he cares about his readers. The object of convenience is to save readers time and effort in assimilating the contents of the audit report. Convenience can take many forms including such things as:

Clear and accurate titles and subtitles
Minimum number of subject matter sublevels
A table of contents, when applicable
Complete paging
Proper handling of exhibits and appendices
A management summary, when applicable

Clear and Accurate Titles

Few things are as awkward and inconvenient for readers of audit reports as poor titles and subtitles. Audit reports are almost always difficult reading. Titles and subtitles are as necessary to readers of audit reports as signs are essential to drivers of modern freeways. A title should be assigned not only to the audit report as a whole but also to *each and every* major and minor subject area covered in the report. All titles should be short, clear and accurate.

One is almost led to believe that some internal auditors consider it inelegant to use a title that actually fits the subject matter. Anyone who doubts this assertion has only to check a sample of the work of his associates, note their titles, attempt to guess at the subject matter that follows and then see what the subject matter really is. Chances are that over half the titles will be vague or misleading. A common failing is to abstract the subject matter when this is not necessary. If the subject is diamonds, for example, the title must be a more abstract term such as jewels, gems or precious stones. It can't simply be diamonds. Another common failing might be called the "shift." This is calling something by a name that actually describes a different but closely related thing. Calling something "planning" when it is really "scheduling" would be an example of this.

Any auditor wishing to improve his audit report writing but who is not sure where to start should simply concentrate on titling. Let him assign a truly appropriate title to his overall report and follow this with a short but descriptive title for each major and minor subject area of the report. The immediate effect will be very positive and it will lead to greater precision in the use of language throughout the report.

There is a very simple test of good titling: the titles themselves should tell a story. One should be able to flip through an entire report and get an excellent idea of what the report is about just from the titles. An auditor can conduct this test on his very next report simply by asking any qualified associate for five or ten minutes of his time. Let his associate study the report titles and subtitles and describe his expectations concerning report content as specifically as he can. If he comes fairly close, it's a sign of good titling. If he is far off the mark, chances are that the titles need to be improved.

Subject Matter Sublevels

Anyone who has read reports where the subject matter was broken down into three or more levels can attest to how awkward and inconvenient this is for the reader. Some types of technical reports may indeed require such detailed sublevels, but internal audit reports seldom do. Short audit reports of two to five pages in length can almost always be fashioned with only one sublevel.

Longer audit reports usually require two sublevels. The most convenient and aesthetically pleasing treatment is to start on a fresh page whenever there is a change in major subject matter. The title of the major subject area is centered at the top of the page, capitalized and underlined. Minor subject-area titles may then be placed along the left-hand margin, in lower case and underlined.

Table of Contents

Most audit reports do not require a table of contents. However it may be useful in a lengthy operational or management audit report. Detailed tables of contents are almost never necessary. The best approach is to include only the major subject areas, thus providing readers with a quick overview of the main lines of the report. To go beyond this is to risk that readers will ignore the table of contents altogether.

Complete Paging

Audit reports should be completely paged. Paging should start with the first page of the report text and should run through the entire Appendix section. Complete paging permits positive location reference to any text, exhibit, appendix or part thereof.

Exhibits and Appendices

It is a mistake to be so proud of charts and exhibits as to compel readers to examine them. The convenience principle requires that readers be given a choice whenever possible. For busy higher-level readers, it is usually possible to cite essential facts and conclusions in the text and save them the time and trouble of studying complex tables or charts. Tables and charts are of interest mainly to those who must verify the correctness of a report or who will be responsible for implementing its recommendations. For this reason, lengthy tables and charts should usually be relegated to the back of the report.

Management Summary

A management summary should be a real summary. It should be no longer than one to three pages. It should contain mainly conclusions and recommendations in the style of "completed staff work" where senior managers are assumed to have a feel for the right solution without the need for detailed proof. Besides, if there are problems with an audit report, someone will let management know in quick order.

Management summaries serve a very real convenience purpose. They greatly reduce the reading time of senior management personnel who must be served quickly and expeditiously. Even readers of a detailed audit report may find a management summary useful in getting the overall gist of a report before wading into its detail.

Attractiveness

Attractiveness is the fourth principle of audit report macrostructure. Attractiveness is culturally determined. A well-structured report does not violate the tastes and preferences of those for whom the report was prepared. It isn't the tastes and preferences of the writer that count, but those of the reader.

Audit reports should have adequate "white space." Solid text, page after page, turns off most readers. A good plan is to start each new major subject area on a fresh page. Within each major subject area, adequate white space should result simply from titling each minor subject area and observing good paragraphing conventions.

Flexibility

Flexibility is the fifth and final principle of audit report macrostructure. This principle is a reminder to the auditor not to follow any structural concept blindly. This is another way of saying that "form follows function." If there is a conflict between a standard structure or format and the needs of the reader, then the former should yield to the latter. The needs of the reader should come first.

REPORT COMPONENTS

A well-structured, well-executed audit report is a deceptively simple-looking document. To fully understand what is going on in an audit report, one must analyze its various components. Audit reports usually have three major components:

1. Introductory
2. Main Body
3. Conclusion

Introductory Component

The purpose of the introductory component is to prepare the reader to understand and accept what is contained in the main body and in the conclusion. The introductory component includes:

Letter of transmittal
Report title
Table of contents (if appropriate)
Background, objectives and scope

It is very useful for the report writer to view these four subcomponents as related to a single purpose—which is to lay the groundwork for the reader's understanding and acceptance.

Letter of Transmittal

The first thing which is read by the report recipient is the letter of transmittal. This gives the letter of transmittal a potential importance often overlooked by writers of audit reports. To the extent that the letter contains substantive information about the report, it provides the first clue to the report's purpose, tone, structure and contents. The writer must carefully avoid writing anything in the letter of transmittal which may risk prejudicing the reader against the report. Given the fact that the purpose of an audit report is to inform and *persuade* the reader, the writer has to take care not to create unnecessary difficulties in the letter of transmittal which may make the task of the report itself more difficult.

In many cases, it will be best to view the letter of transmittal as an *administrative* document only and to exclude all mention of the contents of the report. This will avoid the premature introduction of sensitive material for which the reader has not been sufficiently prepared. Sensitive material should be introduced in the main body of the report where the writer will have more leeway to manage the reader's intellectual and emotional responses.

Report Title

Many internal auditors, especially junior ones, give very little thought to the titles of their reports. Reports are often given the same titles that were assigned when the audits were first planned, even though the audits may have progressed along lines that make their original titles entirely inaccurate or inappropriate.

When viewed as part of the introductory component of an audit report, the title takes on a new significance. The title is seen as a key device for informing the reader of the general subject matter of the report. It can also be used to establish an emotional climate conducive to the acceptance of the report, or at least to avoid an adverse emotional climate. For example, if a manager has requested a review of a particular problem area, it might be inappropriate to title the resulting report "Audit of . . . ."

Table of Contents

Viewing the table of contents as part of an overall introductory component provides a better insight into its purpose and potential usefulness. The table of contents picks up after the letter of transmittal and the report title to extend the reader's preliminary understanding of the report he is about to read. This is why the table of contents should be short. The reader is probably interested in a preliminary glimpse of the overall report contents. However, he is almost certainly not interested in reading a detailed outline. Anyone doubting this need only ask himself when he last had the interest and patience to study a detailed report outline.

Background, Objectives and Scope

The background, objectives and scope statement completes the introductory component of the report. It is here that the reader will learn the specific objective(s) of the audit or study, its scope and any background information required to fully understand the report.

The background, objectives and scope statement should be designed to fit the specific needs of the report and its readers. Too many auditors resort to boilerplate to describe the objectives and scope of their audits. They give the reader things that he can barely understand and withhold information that he might find really useful. Surely this sort of thing cannot be justified under the name of "professionalism," unless professionalism has come to mean uncaring exploitation of the client.

Short reports usually require a short combined statement of objectives and scope without need for any background information. If a statement of objectives leaves no ambiguity concerning scope, then mention of scope should be omitted altogether. In a short report, an adequate statement of objectives (and possibly scope) should seldom take more than four to eight lines of type. Better a short statement that is direct and clear than a long one that obfuscates and seeks to impress.

In a long audit report, the objectives, scope and background section is treated as a major subject area distinct from all others. If the statement is very short, there is no need for minor titles along the left-hand margin. If the statement is lengthy, minor titles should be devised to fit the need. The most typical case is to have a minor title for "Objectives and Scope" and another for "Background."

There are cases when "Background" merits treatment as a major subject area by itself. Reports of control reviews of large computerized information systems are a good case in point. For certain readers to fully understand such reports, it is often necessary to provide a system overview by way of background.

Whatever the requirements may be in the case of a long report, conciseness should remain the operative rule. The fact that a report is categorized as a "long" report should never influence the auditor to stretch any portion of it beyond its necessary length. The auditor must remember that any unnecessary length, whether in a short or long report, is an imposition upon the client and reflects poorly upon the auditor's professional judgment.

Main Body

The main body of an audit report is where the findings are discussed and is therefore that component of a report where the report's principal work is performed. Our discussion of the main body will make reference to two audit report formats: the long format and the short format.

Long Format

The long format is distinguished by the fact that it has two subject matter levels: a major level and a minor level. As we pointed out earlier, major topics are introduced at the top-center of a new page just like the chapters in a book. Minor topics are shown along the left-hand margin of the page.

Short Format

Since short audit reports by definition have only a small number of findings, they require only one level of subject-matter breakdown. The findings in a short report do not have to be grouped. They only have to be sequenced in some sort of logical order. Appropriate titles are devised for each finding and these are entered along the left-hand margin of the page immediately following the objectives and scope statement.

Note that this suggested arrangement does away entirely with the title "Findings and Recommendations" which is so often found in audit reports. Use of this title is probably a holdover from public accounting and has no real place in internal audit reports. It has the undesirable and unnecessary effect of forcing a two-level scheme of subject-matter breakdown when a single-level approach would otherwise be adequate.

Conclusion Component

In addition to an introductory component and a main body, many audit reports also have a conclusion component. It may be located at the end or at the beginning of the report. It may be called the opinion, the conclusion, the summary* or something else altogether. But if it is mainly an *overall* judgment drawn by the auditor from the specific findings in the main body, it is what we term the conclusion component.

In financial audit reports, the conclusion component usually takes the form of an auditor's overall opinion of the area reviewed. This opinion is generally found immediately after the statement of objectives and scope and before the findings and recommendations. Its location here is based mainly on custom but probably serves a useful purpose. Since financial audit reports continue to be prepared on the exception principle, a favorable overall opinion early in the report interjects an element of balance in what is otherwise a rather negative document.

In compliance and certain EDP audit reports, the conclusion component is similar in objective and approach to that in financial audit reports. It provides an opportunity for the auditor to express an overall opinion concerning the adequacy of controls, the effective and efficient use of resources, the achievement of assigned goals and objectives and the quality of management performance.

*Not to be confused with a "management summary."

In operational and management audits, the conclusion component is optional. Its use depends upon whether the auditor feels a need to draw conclusions or offer recommendations of a general nature not tied to specific findings in the report. The conclusion component can be an extremely useful vehicle for suggesting basic reforms such as reorganization, realignment of duties, reassignment of personnel and so forth. The ideas advanced in the conclusion component of an operational or management audit report are not usually treated as formal, numbered recommendations requiring a response. As a result, the auditor feels greater freedom to advance certain ideas since management is not asked to react to them. Management is free to take action now, later or not at all, as it sees fit.

SUMMARY

Macrostructure in audit report writing is determined by five basic principles: grouping, sequence, convenience, attractiveness and flexibility.

The *grouping* principle requires that the auditor identify each of his findings and group them in a manner that will facilitate his writing of the report and the reader's understanding of it. Groups of findings should be given an appropriate title similar to that of a chapter in a book.

The *sequence* principle requires that findings be addressed in an order providing the best possible logical and emotional progression.

The *convenience* principle requires that everything about an audit report be designed with the reader's interest in mind: clear and accurate titles and subtitles; a minimum number of subject-matter sublevels; a short table of contents; complete paging; proper design and location of exhibits and appendices; and the provision of a management summary when applicable.

The *attractiveness* principle requires that an audit report avoid violating the tastes and preferences of those for whom the report was prepared.

The *flexibility* principle requires that the form of an audit report reflect its function. Conflicts between report standards and the needs of the reader should be resolved in favor of the latter.

Audit reports usually have three components: the introductory component, the main body, and the conclusion component.

Included in the introductory component are the letter of transmittal, the report title, the table of contents (if any) and the statement of background, objectives and scope. It is the common purpose of all of these to prepare the reader intellectually and emotionally for what is to be found in the main body of the report.

The main body of an audit report contains the findings and is therefore the component where the report's principal work is performed.

There are two traditional audit formats: the long format and the short format. Long-format reports have a significant number of findings and require two levels of subject-matter breakdown.

Since short-format reports have only a limited number of findings, the grouping principle does not apply. The findings are simply sequenced in a logical order, assigned appropriate titles and presented at a single level of subject-matter breakdown. The traditional title "Findings and Recommendations" should be eliminated since it forces a second level of subject-matter breakdown without providing any compensating benefit.

Most financial and compliance audit reports have a conclusion component. In operational and management reports, the conclusion component is optional depending upon the auditor's need to offer general conclusions and recommendations based upon the findings as a whole.

DISCUSSION

The new internal auditing incorporates a heightened sensitivity to the needs of operating management and auditees. This sensitivity is reflected in a number of ideas discussed in this chapter: satisfaction of the reader's need for order, categories and limits; intellectual and emotional progression; avoidance of criticism; reader convenience; attractiveness and flexibility; and use of a conclusion component to suggest basic reforms without forcing a formal response by management.

The "politics" of the new internal auditing will be considerably more subtle and complex than the politics of conventional auditing. Such a politics will more readily recognize management's prerogative to accept, defer, or reject audit recommendations and will therefore require a deeper appreciation of the communications potential of the audit report.

Microstructure

Fact-finding is more effective than fault-finding.

CARL LOTUS BECKER, *Progress and Power*

AUDIT REPORTS VERSUS COLLEGE PAPERS

Very little in the college career of the novice auditor has prepared him for the challenge of writing an internal audit report. Audit reports have a special structure and discipline not normally applicable to college reports and essays.

Readers of this book may have encountered audit reports written like college papers. Such reports were not uncommon ten years ago when the profession ventured increasingly into operational auditing and had not yet developed a suitable approach to report writing. The difficulties engendered by these early audit reports would be hard to believe today. It was often difficult to determine what the auditors were attempting to say. Reports had to be subjected to special analysis to pinpoint their findings and recommendations. It was not unusual for such reports to set off bitter exchanges between auditees and auditors resulting in victories and defeats on both sides until some sort of peace was reestablished. Needless to say, this sort of thing seldom happens today. The reason it doesn't is that the profession has developed a clearer understanding of what an audit finding is and how it must be presented in order to secure the auditee's concurrence.

THE AUDIT PROCESS

An audit finding can be defined as the end result of the audit process. To understand what an audit finding is, it is first necessary to understand what the audit process is all about. The audit process involves six basic intellectual steps:

1. Defining the audit objective.
2. Identifying appropriate evaluation criteria.
3. Collecting and analyzing facts.
4. Comparing the facts against the evaluation criteria.
5. Drawing a conclusion.
6. Offering a recommendation if appropriate.

Defining the Audit Objective

Every audit task must have an objective. An auditor assigned to review a particular activity is confronted with hundreds of possibilities. The methods for conducting any given audit are so varied that an auditor literally cannot begin his (or her) work unless his mind first focuses upon some sort of objective. This is why internal auditors are so interested in audit programs and checkoff lists. Programs and checkoff lists suggest possible audit objectives and, therefore, are of immense value to internal auditors in planning their work.

An example of a typical audit objective might be to determine whether personnel turnover in a particular organization was normal or excessive.

Identifying Appropriate Evaluation Criteria

Internal auditing is mainly an evaluative function. As such, it seeks to determine whether something is adequate or inadequate, acceptable or unacceptable. To make such a determination, it is necessary to have a standard by which to measure or judge the area under review. An auditor wishing to determine whether personnel turnover is excessive must first have some idea of what excessive is. Is it 5%, 10%, 20% or 30%?

Collecting/Analyzing Facts

An auditor wishing to evaluate personnel turnover must determine what the rate of turnover actually is. Every audit finding ultimately rests upon a foundation of *facts* established by the auditor.

Comparing Facts Against Evaluation Criteria

Once the auditor is in possession of the necessary facts and evaluation criteria, he is then in a position to compare the two. In our example, let us assume that actual turnover is 30% as compared with a "normal" rate of 10%.

Drawing a Conclusion

In the example we are describing, the auditor would probably draw an adverse conclusion: that personnel turnover is, in fact, excessive.

Offering a Recommendation

More often than not, modern internal auditing requires that an internal auditor's adverse conclusion be accompanied by a recommendation designed to correct the problem. Practical and cost-effective recommendations constitute the most valuable service provided to management by internal auditors.

RELEVANCE OF THE AUDIT PROCESS TO REPORT WRITING

The key to acquiring facility in the art of audit report writing lies in understanding two things:

1. An audit report is essentially a collection of findings.
2. Writing about an audit finding follows the same logical pattern as the audit process we have just described.

It turns out that writing the main body of an audit report is really quite simple. All one has to do is to group and sequence the audit findings in a logical manner, and then write up each finding according to a standard "microstructure."

STRUCTURE OF THE AUDIT FINDING

Every audit finding consists of four structural elements:

1. The objective.
2. The "findings" (defined here in the narrow sense as including the observed facts, the evaluation criteria and the basic comparison of the two).
3. The conclusion.
4. The recommendation.

Not only are the above elements present in every audit finding, explicitly or implicitly, but they are usually* written in the order in which they are listed above. This is why a clear understanding of audit report microstructure is a sure cure for writer's block. It tells the writer exactly where to start: with his audit objective. (See Exhibit 8 on the following page.)

Let us demonstrate how thinking in terms of objective, findings, conclusion and recommendation immediately gets the ink flowing. In the case of our example on personnel turnover, the auditor can launch directly into his first draft as follows:

EMPLOYEE TURNOVER

Objective → An analysis was conducted to determine whether employee turnover was excessive.

Findings → Turnover for the period 1983–84 was determined from the department's records of employee hires and separations. Average turnover for the two-year period was computed at 22% per year. This compared with 7% for 1981–82 and with 6.2% for the 1983–84 average of three similar branch operations in the state.

Conclusion → It is concluded that employee turnover is excessive and probably accounts in part for the job scheduling and quality control difficulties referred to earlier.

---

*Usually, but not always. For example, one style of report writing involves starting each finding with a short conclusion statement.

Recommendation → It is recommended that the employee relations department conduct a review of wage rates and working conditions at the branch to identify the causes of the high rate of turnover.

Note how thinking in terms of objective, findings, conclusion and recommendation has permitted the auditor to dispose of his finding in short order and without any apparent difficulty. The auditor did not concern himself with fine points of language in writing his first draft. He simply put down everything he knew about his objective, findings, conclusion and recommendation in four consecutive paragraphs. If he follows this same procedure for every finding, he should have no difficulty in completing a rough draft of his report in less than a day.

EXHIBIT 8. THE AUDIT PROCESS AND THE AUDIT FINDING

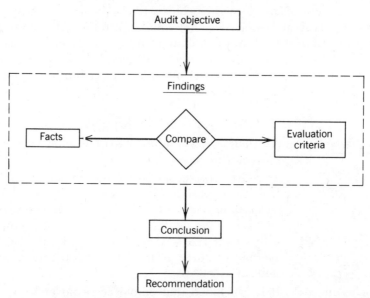

Comment: An audit report is essentially a collection of audit findings (broadly defined). The logic used in writing up a finding is the same as the logic of the audit process itself. The auditor addresses his objective, his findings (narrowly defined), his conclusion and his recommendation, in that order.

INTERSECTION OF TWO STRUCTURES

Let us now return to our original thesis, that an audit report is simply a collection of findings, and see how rich a concept this really is. We are now ready to combine our notions of audit report macrostructure and microstructure into a single, unified model.

In Exhibit 9 (on page 260), we see the introductory component with its four elements; the main body with its major and minor subject areas; and the conclusion. All of these comprise the macrostructure of the report. To the rear, we see the minor subject areas (findings) exploded into four elements: an objective, findings, a conclusion and one or more recommendations. We see how this microstructure of the findings "intersects" the macrostructure of the report to form a three-dimensional whole.

It is easy to see how this view of an audit report is incompatible with the rambling style of writing often associated with certain types of college papers. The principal difference between an audit report and a college paper is that the points made in an audit report are discrete, easily identified and localized. Whereas an argument in a college paper may be introduced, partially developed, set aside, reintroduced and further developed before being disposed of, an audit finding is addressed *in its entirety* in one place.

Mention was made previously of early audit reports which had to be analyzed by auditees in order to be understood. The reason why these early reports were difficult to understand is that the four logical elements of a finding were separated from each other and scattered over various parts of the report. Well-written reports do not pose this difficulty for readers. Once a finding is introduced, it is addressed in its entirety. The auditor's objective is made clear. The facts, observations and criteria upon which the finding is based are forthrightly presented. These are immediately followed by the auditor's conclusion and, if applicable, his recommendation.

WRITING UP THE FINDING

The basic rule in writing up a finding is to separate its four elements by paragraph breaks.

The auditor's *objective* is covered in the first paragraph.

Following the objective, the *findings* are presented in one or more

EXHIBIT 9. AUDIT REPORT STRUCTURE: INTERSECTION OF MACROSTRUCTURE AND MICROSTRUCTURE

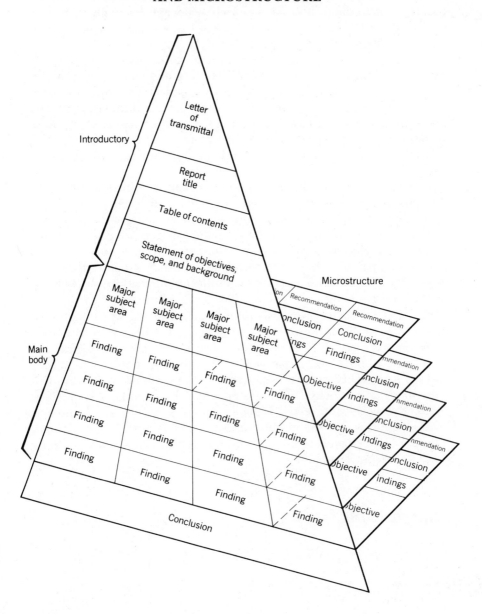

paragraphs as appropriate. Findings must be limited to factual material that is easily supportable and beyond controversy. By starting off with his objective and his findings, the auditor leads his reader into the subject matter in a controlled fashion. There is little or no risk that the reader will be derailed early in the text by statements that are subjective, judgmental or evaluative. The auditor makes his factual case fully before he draws conclusions and offers recommendations. This approach greatly facilitates the writing process. Writing a mixture of factual and evaluative statements is inherently difficult. It is easier to write the facts first and to draw conclusions later.

For purposes of this discussion, *conclusion* is defined as whatever the auditor wishes to say *after* he has presented his factual and non-controversial findings and *before* he offers specific (numbered) recommendations to identified responsible organizations. Opinions, comments and other similar statements would therefore come under our definition of "conclusion." Whereas findings are usually objective, concrete and very specific, conclusions are usually abstract and almost always contain an element of subjectivity. If an individual was observed taking an article belonging to another, his having taken the article would constitute a fact. Whether or not the taking of the article constituted a theft would be a *conclusion* drawn from other facts and circumstances surrounding the taking of the article.

In basic financial and compliance audits, a *recommendation* is a recommendation, and that's about all there is to it. Once an auditor progresses beyond basic auditing, however, he needs to enrich his concept of the recommendation. Selecting just the right wording can spell the difference between success and failure in securing the auditee's acceptance of a recommendation.

A recommendation can be general (you have a problem and you should fix it) or it can be specific (your clerk should take a refresher course in arithmetic). A recommendation can be immediate (money and negotiable instruments should not be left on desk tops overnight) or long-term (a new wing will need to be added to the general office within four years). A recommendation can run from very tentative to very definite:

Consideration should be given to . . .
It is suggested that . . .
It is recommended . . .
It is strongly recommended . . .

Generally, "soft" findings* call for soft recommendations which give management latitude and discretion. The softest kind of recommendation is one that is only implied in the conclusion: the word "recommendation" is not used and there is no recommendation number compelling a response.

EXPLICITNESS VERSUS IMPLICITNESS

We have stressed that all findings are comprised of an objective, findings, a conclusion and one or more recommendations. It is essential to good writing that the auditor think systematically in terms of these four elements of any finding. What is less essential, however, is that the auditor actually include all four elements in his discussion of the finding. There will be times when an auditor's text will not address all four elements of a finding explicitly since one element may be implicit in another:

The objective may be implicit in the title of the minor subject area. If, for example, a minor subject area is titled "cash verification," it will not be necessary for the auditor to state that his objective was to verify a cash fund.

The objective may be implicit in the finding. If an auditor observed a supervisor physically assaulting a subordinate, his report need not specify that his objective was to evaluate the supervisor's employee relations practices.

The conclusion may be implicit in the finding. If an inventory verification disclosed an unexplained shortage of 30%, it may not be necessary to draw the explicit conclusion that inventory control practices appear to be inadequate.

The conclusion may be implicit in the recommendation. If a clerk continues to commit an unacceptable number of errors despite all efforts at retraining, a recommendation that he be assigned to other duties need not be preceded by the explicit conclusion that he is not suited for his present assignment.

The recommendation may be implicit in the conclusion. If an auditor has conclusive proof that an employee has stolen company property, explicitly recommending disciplinary action may be entirely unnecessary.

*Highly judgmental findings for which compelling proof is lacking.

There are a number of reasons why an auditor may choose to omit explicit mention of one or more of the four elements of a finding. He may do so for reasons of conciseness, report format, writing style or auditee relations. The important thing is not whether all four elements are explicitly addressed in the report text. What matters is that the auditor think in terms of the four elements of a finding and ensure that his text is sufficiently clear, explicitly or implicitly, with respect to all four elements.

QUALITY ASSURANCE

Clarity and completeness in the presentation of an audit finding is not only good for the reader: it also benefits the audit organization as well. Good microstructure protects the audit organization from errors and their embarrassing consequences. The auditor's finding is clearly laid out for audit supervision and management: the underlying objective, the essential facts and observations, the applicable evaluation criteria, the conclusion and the recommendation. If the auditor is known to have good work habits, one hardly needs to examine his workpapers. Everything that matters in in full view in the report. The report convinces the reviewer, and it will convince the auditee. The report is *authoritative*. Good microstructure is therefore seen as promoting authoritativeness in an audit report.

SUMMARY

Audit reports have a special structure and discipline not normally required in other types of writing.

An audit finding can be defined as the end result of the audit process.

An audit report can be viewed simply as a collection of audit findings.

Microstructure refers to the structure of the individual audit finding. The conceptual structure of every audit finding is essentially the same. A clear understanding of audit report microstructure helps to eliminate writer's block.

The structure of the audit finding reflects the nature of the audit process. Every finding involves an objective, a set of observed facts, appropriate evaluation criteria, a comparison of the observed facts against the evaluation criteria, a conclusion and a recommendation.

All of the elements of a particular audit finding must be presented together in one place; they must not be scattered over various parts of the report.

All four elements of an audit finding need not be included explicitly in the report text. A particular element may be omitted if it is implicitly contained in another.

Good report microstructure facilitates report quality control by the auditor, audit supervision and audit management. For this reason, good microstructure supports the essential quality of authoritativeness in an audit report.

DISCUSSION

An interesting aspect of the new internal auditing is that it more clearly acknowledges the role of auditees and operating management in quality control of the audit product. Internal auditing's partnership with management extends all the way from initial audit planning to the joint evaluation of audit results.

Good report microstructure helps to make audit findings clearer to auditees and operating management. If a finding is sound, it will be accepted more readily. If it contains a flaw, the flaw will be eliminated with less difficulty. Viewed in this light, report microstructure is seen as a valuable technique serving the ends of the new internal auditing.

CHAPTER 16

Completed Staff Work

It's the only way to fly.

WESTERN AIRLINES COMMERCIAL

A WELL-KEPT SECRET

The expression "completed staff work" is unknown to the vast majority of well-educated business professionals. When asked, internal auditors can easily define each of the three words in the expression, and can usually hazard a guess as to what the words may mean in combination. But the fact remains that hardly anyone understands completed staff work as a specialized technical concept. It's one of the most useful concepts any business professional could learn—and it's also one of the best-kept secrets there is.

A VERY OLD CONCEPT

The evidence indicates that the idea and practice of completed staff work has been in existence a very long time. The author first learned of the concept in a paper written by a U.S. Navy captain which was apparently given wide circulation in military circles. The paper pointed out that the concept has been in use for hundreds of years. The reason it is not widely recognized is that it represents a way of working which very few people are privileged to adopt. Typically, completed staff work is performed by a select group of trusted and highly experienced staff assistants to powerful figures in large organizations. Organizations known to utilize completed staff work are governments, armed services, large corporations and other organizations with complex and wide-ranging interests such as the Catholic church.

WHAT THE CONCEPT IS

Completed staff work consists in performing all aspects of a staff assignment, without any assistance from one's superior, so that all that is required from the superior is approval of the work product or proposed course of action.

Completed staff work has been described as involving only two meetings with the boss: one to receive the assignment and another to deliver the finished product—neatly tied with a ribbon.

An Example

A classic example of completed staff work which was cited in the Navy paper mentioned earlier was the plan for the attack on Pearl Harbor during World War II. The brilliant Japanese officer who developed this plan had numerous factors to consider:

Current/projected overall military situation
Strategic targets on the Island of Oahu
Enemy defense capability
Enemy pursuit/retaliation capability
Date/time/weather
Requirements for ships, aircraft, personnel, supplies and so forth
Special training requirements
Navigation and refueling

Sailing instructions, rendezvous points and so forth

Task force command structure

Order of battle

Tactical intelligence and communications

Other factors

Planning a successful attack on Pearl Harbor involved identifying and resolving all problems *for* the commander. It did not involve referring problems to the commander to be solved *by* him.

Relationship Between Superior and Subordinate

Completed staff work represents the highest form of staff work. It requires very advanced knowledge and skills usually acquired over many years in various line and staff assignments. It also requires a very high degree of rapport, respect and confidence between superior and subordinate. This is why individuals who must do completed staff work are never foisted upon a superior. They are invariably selected by him on the basis of successful past association.

A subordinate's ability to do completed staff work can be very threatening to a low-level manager or supervisor who may feel that his value and importance can only be demonstrated through constant involvement in the work of subordinates. However, true executives with broad responsibilities and busy schedules have little choice but to demand initiative and self-sufficiency from subordinates. Such executives can, in a single day, generate a number of assignments each of which may require many months of effort to complete. For them to involve themselves in the details of these assignments would be literally impossible.

Conversely, a superior's need for completed staff work can be very threatening to a subordinate who is not intellectually or emotionally equipped to work in this mode. Completed staff work can be extremely risky for those who aren't up to it. The penalty for failure is rejection of the entire work product. Repeated failures inevitably lead to dismissal. For the individual with advanced knowledge and skills, however, completed staff work provides the ultimate in challenge, achievement, satisfaction and self-realization. For the true professional, it's "the only way to fly."

Review of Completed Staff Work

An interesting and surprising characteristic of completed staff work is that review of the end product by the superior is a relatively simple matter. The emphasis is on the solution or recommendation itself—not on how it was arrived at. The superior does not require detailed proof that the solution or recommendation is the correct one. Once it is described, the superior can tell intuitively whether or not it is correct.

The mind of a competent and experienced superior acts as a template through which the solution or recommendation must pass. Any excessive "looseness" or "tightness" of fit triggers an immediate reaction. The apparent ease with which a superior can confirm that a proposal is sound, or demonstrate that it is not, can be baffling and frustrating to junior personnel who may have worked months to complete an assignment. However, the process is really not so mysterious if one recalls modern discoveries that the human mind has information processing capabilities exceeding those of even the most sophisticated computers.

Relevance to Internal Auditing

Most readers with any experience in internal auditing will have already surmised why this chapter on completed staff work was included in a treatise on audit report writing. They will already have concluded that the field of internal auditing provides an excellent opportunity for even relatively junior personnel to move into the mode of completed staff work the moment that their experience, ability and drive permit.

Whereas most types of work can involve waiting a long time for the opportunity to demonstrate one's abilities, internal auditing provides a fast track for the truly gifted. Any auditor who completes an assignment on time and with apparent ease will almost invariably attract a more challenging assignment the next time around. Most supervisors are so busy providing support and assistance to auditors experiencing difficulty that they are usually eager to let the occasional go-getter work on his own with only light supervision. It follows that internal auditing provides an opportunity for an individual to develop his skills and abilities at a very rapid rate. If that individual is acquainted with the principles of completed staff work, he has the added advantage of knowing precisely where he should be heading. In many cases, he will be doing exactly the opposite of what his peers are doing.

A Personal Style

The concept of completed staff work can be used by the ambitious internal auditor to develop a success-oriented personal style. The essence of completed staff work is initiative. Its opposite is passivity.

The auditor with initiative understands that formal training programs can do little more than stimulate personal development. Ultimately, the internal auditor must accept most of the responsibility for his own development. He should avail himself of all of the developmental opportunities provided by his employer and then fill in any remaining gaps on his own.

The truly professional internal auditor is an avid reader of the professional literature—on his own time if need be. He joins the IIA and, if necessary, pays his tax-deductible membership fee out of his own pocket. He attends chapter meetings, makes contacts and volunteers to serve on committees. He studies for the CIA examination, takes the exam and passes it. He makes sure that he has read all of the important books and research works on internal auditing. He maintains a reference library of all basic IIA pronouncements including the new SIASs.

On the job, the professional internal auditor does not shy away from special assignments, but seeks them out. He cheerfully assists his boss in performing administrative tasks. If he is fully trained in financial auditing, he looks for opportunities to do operational, EDP and management audits. He goes out of his way to acquire competence in computer systems, including the use of remote terminals and personal computers.

The professional internal auditor recognizes the need to understand many things besides internal auditing. He studies the economic, financial and operational characteristics of his industry. He determines his company's position in the industry, its strategy, objectives and goals. He studies his company's organization and seeks to become personally acquainted with key personnel and sources of information. In a word, the professional internal auditor is constantly grooming himself to perform completed staff work.

An Internal Consultant

The auditor who has developed his knowledge and skills in the manner described above eagerly tackles the toughest assignments, confident of his ability to handle difficult technical and human relations problems. He grasps the essential objectives and scope of his assignments quickly and is able to develop work plans with little assistance from his superiors. He works effectively and efficiently without the need for external motivation or moral support. Although he is sociable and sensitive to the needs of others, he manages to keep busy and never wastes time.

The professional internal auditor can describe his findings effectively in terms of relevance, materiality and impact. He can demonstrate the feasibility and practicality of his recommendations and can enlist the support of key decision makers. His reports are well organized, concise and letter perfect. All they require is the supervisor's signature.

The professional auditor qualifies to be considered an internal consultant within his company. He is among the best-paid auditors in his department and is high on the eligibility list for advancement to surpervision and management within auditing or elsewhere in his company.

SUMMARY

Completed staff work consists in performing all aspects of a staff assignment, without any assistance from one's superior, so that all that is required from the superior is approval of the work product.

Completed staff work requires that all problems be identified and resolved *for* the superior. It does not involve referring problems to the superior to be solved *by* him.

Completed staff work implies a high degree of rapport, respect and confidence between superior and subordinate.

The review of completed staff work by the superior is a relatively simple matter. Once the solution or recommendation is described, the superior can tell intuitively whether or not it is correct.

Internal auditing provides an opportunity for relatively junior personnel to work in the mode of completed staff work early in their careers.

Completed staff work provides a model for the development of a success-oriented personal style. The essence of completed staff work is the exercise of initiative.

Auditors trained in the discipline of completed staff work are prepared to serve as internal consultants within their organizations.

DISCUSSION

The new internal auditing will require very special people if it is to fulfill its mission of service to the organization. The new internal auditor will not be a carbon copy of someone else. He will bring a certain uniqueness to his organization which, if added to the uniqueness of his associates, will produce a highly desirable diversity of backgrounds and abilities which will be needed by internal audit staffs of the 1980s and 1990s.

If, in addition, the new internal auditor pursues the concept of completed staff work, internal audit departments will possess staff capabilities unmatched by any other group in their organizations. This result will tend to attract favorable salary treatment of internal auditors and will also make them top-ranking candidates for advancement to desirable positions outside internal auditing. Internal auditors today are at the right place at the right time. Let them make the most of it.

Conclusion

My object all sublime
I shall achieve in time.

W. S. GILBERT, *The Mikado*

The task which we set for ourselves in the Introduction is now complete. We have explored the audit environment in considerable detail in order to identify clues to the present and future direction of the internal audit profession.

What we have observed may not conform to hopes and expectations entertained by many of us in the past. There was a time when internal auditing saw its principal challenge as demonstrating to senior management and the board audit committee that it was technically competent to perform a variety of useful tasks. It was hoped that senior management and the board audit committee would then provide sufficient resources and support to enable internal auditing to vigorously eradicate ineffectiveness, inefficiency and weaknesses in internal control on a broad front. This expectation does not appear to be warranted by our observations. What we have seen is a board audit committee reluctant to engage in controversy and cautious in its support of the internal audit function. We have also seen a senior management defensive of its prerogative to manage, fearful of allowing uncontrolled communications to the board and sensitive to complaints from below concerning the occasional harsh aspects of internal auditing. Former hopes for the development of the internal audit function are seen to have been based upon unrealistic expectations concerning unity and strength of command at the top. They also reflected an exaggerated estimate of the virtue and competence likely to be displayed by an internal audit function exempt from normal checks and balances. Wise senior managers know that no one is exempt from the Machiavellian dictum that "power corrupts, and absolute power corrupts absolutely."

We have seen that most board audit committees currently view their mandate as being restricted to the areas of internal accounting control and corporate governance, and that all internal audit activities outside these areas find their natural sponsor in senior management. Our examination of the concept of audit independence revealed that it does not apply to auditing's relationship to senior management and the board. Senior management and the board are the source, not the object, of audit independence. Audit independence is seen to derive from organizational status and organizational separation and to apply to auditing's relationship to areas under review.

We have seen that the IIA Code of Ethics enjoins the internal auditor to wholly support the interests and welfare of his employer, except that the internal auditor may not be a part of any illegal or improper activity. The Code does not enlist the internal auditor in performing any duties or responsibilities apart from those imposed by his employer. The internal auditor has no special mandate to assist law enforcement or regulatory agencies independently from his employer.

We have seen that the internal auditor operates in the power field of the corporation. The internal auditor has no choice but to view all members of the corporation as friends and economic allies whose efforts synergize with his own to produce extraordinary benefits for all. The internal auditor is shedding his self-image as a technician-warrior tilting against perceived negative forces within the corporation. His newfound consciousness as a member of the corporation's leadership team are opening up ways of contributing to corporate goals and objectives through alliance with positive forces in the organization.

The internal auditor has been typecast as a policeman or watchdog. Too many auditees and operating managers view interaction with the internal audit function as posing a threat to their careers. Sensing this, many internal auditors are abandoning their adversary assumptions, modifying their disclosure practices and seeking admittance to the mainstream corporate culture.

Fear and mistrust of the internal audit function is not limited to lower-level auditees and operating managers. It also infects senior management, and to a certain degree, the board audit committee itself. This all-pervasive fear and mistrust is the single most significant factor limiting the effectiveness of the internal audit function today. Its cause is rooted in disclosure practices inherited from the past.

Out of the environment which we have just described is emerging a new internal auditing and a new internal auditor. The motto of the new internal auditing is "partnership with management"—all levels of management. The new internal auditing assumes that the profession has already won its struggle for recognition and acceptance by senior management and the board, as evidenced by its new reporting relationship. It proposes to cement its relationship with senior management by focusing on common interests and objectives, respecting management's right to maintain the initiative, cooperating with established modes of leadership and engaging in judicious disclosure practices. The new internal auditing also proposes to improve its relationship with operating managers and auditees by boldly soliciting their confidence and trust and asking only that they actively participate in identifying and implementing needed operational and control improvements. The new internal auditing sees itself as being able to do its job, honor its primary loyalty to senior management and the board and yet avoid causing damage to the careers of most people with whom it comes into contact. The new internal auditing proposes to work with auditees and operating managers to make things work better, and to avoid disclosing matters which have been resolved and which no longer constitute a problem.

The new internal auditing understands that it must continue to perform such harsh assignments as senior management may issue from time to time. Also, in conformance with the IIA Code of Ethics, the new internal auditing will never fail to communicate to senior management and the board the things they need to know. However, the new internal auditing understands that senior management's support of the audit function depends to a significant extent upon the degree of acceptance at the lower levels of the organization. Accordingly, the new internal auditing will accept engagements from clients below the level of senior management provided such engagements are consistent with corporate objectives, ensure quality of work product, do not conflict with the IIA Code of Ethics and do not impinge upon the independence of the regular audit program.

The new internal auditing involves a "politics of communication" which ultimately reduces the relative importance of the final audit report. Agreement on findings and recommendations with operating managers and auditees, during the audit, renders the substance of the final audit report largely anticlimactic. The final report is no longer a disclosure of problems requiring the attention of upper management. Rather it is a record of joint accomplishment by auditees, operating management and internal auditing. Notwithstanding the changed character and reduced importance of the audit report, the new internal auditing will be associated with reports that are well structured, well written and reflective of a consistent and benign philosophy of auditing and audit relations.

As was said in the Introduction, the new internal auditing may not be right for everyone. The new internal auditing is not so much right as it is valid. It is valid because its elements exist here and now. This book has described a particular audit environment and the response it has elicited in some organizations. Readers who have seen their own audit environments reflected in these pages have either already moved toward the new internal auditing or are thinking of doing so. The virtue of this book, if it has any, is that it may have provided a systematic rationale for the new internal auditing and may therefore accelerate and facilitate its adoption by those who are ready for it. For those who are not ready, the book has hopefully provided concepts and criteria which may someday enable them to detect early warning signs of environmental change. If the book has accomplished either of these two things for practicing internal auditors, it has been worth the doing.

Appendices

A P P E N D I X A*

Foreign Corrupt Practices Act of 1977 Public Law 95–213 [S. 305]; Dec. 19, 1977

An Act to amend the Securities Exchange Act of 1934 to make it unlawful for an issuer of securities registered pursuant to section 12 of such Act or an issuer required to file reports pursuant to section 15(d) of such Act to make certain payments to foreign officials and other foreign persons, to require such issuers to maintain accurate records, and for other purposes.

Securities Exchange Act of 1934, amendment. Foreign Corrupt Practices Act of 1977. 15 USC 78a note.

Be it enacted by the Senate and House of Representatives of the United States of America in Congress assembled,

TITLE I—FOREIGN CORRUPT PRACTICES

Short Title

SEC. 101. This title may be cited as the "Foreign Corrupt Practices Act of 1977."

*United States code, *Congressional and Administrative News*, 95th Congress—First Session, 1977, Vol. 1, [91 Stat. pages 1494 to 1500]. By permission of West Publishing Co., St. Paul, Minnesota.

Accounting Standards

Assets, transactions and dispositions. 15 USC 78m.

15 USC 78*l*. *Post*, p. 1500. Records, maintenance.

SEC. 102. Section 13(b) of the Securities Exchange Act of 1934 (15 U.S.C. 78q(b)) is amended by inserting "(1)" after "(b)" and by adding at the end thereof the following:

"(2) Every issuer which has a class of securities registered pursuant to section 12 of this title and every issuer which is required to file reports pursuant to section 15(d) of this title shall—

Internal accounting controls, establishment.

"(A)   make and keep books, records, and accounts, which, in reasonable detail, accurately and fairly reflect the transactions and dispositions of the assets of the issuer; and

"(B)   devise and maintain a system of internal accounting controls sufficient to provide reasonable assurances that—

"(i)   transactions are executed in accordance with management's general or specific authorization;

"(ii)   transactions are recorded as necessary (I) to permit preparation of financial statements in conformity with generally accepted accounting principles or any other criteria applicable to such statements, and (II) to maintain accountability for assets;

"(iii)   access to assets is permitted only in accordance with management's general or specific authorization; and

"(iv)   the recorded accountability for assets is compared with the existing assets at reasonable intervals and appropriate action is taken with respect to any differences.

Exemption directive, issuance and expiration.

"(3) (A) With respect to matters concerning the national security of the United States, no duty or liability under paragraph (2) of this subsection shall be imposed upon any person acting in cooperation with the head of any Federal department or agency responsible for such matters if such act in cooperation with such head of a department or agency was done upon the specific, written directive of the head of such department or agency pursuant to Presidential authority to issue such directives. Each directive issued under this paragraph shall set forth the specific facts and circumstances with respect to which the provisions of this paragraph are to be invoked. Each such directive shall, unless renewed in writing, expire one year after the date of issuance.

File mainte-
nance.
Annual summary,
transmittal to congres-
sional committees.

"(B) Each head of a Federal department or agency of the United States who issues a directive pursuant to this paragraph shall maintain a complete file of all such directives and shall, on October 1 of each year, transmit a summary of matters covered by such directives in force at any time during the previous year to the Permanent Select Committee on Intelligence of the House of Representatives and the Select Committee on Intelligence of the Senate.".

Foreign Corrupt Practices by Issuers

SEC. 103. (a) The Securities Exchange Act of 1934 is amended by inserting after section 30 the following new section:

"Foreign Corrupt Practices by Issuers

15 USC
78dd-1.
15 USC 78*l*.
Post, p. 1500.

"SEC. 30A. (a) It shall be unlawful for any issuer which has a class of securities registered pursuant to section 12 of this title or which is required to file reports under section 15(d) of this title, or for any officer, director, employee, or agent of such issuer or any stockholder thereof acting on behalf of such issuer, to make use of the mails or any means or instrumentality of interstate commerce corruptly in furtherance of an offer, payment, promise to pay, or authorization of the payment of any money, or offer, gift, promise to give, or authorization of the giving of anything of value to—

"(1) any foreign official for purposes of—

"(A) influencing any act or decision of such foreign official in his official capacity, including a decision to fail to perform his official functions; or

"(B) inducing such foreign official to use his influence with a foreign government or instrumentality thereof to affect or influence any act or decision of such government or instrumentality,

in order to assist such issuer in obtaining or retaining business for or with, or directing business to, any person;

"(2) any foreign political party or official thereof or any candidate for foreign political office for purposes of—

"(A) influencing any act or decision of such party, official, or candidate in its or his official capacity, including a decision to fail to perform its or his official functions; or

"(B) inducing such party, official, or candidate to use its or his influence with a foreign government or instrumentality thereof to affect or influence any act or decision of such government or instrumentality.

in order to assist such issuer in obtaining or retaining business for or with, or directing business to, any person; or

"(3) any person, while knowing or having reason to know that all or a portion of such money or thing of value will be offered, given, or promised, directly or indirectly, to any foreign official, to any foreign political party or official thereof, or to any candidate for foreign political office, for purposes of—

"(A) influencing any act or decision of such foreign official, political party, party official, or candidate in his or its official capacity, including a decision to fail to perform his or its official functions; or

"(B) inducing such foreign official political party, party official, or candidate to use his or its influence with a foreign government or instrumentality thereof to affect or influence any act or decision of such government or instrumentality,

in order to assist such issuer in obtaining or retaining business for or with, or directing business to, any person.

"Foreign official."

"(b) As used in this section, the term 'foreign official' means any officer or employee of a foreign government or any department, agency, or instrumentality thereof, or any person acting in an official capacity for or on behalf of such government or department, agency, or instrumentality. Such term does not include any employee of a foreign government or any department, agency, or instrumentality thereof whose duties are essentially ministerial or clerical.".

Penalties.
Ante, p. 1495.

(b) (1) Section 32(a) of the Securities Exchange Act of 1934 (15 U.S.C. 78ff(a)) is amended by inserting "(other than section 30A)" immediately after "title" the first place it appears.

(2) Section 32 of the Securities Exchange Act of 1934 (15 U.S.C. 78ff) is amended by adding at the end thereof the following new subsection:

"(c) (1) Any issuer which violates section 30A(a) of this title shall, upon conviction, be fined not more than $1,000,000.

"(2) Any officer or director of an issuer, or any stockholder acting on behalf of such issuer, who willfully violates section 30A(a) of this title shall, upon conviction, be fined not more than $10,000, or imprisoned not more than five years, or both.

"(3) Whenever an issuer is found to have violated section 30A(a) of this title, any employee or agent of such issuer who is a United States citizen, national, or resident or is otherwise subject to the jurisdiction of the United States (other than an officer, director, or stockholder of such issuer), and who willfully carried out the act or practice constituting such violation shall, upon conviction, be fined not more than $10,000, or imprisoned not more than five years, or both.

"(4) Whenever a fine is imposed under paragraph (2) or (3) of this subsection upon any officer, director, stockholder, employee, or agent of an issuer, such fine shall not be paid, directly or indirectly, by such issuer.".

Foreign Corrupt Practices by Domestic Concerns

15 USC
78dd-2.

SEC. 104. (a) It shall be unlawful for any domestic concern, other than an issuer which is subject to section 30A of the Securities Exchange Act of 1934, or any officer, director, employee, or agent of such domestic concern or any stockholder thereof acting on behalf of such domestic concern, to make use of the mails or any means or instrumentality of interstate commerce corruptly in furtherance of an offer, payment, promise to pay, or authorization of the payment of any money, or offer, gift, promise to give, or authorization of the giving of anything of value to—

(1) any foreign official for purposes of—

(A) influencing any act or decision of such foreign official in his official capacity, including a decision to fail to perform his official functions; or

(B) inducing such foreign official to use his influence with a foreign government or instrumentality thereof to affect or influence any act or decision of such government or instrumentality,

in order to assist such domestic concern in obtaining or retaining business for or with, or directing business to, any person;

(2) any foreign political party or official thereof or any candidate for foreign political office for purposes of—

(A) influencing any act or decision of such party, official, or candidate in its or his official capacity, including a decision to fail to perform its or his official functions; or

(B) inducing such party, official, or candidate to use its or his influence with a foreign government or instrumentality thereof to affect or influence any act or decision of such government or instrumentality,

in order to assist such domestic concern in obtaining or retaining business for or with, or directing business to, any person; or

(3) any person, while knowing or having reason to know that all or a portion of such money or thing of value will be offered, given, or promised, directly or indirectly, to any foreign official, to any foreign political party or official thereof, or to any candidate for foreign political office, for purposes of—

(A) influencing any act or decision of such foreign official, political party, party official, or candidate in his or its official capacity, including a decision to fail to perform his or its official functions; or

(B) inducing such foreign official, political party, party official, or candidate to use his or its influence with a foreign government or instrumentality thereof to affect or influence any act or decision of such government or instrumentality,

in order to assist such domestic concern in obtaining or retaining business for or with, or directing business to, any person.

Penalties.

(b) (1) (A) Except as provided in subparagraph (B), any domestic concern which violates subsection (a) shall, upon conviction, be fined not more than $1,000,000.

(B) Any individual who is a domestic concern and who willfully violates subsection (a) shall, upon conviction, be fined not more than $10,000, or imprisoned not more than five years, or both.

(2) Any officer or director of a domestic concern, or stockholder acting on behalf of such domestic concern, who willfully violates subsection (a) shall, upon conviction, be fined not more than $10,000, or imprisoned not more than five years, or both.

(3) Whenever a domestic concern is found to have vio-

lated subsection (a) of this section, any employee or agent of such domestic concern who is a United States citizen, national, or resident or is otherwise subject to the jurisdiction of the United States (other than an officer, director, or stockholder acting on behalf of such domestic concern), and who willfully carried out the act or practice constituting such violation shall, upon conviction, be fined not more than $10,000, or imprisoned not more than five years, or both.

(4) Whenever a fine is imposed under paragraph (2) or (3) of this subsection upon any officer, director, stockholder, employee, or agent of a domestic concern, such fine shall not be paid, directly or indirectly, by such domestic concern.

Civil action.

(c) Whenever it appears to the Attorney General that any domestic concern, or officer, director, employee, agent, or stockholder thereof, is engaged, or is about to engage, in any act or practice constituting a violation of subsection (a) of this section, the Attorney General may, in his discretion, bring a civil action in an appropriate district court of the United States to enjoin such act or practice, and upon a proper showing a permanent or temporary injunction or a temporary restraining order shall be granted without bond.

Definitions.

(d) As used in this section:

(1) The term "domestic concern" means (A) any individual who is a citizen, national, or resident of the United States; or (B) any corporation, partnership, association, joint-stock company, business trust, unincorporated organization, or sole proprietorship which has its principal place of business in the United States, or which is organized under the laws of a State of the United States or a territory, possession, or commonwealth of the United States.

(2) The term "foreign official" means any officer or employee of a foreign government or any department, agency, or instrumentality thereof, or any person acting in an official capacity for or on behalf of any such government or department, agency, or instrumentality. Such term does not include any employee of a foreign government or any depart-

ment, agency, or instrumentality thereof whose duties are essentially ministerial or clerical.

(3)   The term "interstate commerce" means trade, commerce, transportation, or communication among the several States, or between any foreign country and any State or between any State and any place or ship outside thereof. Such term includes the intrastate use of (A) a telephone or other interstate means of communication, or (B) any other interstate intrumentality.

TITLE II—DISCLOSURE

Domestic and Foreign Investment Improved Disclosure Act of 1977. 15 USC 78a note.
Equity security acquisition, statement, filing. Contents.

15 USC 78*l.*
15 USC 80a-51.

SEC. 201. This title may be cited as the "Domestic and Foreign Investment Improved Disclosure Act of 1977."

SEC. 202. Section 13(d) (1) of the Securities Exchange Act of 1934 (15 U.S.C. 78m) is amended to read as follows:

"(d) (1) Any person who, after acquiring directly or indirectly the beneficial ownership of any equity security of a class which is registered pursuant to section 12 of this title, or any equity security of an insurance company which would have been required to be so registered except for the exemption contained in section 12(g) (2) (G) of this title, or any equity security issued by a closed-end investment company registered under the Investment Company Act of 1940, is directly or indirectly the beneficial owner of more than 5 per centum of such class shall, within ten days after such acquisition, send to the issuer of the security at its principal executive office, by registered or certified mail, send to each exchange where the security is traded, and file with the Commission, a statement containing such of the following information, and such additional information, as the Commission may by rules and regulations, prescribe as necessary or appropriate in the public interest or for the protection of investors—

"(A) the background, and identity, residence, and citizenship of, and the nature of such beneficial ownership by, such person and all other persons by whom or on whose behalf the purchases have been or are to effected;

"(B) the source and amount of the funds or other consideration used or to be used in making the purchases, and if any part of the purchase price is represented or is to be represented by funds or other consideration borrowed or otherwise obtained for the purpose of acquiring, holding, or trading such security, a description of the transaction and the names of the parties thereto, except that where a source of funds is a loan made in the ordinary course of business by a bank, as defined in section 3(a) (6) of this title, if the person filing such statement so requests, the name of the bank shall not be made available to the public;

"(C) if the purpose of the purchases or prospective purchases is to acquire control of the business of the issuer of the securities, any plans or proposals which such persons may have to liquidate such issuer, to sell its assets to or merge it with any other persons, or to make any other major change in its business or corporate structure;

"(D) the number of shares of such security which are beneficially owned, and the number of shares concerning which there is a right to acquire, directly or indirectly, by (i) such person, and (ii) by each associate of such person, giving the background, identity, residence, and citizenship of each such associate; and

"(E) information as to any contracts, arrangements, or understandings with any person with respect to any securities of the issuer, including but not limited to transfer of any of the securities, joint ventures, loan or option arrangements, puts or calls, guaranties of loans, guaranties against loss or guaranties of profits, division of losses or profits, or the giving or withholding of proxies, naming the persons with whom such contracts arrangements, or understandings have been entered into, and giving the details thereof.".

Equity
security
ownership,
statement,
filing.

SEC. 203. Section 13 of the Securities Exchange Act of 1934, as amended (15 U.S.C. 78m), is amended by adding at the end thereof the following new subsection:

"(g) (1) Any person who is directly or indirectly the beneficial owner of more than 5 per centum of any security of a class described in subsection (d) (1) of this section shall send to the issuer of the security and shall file with the Commission a statement setting forth, in such form and at such time as the Commission may, by rule, prescribe—

"(A) such person's identity, residence, and citizenship; and

"(B) the number and description of the shares in which such person has an interest and the nature of such interest.

"(2) If any material change occurs in the facts set forth in the statement sent to the issuer and filed with the Commission, an amendment shall be transmitted to the issuer and shall be filed with the Commission, in accordance with such rules and regulations as the Commission may prescribe as necessary or appropriate in the public interest or for the protection of investors.

"(3) When two or more persons act as a partnership, limited partnership, syndicate, or other group for the purpose of acquiring, holding, or disposing of securities of an issuer, such syndicate or group shall be deemed a 'person' for the purposes of this subsection.

"(4) In determining, for purposes of this subsection, any percentage of a class of any security, such class shall be deemed to consist of the amount of the outstanding securities of such class, exclusive of any securities of such class held by or for the account of the issuer or a subsidiary of the issuer.

"(5) In exercising its authority under this subsection, the Commission shall take such steps as it deems necessary or appropriate in the public interest or for the protection of investors (A) to achieve centralized reporting of information regarding ownership, (B) to avoid unnecessarily duplicative reporting by and minimize the compliance burden on persons required to report, and (C) to tabulate and
promptly make available the information contained in any report filed pursuant to this subsection in a manner which will, in the view of the Commission, maximize the usefulness of the information to other Federal and State agencies and the public.

"(6) The Commission may, by rule or order, exempt, in whole or in part, any person or class of persons from any or all of the reporting requirements of this subsection as it deems necessary or appropriate in the public interest or for the protection of investors.

"(h) The Commission shall report to the Congress within thirty months of the date of enactment of this subsection with respect to (1) the effectiveness of the ownership reporting requirements contained in this title, and (2) the desirability and the feasibility of reducing or otherwise modifying the 5 per centum threshold used in subsections (d) (1) and (g) (1) of this section, giving appropriate consideration to—

Ante, p. 1498.

> "(A)   the incidence of avoiding of reporting by beneficial owners using multiple holders of record;
>
> "(B)   the cost of compliance to persons required to report;
>
> "(C)   the cost to issuers and others of processing and disseminating the reported information;
>
> "(D)   the effect of such action on the securities markets, including the system for the clearance and settlement of securities transactions;
>
> "(E)   the benefits to investors and to the public;
>
> "(F)   any bona fide interests of individuals in the privacy of their financial affairs;
>
> "(G)   the extent to which such reported information gives or would give any person an undue advantage in connection with activities subject to sections 13(d) and 14(d) of this title:
>
> "(H)   the need for such information in connection with the administration and enforcement of this title; and
>
> "(I)   such other matters as the Commission may deem relevant, including the information obtained pursuant to section 13(f) of this title.".

15 USC 78n.

"Held of record," definition.
15 USC 78*o*.

SEC. 204. Section 15(d) of the Securities Exchange Act of 1934 is amended by inserting immediately before the last sentence the following new sentence: "The Commission may, for the purpose of this subsection, define by rules and regulations the term 'held of record' as it deems necessary or appropriate in the public interest or for the protection of investors in order to prevent circumvention of the provisions of this subsection."

Approved December 19, 1977.

LEGISLATIVE HISTORY:
HOUSE REPORTS: No. 95-640 accompanying H.R. 3815 (Comm. on Interstate and Foreign Commerce) and No. 95-831 (Comm. of Conference).
SENATE REPORT No. 95-114 (Comm. on Banking, Housing, and Urban Affairs).
CONGRESSIONAL RECORD, Vol. 123 (1977):
  May. 5, considered and passed Senate.
  Nov. 1, considered and passed House, amended, in lieu of H.R. 3815.
  Dec. 6, Senate agreed to conference report.
  Dec. 7, House agreed to conference report.
WEEKLY COMPILATION OF PRESIDENTIAL DOCUMENTS, Vol. 13, No. 52: Dec. 20, Presidential statement.

Statement of Responsibilities of Internal Auditing

As originally appeared on July 15, 1947

Responsibilities of the Internal Auditor

FOREWORD

This statement of the Responsibilities of the Internal Auditor was prepared by the Research Committee and approved by the Board of Directors of THE INSTITUTE OF INTERNAL AUDITORS, INC. *at its meeting of July 15, 1947. In taking this action the Board was desirous of lending its full support and that of* THE INSTITUTE *to the Statement. It was not intended, however, that the treatment of the various matters in the Statement was con-*

sidered in any sense to be final or fixed. Rather it was recognized that the principles and concepts relating to internal auditing are evolving constantly. The approval therefore represented essentially an endorsement of what the Board believes to be a fair and considered statement of the responsibilities of the internal auditor at its present stage of development. The Statement is therefore subject to such further modification in the future as may appear to be warranted in the light of new conditions and needs and through further development in the professional stature of the internal auditor.

NATURE OF INTERNAL AUDITING

Internal auditing is the independent appraisal activity within an organization for the review of the accounting, financial, and other operations as a basis for protective and constructive service to management. It is a type of control which functions by measuring and evaluating the effectiveness of other types of control. It deals primarily with accounting and financial matters but it may also properly deal with matters of an operating nature.

OBJECTIVES AND RELATED ACTIVITIES

The overall objective of internal auditing is to assist management in achieving the most efficient administration of the operations of the organization. This total objective has two major phases, as follows:

(1) The protection of the interests of the organization, including the pointing out of existing deficiencies to provide a basis for appropriate corrective action.

The attainment of this objective involves such activities of the internal auditor as:

(a) Ascertaining the degree of reliability of accounting and statistical data developed within the organization.

(b) Ascertaining the extent to which company assets are properly accounted for and safeguarded from losses of all kinds.

(c) Ascertaining the extent of compliance with established policies, plans, and procedures.

(2) The furtherance of the interests of the organization, including the recommendation of changes for the improvement of the various phases of the operations.

The attainment of this objective involves such activities of the internal auditor as:

(a) Reviewing and appraising the policies and plans of the organization in the light of the related data and other evidence.

(b) Reviewing and appraising the internal records and procedures of the organization in terms of their adequacy and effectiveness.

(c) Reviewing and appraising performance under the policies, plans and procedures.

SCOPE OF AUTHORITY AND RESPONSIBILITY

Internal auditing is a staff or advisory function rather than a line or operating function. Therefore the internal auditor does not exercise direct authority over other persons in the organization.

The internal auditor should be free to review and appraise policies, plans and procedures but his review and appraisal does not in any way relieve other persons in the organization of the primary responsibilities assigned to them.

INDEPENDENCE

Independence is basic to the effectiveness of the internal auditing program. This independence has two major aspects, as follows:

(1) The head of the internal auditing department should be made responsible to an officer of sufficient rank in the organization as will assure adequate consideration and action on the findings or recommendations. The organizational status of the internal auditor and the support accorded to him by management are major determinants of the range and value of the services which management will obtain from the internal auditing function.

(2) Internal auditing should not include responsibilities for procedures which are essentially a part of the regular operations of a

complete and adequate accounting system or of a properly organized operating department. In some instances management
may assign current operating responsibilities to the internal auditing department, but in such cases the execution of the current
operating responsibilities should be performed by separate personnel and be subjected to the same review and appraisal as is accorded other operations.

SECOND VERSION (FIRST REVISION)

As approved on May 30, 1957
(but incorporating a revised foreword approved on January 17, 1964)

Statement of Responsibilties of the Internal Auditor

FOREWORD

The first Statement of Responsibilities of the Internal Auditor was developed by the Research Committee and approved by the Board of Directors of THE INSTITUTE OF INTERNAL AUDITORS *on July 15, 1947. In the Foreword to that Statement recognition was given to the fact that "new conditions and needs and further development in the professional stature of the internal auditor" might well require future revisions.*

The evolution and growth of the internal auditing profession since the issuance of the first Statement necessitated the development of a revised Statement by the Research Committee to express the broader concepts of modern internal auditing.

This present Statement was approved by the Board of Directors on May 30, 1957.

NATURE OF INTERNAL AUDITING

Internal auditing is an independent appraisal activity within an organization for the review of accounting, financial and other operations as a basis for service to management. It is a managerial control, which functions by measuring and evaluating the effectiveness of other controls.

OBJECTIVE AND SCOPE OF INTERNAL AUDITING

The over-all objective of internal auditing is to assist all members of management in the effective discharge of their responsibilities, by furnishing them with objective analyses, appraisals, recommendations and pertinent comments concerning the activities reviewed. The internal auditor therefore should be concerned with any phase of business activity wherein he can be of service to management. The attainment of this over-all objective of service to management should involve such activities as:

- Reviewing and appraising the soundness, adequacy and application of accounting, financial and operating controls.
- Ascertaining the extent of compliance with established policies, plans and procedures.
- Ascertaining the extent to which company assets are accounted for, and safeguarded from losses of all kinds.
- Ascertaining the reliability of accounting and other data developed within the organization.
- Appraising the quality of performance in carrying out assigned responsibilities.

AUTHORITY AND RESPONSIBILITY

Internal auditing is a staff function rather than a line function. Therefore the internal auditor does not exercise direct authority over other persons in the organization whose work he reviews.

The internal auditor should be free to review and appraise policies, plans, procedures, and records; but his review and appraisal does not in any way relieve other persons in the organization of the responsibilities assigned to them.

INDEPENDENCE

Independence is essential to the effectiveness of the internal auditing program. This independence has two major aspects.

(1) The organizational status of the internal auditor and the support accorded to him by management are major determinants of the range and value of the services which management will obtain from the internal auditing function. The head of the internal auditing department, therefore, should be responsible to an officer of sufficient rank in the organization as will assure a broad scope of activities, and adequate consideration of and effective action on the findings or recommendations made by him.

(2) Since complete objectivity is essential to the audit function, internal auditors should not develop and install procedures, prepare records, or engage in any other activity which they normally would be expected to review and appraise.

THIRD VERSION (SECOND REVISION)

As approved on June 30, 1971

Statement of Responsibilities
of the Internal Auditor

NATURE

Internal auditing is an independent appraisal activity within an organization for the review of operations as a service to management. It is a managerial control which functions by measuring and evaluating the effectiveness of other controls.

OBJECTIVE AND SCOPE

The objective of internal auditing is to assist all members of management in the effective discharge of their responsibilities by furnishing them with analyses, appraisals, recommendations, and pertinent comments concerning the activities reviewed. The internal auditor is concerned with any phase of business activity where he may be of service to management. This involves going beyond the accounting and financial records to obtain a full understanding of the operations under review. The attainment of this overall objective involves such activities as:

- Reviewing and appraising the soundness, adequacy, and application of accounting, financial, and other operating controls and promoting effective control at reasonable cost.
- Ascertaining the extent of compliance with established policies, plans, and procedures.
- Ascertaining the extent to which company assets are accounted for and safeguarded from losses of all kinds.
- Ascertaining the reliability of management data developed within the organization.
- Appraising the quality of performance in carrying out assigned responsibilities.
- Recommending operating improvements.

RESPONSIBILITY AND AUTHORITY

The responsibilities of internal auditing in the organization should be clearly established by management policy. The related authority should provide the internal auditor full access to all of the organization's records, properties, and personnel relevant to the subject under review. The internal auditor should be free to review and appraise policies, plans, procedures, and records.

The internal auditor's responsibilities should be:

- To inform and advise management and to discharge this responsibility in a manner that is consistent with the *Code of Ethics* of The Institute of Internal Auditors.
- To coordinate his activities with others so as to best achieve his audit objectives and the objectives of the organization.

In performing his functions, an internal auditor has no direct responsibility for nor authority over any of the activities which he reviews. Therefore, the internal audit review and appraisal do not in any way relieve other persons in the organization of the responsibilities assigned to them.

INDEPENDENCE

Independence is essential to the effectiveness of internal auditing. This independence is obtained primarily through organizational status and objectivity:

- The organizational status of the internal auditing function and the support accorded to it by management are major determinants of its range and value. The head of the internal auditing function, therefore, should be responsible to an officer whose authority is sufficient to assure both a broad range of audit coverage and the adequate consideration of and effective action on the audit findings and recommendations.
- Objectivity is essential to the audit function. Therefore, an internal auditor should not develop and install procedures, prepare records, or engage in any other activity which he would normally review and appraise and which could reasonably be construed to compromise his independence. His objectivity need not be adversely affected, however, by his determination and recommendation of the standards of control to be applied in the development of the systems and procedures under his review.

FOURTH VERSION (THIRD REVISION)

As approved on June 30, 1976

Statement of Responsibilities of Internal Auditors

NATURE

Internal auditing is an independent appraisal activity within an organization for the review of operations as a service to management. It is a managerial control which functions by measuring and evaluating the effectiveness of other controls.

OBJECTIVE AND SCOPE

The objective of internal auditing is to assist all members of management in the effective discharge of their responsibilities by furnishing them with analyses, appraisals, recommendations, and pertinent comments concerning the activities reviewed. Internal auditors are concerned with any phase of business activity where they may be of service to management. This involves going beyond the accounting and financial records to obtain a full understanding of the operations under review. The attainment of this overall objective involves such activities as:

- Reviewing and appraising the soundness, adequacy, and application of accounting, financial, and other operating controls and promoting effective control at reasonable cost.
- Ascertaining the extent of compliance with established policies, plans, and procedures.
- Ascertaining the extent to which company assets are accounted for and safeguarded from losses of all kinds.
- Ascertaining the reliability of management data developed within the organization.

- Appraising the quality of performance in carrying out assigned responsibilities.
- Recommending operating improvements.

RESPONSIBILITY AND AUTHORITY

The responsibilities of internal auditing in the organization should be clearly established by management policy. The related authority should provide the internal auditor full access to all of the organization's records, properties, and personnel relevant to the subject under review. The internal auditor should be free to review and appraise policies, plans, procedures, and records.

The internal auditor's responsibilities should be:

- To inform and advise management and to discharge this responsibility in a manner that is consistent with the Code of Ethics of The Institute of Internal Auditors.
- To coordinate internal audit activities with others so as to best achieve the audit objectives and the objectives of the organization.

In performing their functions, internal auditors have no direct responsibilities for nor authority over any of the activities reviewed. Therefore, the internal audit review and appraisal do not in any way relieve other persons in the organization of the responsibilities assigned to them.

INDEPENDENCE

Independence is essential to the effectiveness of internal auditing. This independence is obtained primarily through organizational status and objectivity:

- The organizational status of the internal auditing function and the support accorded to it by management are major determinants of its range and value. The head of the internal auditing function, therefore, should be responsible to an officer whose authority is sufficient to assure both a broad range of audit coverage and the adequate consideration of and effective action on the audit findings and recommendations.

■ Objectivity is essential to the audit function. Therefore, an internal auditor should not develop and install procedures, prepare records, or engage in any other activity which he would normally review and appraise and which could reasonably be construed to compromise the independence of the internal auditor. The internal auditor's objectivity need not be adversely affected, however, by determining and recommending standards of control to be applied in the development of the systems and procedures being reviewed.

FIFTH VERSION (FOURTH REVISION)

As approved on December 4, 1981

Statement of Responsibilities of Internal Auditing

The purpose of this statement is to provide in summary form a general understanding of the role and responsibilities of internal auditing. For more specific guidance, readers should refer to the *Standards for the Professional Practice of Internal Auditing*.

NATURE

Internal auditing is an independent appraisal activity established within an organization as a service to the organization. It is a control which functions by examining and evaluating the adequacy and effectiveness of other controls.

OBJECTIVE AND SCOPE

The objective of internal auditing is to assist members of the organization in the effective discharge of their responsibilities. To this end, internal auditing furnishes them with analyses, appraisals, recommendations, counsel, and information concerning the activities reviewed. The audit objective includes promoting effective control at reasonable cost.

The scope of internal auditing encompasses the examination and evaluation of the adequacy and effectiveness of the organization's system of internal control and the quality of performance in carrying out assigned responsibilities. The scope of internal auditing includes:

- Reviewing the reliability and integrity of financial and operating information and the means used to identify, measure, classify, and report such information.
- Reviewing the systems established to ensure compliance with those policies, plans, procedures, laws, and regulations which

could have a significant impact on operations and reports, and determining whether the organization is in compliance.

- Reviewing the means of safeguarding assets and, as appropriate, verifying the existence of such assets.
- Appraising the economy and efficiency with which resources are employed.
- Reviewing operations or programs to ascertain whether results are consistent with established objectives and goals and whether the operations or programs are being carried out as planned.

RESPONSIBILITY AND AUTHORITY

Internal auditing functions under the policies established by management and the board. The purpose, authority and responsibility of the internal auditing department should be defined in a formal written document (charter), approved by management, and accepted by the board. The charter should make clear the purposes of the internal auditing department, specify the unrestricted scope of its work, and declare that auditors are to have no authority or responsibility for the activities they audit.

The responsibility of internal auditing is to serve the organization in a manner that is consistent with the *Standards for the Professional Practice of Internal Auditing* and with professional standards of conduct such as the *Code of Ethics* of The Institute of Internal Auditors, Inc. This responsibility includes coordinating internal audit activities with others so as to best achieve the audit objectives and the objectives of the organization.

INDEPENDENCE

Internal auditors should be independent of the activities they audit. Internal auditors are independent when they can carry out their work freely and objectively. Independence permits internal auditors to render the impartial and unbiased judgments essential to the proper conduct of audits. It is achieved through organizational status and objectivity.

Organizational status should be sufficient to assure a broad range of audit coverage, and adequate consideration of and effective action on audit findings and recommendations.

Objectivity requires that internal auditors have an independent mental attitude, and an honest belief in their work product. Drafting procedures, designing, installing, and operating systems, are not audit functions. Performing such activities is presumed to impair audit objectivity.

APPENDIX C

Ethics

THE INSTITUTE OF INTERNAL AUDITORS, INC. CODE OF ETHICS

Introduction

Recognizing that ethics are an important consideration in the practice of internal auditing and that the moral principles followed by members of *The Institute of Internal Auditors, Inc.,* should be formalized, the Board of Directors at its regular meeting in New Orleans on December 13, 1968, received and adopted the following resolution:

> *WHEREAS* the members of *The Institute of Internal Auditors, Inc.* represent the profession of internal auditing; and
>
> *WHEREAS* managements rely on the profession of internal auditing to assist in the fulfillment of their management stewardship; and
>
> *WHEREAS* said members must maintain high standards of conduct, honor and character in order to carry on proper and meaningful internal auditing practice;
>
> *THEREFORE BE IT RESOLVED* that a Code of Ethics be now set forth, outlining the standard of professional behavior for the guidance of each member of *The Institute of Internal Auditors, Inc.*

305

In accordance with this resolution, the Board of Directors further approved of the principles set forth.

Interpretation of Principles

The provisions of this Code of Ethics cover basic principles in the various disciplines of internal auditing practice. Members shall realize that individual judgment is required in the application of these principles. They have a responsibility to conduct themselves so that their good faith and integrity should not be open to question. While having due regard for the limit of their technical skills, they will promote the highest possible internal auditing standards to the end of advancing the interest of their company or organization.

Articles

I.   Members shall have an obligation to exercise honesty, objectivity, and diligence in the performance of their duties and responsibilities.

II. Members, in holding the trust of their employers, shall exhibit loyalty in all matters pertaining to the affairs of the employer or to whomever they may be rendering a service. However, members shall not knowingly be a part to any illegal or improper activity.

III. Members shall refrain from entering into any activity which may be in conflict with the interest of their employers or which would prejudice their ability to carry out objectively their duties and responsibilities.

IV. Members shall not accept a fee or a gift from an employee, a client, a customer, or a business associate of their employer without the knowledge and consent of their senior management.

V.   Members shall be prudent in the use of information acquired in the course of their duties. They shall not use confidential information for any personal gain nor in a manner which would be detrimental to the welfare of their employer.

VI. Members, in expressing an opinion, shall use all reasonable care to obtain sufficient factual evidence to warrant such expression. In their reporting, members shall reveal such material facts known to them, which, if not revealed, could either distort the report of the results of operations under review or conceal unlawful practice.

VII.   Members shall continually strive for improvement in the proficiency and effectiveness of their service.

VIII.   Members shall abide by the bylaws and uphold the objectives of *The Institute of Internal Auditors, Inc.* In the practice of their profession, they shall be ever mindful of their obligation to maintain the high standard of competence, morality, and dignity which *The Institute of Internal Auditors, Inc.*, and its members have established.

CERTIFIED INTERNAL AUDITOR CODE OF ETHICS

The Certified Internal Auditor has an obligation to the profession, management, and stockholders and to the general public to maintain high standards of professional conduct. In recognition of this obligation, The Institute of Internal Auditors, Inc., adopted this Code of Ethics for Certified Internal Auditors.

Adherence to this Code, which is based on the Code of Ethics for members of The Institute, is a prerequisite to maintaining the designation Certified Internal Auditor. A Certified Internal Auditor who is judged by the Board of Directors of The Institute to be in violation of the provisions of the Code shall forfeit the Certified Internal Auditor designation.

Preamble

The provisions of this Code of Ethics cover basic principles in the various disciplines of internal auditing practice. Certified Internal Auditors shall realize that their individual judgment is required in the application of these principles. They have a responsibility to conduct themselves in a manner so that their good faith and integrity should not be open to question. Furthermore, they shall use the "Certified Internal Auditor" designation with discretion and in a dignified manner, fully aware of what the designation denotes and in a manner consistent with all statutory requirements. While having due regard for the limit of their technical skills, they will promote the highest possible internal auditing standards to the end of advancing the interest of their company or organization.

Articles

I. Certified Internal Auditors shall have an obligation to exercise honesty, objectivity and diligence in the performance of their duties and responsiblities.

II. Certified Internal Auditors, in holding the trust of their employer, shall exhibit loyalty in all matters pertaining to the affairs of the employer or to whomever they may be rendering a service. However, a Certified Internal Auditor shall not knowingly be a party to any illegal or improper activity.

III. Certified Internal Auditors shall refrain from entering into any activity which may be in conflict with the interest of their employer or which would prejudice their ability to carry out objectively their duties and responsibilties.

IV. Certified Internal Auditors shall not accept a fee or a gift from an employee, a client, a customer or a business associate of their employer without the knowledge and consent of senior management.

V. Certified Internal Auditors shall be prudent in their use of information acquired in the course of their duties. They shall not use confidential information for any personal gain or in a manner which would be detrimental to the welfare of their employer.

VI. Certified Internal Auditors, in expressing an opinion, shall use all reasonable care to obtain sufficient factual evidence to warrant such expression. In reporting, Certified Internal Auditors shall reveal such material facts known to them which, if not revealed, could either distort the report of the results of operations under review or conceal unlawful practice.

VII. Certified Internal Auditors shall continually strive for improvements in the proficiency and effectiveness of their service.

CERTIFIED INTERNAL AUDITOR PLEDGE

In all of my professional dealings, I will maintain high standards of conduct and exercise honesty, objectivity, and diligence in the discharge of my responsibilities.

I will not engage in any activity which may be in conflict with my employer's interest, and I will preserve the confidentiality of the information acquired in the performance of my duties.

I will use all reasonable care to obtain sufficient evidence to warrant any expression of opinion, and I will reveal all material facts known to me.

I will continually strive to improve the proficiency and effectiveness with which I carry out my responsibilities, and I reaffirm my pledge to uphold the Code of Ethics for Certified Internal Auditors.

A P P E N D I X   D

Standards for the Professional Practice of Internal Auditing

CONTENTS

INTRODUCTION

Internal auditing is an independent appraisal function established within an organization to examine and evaluate its activities as a service to the organization. The objective of internal auditing is to assist members of the organization in the effective discharge of their responsibilities. To this end, internal auditing furnishes them with analyses, appraisals, recommendations, counsel and information concerning the activities reviewed.

The members of the organization assisted by internal auditing include those in management and the board of directors. Internal auditors owe a responsibility to both, providing them with information about the adequacy and effectiveness of the organization's system of internal control and the quality of performance. The information furnished to each may differ in format and detail, depending upon the requirements and requests of management and the board.

The internal auditing department is an integral part of the organization and functions under the policies established by management and the board. The statement of purpose, authority, and responsibility (charter) for the internal auditing department, approved by management and accepted by the board, should be consistent with these Standards for the Professional Practice of Internal Auditing.

The charter should make clear the purposes of the internal auditing department, specify the unrestricted scope of its work, and declare that auditors are to have no authority or responsibility for the activities they audit.

Throughout the world internal auditing is performed in diverse environments and within organizations which vary in purpose, size and structure. In addition, the laws and customs within various countries differ from one another. These differences may affect the practice of internal auditing in each environment. The implementation of these Standards, therefore, will be governed by the environment in which the internal auditing department carries out its assigned responsibilities, but compliance with the concepts enunciated by these Standards is essential before the responsibilities of internal auditors can be met.

"Independence," as used in these Standards, requires clarification. Internal auditors must be independent of the activities they audit. Such independence permits internal auditors to perform their work freely and objectively. Without independence, the desired results of internal auditing cannot be realized.

In setting these Standards, the following developments were considered:

1. Boards of directors are being held increasingly accountable for the adequacy and effectiveness of their organizations' systems of internal control and quality of performance.
2. Members of management are demonstrating increased acceptance of internal auditing as a means of supplying objective analyses, appraisals, recommendations, counsel and information on the organization's controls and performance.
3. External auditors are using the results of internal audits to complement their own work where the internal auditors have provided suitable evidence of independence and adequate, professional audit work.

In the light of such developments, the purposes of these Standards are to:

1. Impart an understanding of the role and responsibilities of internal auditing to all levels of management, boards of directors, public bodies, external auditors and related professional organizations.
2. Establish the basis for the guidance and measurement of internal auditing performance.
3. Improve the practice of internal auditing.

The Standards differentiate among the varied responsibilities of the organization, the internal auditing department, the director of internal auditing, and internal auditors.

The five general Standards are expressed in italicized statements in upper case. Following each of these standards are specific standards expressed in italicized statements in lower case. Accompanying each specific standard are guidelines describing suitable means of meeting that standard. The Standards encompass:

1. The independence of the internal auditing department from the activities audited, and the objectivity of internal auditors.
2. The proficiency of internal auditors and the professional care they should exercise.
3. The scope of internal auditing work.

4. The performance of internal auditing assignments.
5. The management of the internal auditing department.

The Standards and the accompanying guidelines employ three terms which have been given specific meanings. These are as follows:

The term "board" includes boards of directors, audit committees of such boards, heads of agencies or legislative bodies to whom internal auditors report, boards of governors or trustees of nonprofit organizations and any other designated governing bodies of organizations.

The terms "director of internal auditing" and "director" identify the top position in an internal auditing department.

The term "internal auditing department" includes any unit or activity within an organization which performs internal auditing functions.

SUMMARY OF GENERAL AND SPECIFIC STANDARDS FOR THE PROFESSIONAL PRACTICE OF INTERNAL AUDITING

100 *INDEPENDENCE*—INTERNAL AUDITORS SHOULD BE INDEPENDENT OF THE ACTIVITIES THEY AUDIT.

> **110** *ORGANIZATIONAL STATUS*—The organizational status of the internal auditing department should be sufficient to permit the accomplishment of its audit responsibilities.
>
> **120** *OBJECTIVITY*—Internal auditors should be objective in performing audits.

200 *PROFESSIONAL PROFICIENCY*—INTERNAL AUDITS SHOULD BE PERFORMED WITH PROFICIENCY AND DUE PROFESSIONAL CARE.

> **The Internal Auditing Department**
>
> **210** *STAFFING*—The internal auditing department should provide assurance that the technical proficiency and educational background of internal auditors are appropriate for the audits to be performed.
>
> **220** *KNOWLEDGE, SKILLS AND DISCIPLINES*—The internal auditing department should possess or should obtain the knowledge, skills and disciplines needed to carry out its audit responsibilities.
>
> **230** *SUPERVISION*—The internal auditing department should provide assurance that internal audits are properly supervised.
>
> **The Internal Auditor**
>
> **240** *COMPLIANCE WITH STANDARDS OF CONDUCT*—Internal auditors should comply with professional standards of conduct.
>
> **250** *KNOWLEDGE, SKILLS AND DISCIPLINES*—Internal auditors should possess the knowledge, skills, and disciplines essential to the performance of internal audits.
>
> **260** *HUMAN RELATIONS AND COMMUNICATIONS*—Internal auditors should be skilled in dealing with people and in communicating effectively.

270 *CONTINUING EDUCATION*—Internal auditors should maintain their technical competence through continuing education.

280 *DUE PROFESSIONAL CARE*—Internal auditors should exercise due professional care in performing internal audits.

300 **SCOPE OF WORK**—THE SCOPE OF THE INTERNAL AUDIT SHOULD ENCOMPASS THE EXAMINATION AND EVALUATION OF THE ADEQUACY AND EFFECTIVENESS OF THE ORGANIZATION'S SYSTEM OF INTERNAL CONTROL AND THE QUALITY OF PERFORMANCE IN CARRYING OUT ASSIGNED RESPONSIBILITIES.

310 *RELIABILITY AND INTEGRITY OF INFORMATION*—Internal auditors should review the reliability and integrity of financial and operating information and the means used to identify, measure, classify and report such information.

320 *COMPLIANCE WITH POLICIES, PLANS, PROCEDURES, LAWS AND REGULATIONS*—Internal auditors should review the systems established to ensure compliance with those policies, plans, procedures, laws and regulations which could have a significant impact on operations and reports, and should determine whether the organization is in compliance.

330 *SAFEGUARDING OF ASSETS*—Internal auditors should review the means of safeguarding assets and, as appropriate, verify the existence of such assets.

340 *ECONOMICAL AND EFFICIENT USE OF RESOURCES*—Internal auditors should appraise the economy and efficiency with which resources are employed.

350 *ACCOMPLISHMENT OF ESTABLISHED OBJECTIVES AND GOALS FOR OPERATIONS OR PROGRAMS*—Internal auditors should review operations or programs to ascertain whether results are consistent with established objectives and goals and whether the operations or programs are being carried out as planned.

400 **PERFORMANCE OF AUDIT WORK**—AUDIT WORK SHOULD INCLUDE PLANNING THE AUDIT, EXAMINING AND EVALUATING INFORMATION, COMMUNICATING RESULTS AND FOLLOWING UP.

410 *PLANNING THE AUDIT*—Internal auditors should plan each audit.

420 *EXAMINING AND EVALUATING INFORMATION* — Internal auditors should collect, analyze, interpret and document information to support audit results.

430 *COMMUNICATING RESULTS*—Internal auditors should report the results of their audit work.

440 *FOLLOWING UP*—Internal auditors should follow up to ascertain that appropriate action is taken on reported audit findings.

500 ***MANAGEMENT OF THE INTERNAL AUDITING DEPART-MENT*—THE DIRECTOR OF INTERNAL AUDITING SHOULD PROPERLY MANAGE THE INTERNAL AUDITING DEPARTMENT.**

510 *PURPOSE, AUTHORITY AND RESPONSIBILITY*—The director of internal auditing should have a statement of purpose, authority and responsibility for the internal auditing department.

520 *PLANNING*—The director of internal auditing should establish plans to carry out the responsibilities of the internal auditing department.

530 *POLICIES AND PROCEDURES*—The director of internal auditing should provide written policies and procedures to guide the audit staff.

540 *PERSONNEL MANAGEMENT AND DEVELOPMENT*—The director of internal auditing should establish a program for selecting and developing the human resources of the internal auditing department.

550 *EXTERNAL AUDITORS*—The director of internal auditing should coordinate internal and external audit efforts.

560 *QUALITY ASSURANCE*—The director of internal auditing should establish and maintain a quality assurance program to evaluate the operations of the internal auditing department.

100 Independence

INTERNAL AUDITORS SHOULD BE INDEPENDENT OF THE ACTIVITIES THEY AUDIT

.01 Internal auditors are independent when they can carry out their work freely and objectively. Independence permits internal auditors to render the impartial and unbiased judgments essential to the proper conduct of audits. It is achieved through organizational status and objectivity.

110 ORGANIZATIONAL STATUS

The organizational status of the internal auditing department should be sufficient to permit the accomplishment of its audit responsibilities.

.01   Internal auditors should have the support of management and of the board of directors so that they can gain the cooperation of auditees and perform their work free from interference.

.1   The director of the internal auditing department should be responsible to an individual in the organization with sufficient authority to promote independence and to ensure broad audit coverage, adequate consideration of audit reports and appropriate action on audit recommendations.

.2   The director should have direct communication with the board. Regular communication with the board helps assure independence and provides a means for the board and the director to keep each other informed on matters of mutual interest.

.3   Independence is enhanced when the board concurs in the appointment or removal of the director of the internal auditing department.

.4   The purpose, authority and responsibility of the internal auditing department should be defined in a formal written document (charter). The director should seek approval of the charter by management as well as acceptance by the board. The charter should (a) establish the department's position within the organization; (b) authorize access to records, personnel and physical properties relevant to the performance of audits; and (c) define the scope of internal auditing activities.

.5   The director of internal auditing should submit annually to management for approval and to the board for its information a summary of the department's audit work schedule, staffing plan and financial budget. The director should also submit all significant interim changes for approval and information. Audit work schedules, staffing plans and financial budgets should inform management and the board of the scope of internal auditing work and of any limitations placed on that scope.

.6 The director of internal auditing should submit activity reports to management and to the board annually or more frequently as necessary. Activity reports should highlight significant audit findings and recommendations and should inform management and the board of any significant deviations from approved audit work schedules, staffing plans and financial budgets, and the reasons for them.

120 OBJECTIVITY

Internal auditors should be objective in performing audits.

.01 Objectivity is an independent mental attitude which internal auditors should maintain in performing audits. Internal auditors are not to subordinate their judgment on audit matters to that of others.

.02 Objectivity requires internal auditors to perform audits in such a manner that they have an honest belief in their work product and that no significant quality compromises are made. Internal auditors are not to be placed in situations in which they feel unable to make objective professional judgments.

.1 Staff assignments should be made so that potential and actual conflicts of interest and bias are avoided. The director should periodically obtain from the audit staff information concerning potential conflicts of interest and bias.

.2 Internal auditors should report to the director any situations in which a conflict of interest or bias is present or may reasonably be inferred. The director should then reassign such auditors.

.3 Staff assignments of internal auditors should be rotated periodically whenever it is practicable to do so.

.4 Internal auditors should not assume operating responsibilities. But if on occasion management directs internal auditors to perform nonaudit work, it should be understood that they are not functioning as internal auditors. Moreover, objectivity is presumed to be impaired when internal auditors audit any activity for which they had authority or responsibility. This impairment should be considered when reporting audit results.

.5   Persons transferred to or temporarily engaged by the internal auditing department should not be assigned to audit those activities they previously performed until a reasonable period of time has elapsed. Such assignments are presumed to impair objectivity and should be considered when supervising the audit work and reporting audit results.

.6   The results of internal auditing work should be reviewed before the related audit report is released to provide reasonable assurance that the work was performed objectively.

.03   The internal auditor's objectivity is not adversely affected when the auditor recommends standards of control for systems or reviews procedures before they are implemented. Designing, installing and operating systems are not audit functions. Also, the drafting of procedures for systems is not an audit function. Performing such activities is presumed to impair audit objectivity.

200 Professional Proficiency

INTERNAL AUDITS SHOULD BE PERFORMED WITH PROFICIENCY AND DUE PROFESSIONAL CARE

.01   Professional proficiency is the responsibility of the internal auditing department and each internal auditor. The department should assign to each audit those persons who collectively possess the necessary knowledge, skills and disciplines to conduct the audit properly.

The Internal Auditing Department

210 STAFFING

The internal auditing department should provide assurance that the technical proficiency and educational background of internal auditors are appropriate for the audits to be performed.

.01 The director of internal auditing should establish suitable criteria of education and experience for filling internal auditing positions, giving due consideration to scope of work and level of responsibility.

.02 Reasonable assurance should be obtained as to each prospective auditor's qualifications and proficiency.

220 KNOWLEDGE, SKILLS AND DISCIPLINES

The internal auditing department should possess or should obtain the knowledge, skills and disciplines needed to carry out its audit responsibilities.

.01 The internal auditing staff should collectively possess the knowledge and skills essential to the practice of their profession within their organization. These attributes include proficiency in applying internal auditing standards, procedures and techniques.

.02 The internal auditing department should have employees or use consultants who are qualified in such disciplines as accounting, economics, finance, statistics, electronic data processing, engineering, taxation and law as needed to meet audit responsibilities. Each member of the department, however, need not be qualified in all of these disciplines.

230 SUPERVISION

The internal auditing department should provide assurance that internal audits are properly supervised.

.01 The director of internal auditing is responsible for providing appropriate audit supervision. Supervision is a continuing process, beginning with planning and ending with the conclusion of the audit assignment.

.02 Supervision includes:

.1 Providing suitable instructions to subordinates at the outset of the audit and approving the audit program.

.2 Seeing that the approved audit program is carried out unless deviations are both justified and authorized.

.3   Determining that audit working papers adequately support the audit findings, conclusions and reports.

.4   Making sure that audit reports are accurate, objective, clear, concise, constructive and timely.

.5   Determining that audit objectives are being met.

.03   Appropriate evidence of supervision should be documented and retained.

.04   The extent of supervision required will depend on the proficiency of the internal auditors and the difficulty of the audit assignment.

.05   All internal auditing assignments, whether performed by or for the internal auditing department, remain the responsibility of its director.

The Internal Auditor

240   COMPLIANCE WITH STANDARDS OF CONDUCT

Internal auditors should comply with professional standards of conduct.

.01   The Code of Ethics of The Institute of Internal Auditors sets forth standards of conduct and provides a basis for enforcement among its members. The Code calls for high standards of honesty, objectivity, diligence and loyalty to which internal auditors should conform.

250   KNOWLEDGE, SKILLS AND DISCIPLINES

Internal auditors should possess the knowledge, skills and disciplines essential to the performance of internal audits.

.01   Each internal auditor should possess certain knowledge and skills as follows:

.1   Proficiency in applying internal auditing standards, procedures and techniques is required in performing internal audits. Proficiency means the ability to apply knowledge to situations likely to be encountered and to deal with them without extensive recourse to technical research and assistance.

.2 Proficiency in accounting principles and techniques is required of auditors who work extensively with financial records and reports.

.3 An understanding of management principles is required to recognize and evaluate the materiality and significance of deviations from good business practice. An understanding means the ability to apply broad knowledge to situations likely to be encountered, to recognize significant deviations and to be able to carry out the research necessary to arrive at reasonable solutions.

.4 An appreciation is required of the fundamentals of such subjects as accounting, economics, commercial law, taxation, finance, quantitative methods and computerized information systems. An appreciation means the ability to recognize the existence of problems or potential problems and to determine the further research to be undertaken or the assistance to be obtained.

260 HUMAN RELATIONS AND COMMUNICATIONS

Internal auditors should be skilled in dealing with people and in communicating effectively.

.01 Internal auditors should understand human relations and maintain satisfactory relationships with auditees.

.02 Internal auditors should be skilled in oral and written communications so that they can clearly and effectively convey such matters as audit objectives, evaluations, conclusions and recommendations.

270 CONTINUING EDUCATION

Internal auditors should maintain their technical competence through continuing education.

.01 Internal auditors are responsible for continuing their education in order to maintain their proficiency. They should keep informed about improvements and current developments in internal auditing standards, procedures, and techniques. Continuing education may be obtained through membership and participation in professional societies; attendance at conferences, seminars, college courses, and in-house training programs; and participation in research projects.

280   DUE PROFESSIONAL CARE

Internal auditors should exercise due professional care in performing internal audits.

.01   In exercising due professional care, internal auditors should be alert to the possibility of wrongdoing, errors and omissions, inefficiency, waste, ineffectiveness and conflicts of interest. They should also be alert to those conditions and activities where irregularities are most likely to occur.

.02   The possibility of material irregularities or noncompliance should be considered whenever the internal auditor undertakes an internal auditing assignment.

.03   When an internal auditor suspects wrongdoing, the appropriate authorities within the organization should be informed. The internal auditor may recommend whatever investigation is considered necessary in the circumstances. Thereafter, the auditor should follow up to see that the internal auditing department's responsibilities have been met.

300   Scope of Work

THE SCOPE OF THE INTERNAL AUDIT SHOULD ENCOMPASS THE EXAMINATION AND EVALUATION OF THE ADEQUACY AND EFFECTIVENESS OF THE ORGANIZATION'S SYSTEM OF INTERNAL CONTROL, AND THE QUALITY OF PERFORMANCE IN CARRYING OUT ASSIGNED RESPONSIBILITIES

.01   The scope of internal auditing work, as specified in this standard, encompasses what audit work should be performed. It is recognized, however, that management and the board of directors provide general direction as to the scope of work and the activities to be audited.

.02   The purpose of the review for adequacy of the system of internal control is to ascertain whether the system established provides reasonable assurance that the organization's objectives and goals will be met efficiently and economically.

.03   The purpose of the review for effectiveness of the system of internal control is to ascertain whether the system is functioning as intended.

.04   The purpose of the review for quality of performance is to ascertain whether the organization's objectives and goals have been achieved.

.05   The primary objectives of internal control are to ensure:

.1   The reliability and integrity of information.

.2   Compliance with policies, plans, procedures, laws and regulations.

.3   The safeguarding of assets.

.4   The economical and efficient use of resources.

.5   The accomplishment of established objectives and goals for operations or programs.

310   RELIABILITY AND INTEGRITY OF INFORMATION

Internal auditors should review the reliability and integrity of financial and operating information and the means used to identify, measure, classify and report such information.

.01   Information systems provide data for decision making, control and compliance with external requirements. Therefore, internal auditors should examine information systems and, as appropriate, ascertain whether:

.1   Financial and operating records and reports contain accurate, reliable, timely, complete and useful information.

.2   Controls over record keeping and reporting are adequate and effective.

320   COMPLIANCE WITH POLICIES, PLANS, PROCEDURES, LAWS AND REGULATIONS

Internal auditors should review the systems established to ensure compliance with those policies, plans, procedures, laws and regulations which could have a significant impact on operations and reports, and should determine whether the organization is in compliance.

.01 Management is responsible for establishing the systems designed to ensure compliance with such requirements as policies, plans, procedures and applicable laws and regulations. Internal auditors are responsible for determining whether the systems are adequate and effective and whether the activities audited are complying with the appropriate requirements.

330   SAFEGUARDING OF ASSETS

Internal auditors should review the means of safeguarding assets and, as appropriate, verify the existence of such assets.

.01 Internal auditors should review the means used to safeguard assets from various types of losses such as those resulting from theft, fire, improper or illegal activities and exposure to the elements.

.02 Internal auditors, when verifying the existence of assets, should use appropriate audit procedures.

340   ECONOMICAL AND EFFICIENT USE OF RESOURCES

Internal auditors should appraise the economy and efficiency with which resources are employed.

.01 Management is responsible for setting operating standards to measure an activity's economical and efficient use of resources. Internal auditors are responsible for determining whether:

.1 Operating standards have been established for measuring economy and efficiency.

.2 Established operating standards are understood and are being met.

.3 Deviations from operating standards are identified, analyzed and communicated to those responsible for corrective action.

.4 Corrective action has been taken.

.02 Audits related to the economical and efficient use of resources should identify such conditions as:

.1 Underutilized facilities.

.2 Nonproductive work.

.3 Procedures which are not cost-justified.

.4 Overstaffing or understaffing.

350 ACCOMPLISHMENT OF ESTABLISHED OBJECTIVES AND GOALS FOR OPERATIONS OR PROGRAMS

Internal auditors should review operations or programs to ascertain whether results are consistent with established objectives and goals and whether the operations or programs are being carried out as planned.

.01 Management is responsible for establishing operating or program objectives and goals, developing and implementing control procedures, and accomplishing desired operating or program results. Internal auditors should ascertain whether such objectives and goals conform with those of the organization and whether they are being met.

.02 Internal auditors can provide assistance to managers who are developing objectives, goals and systems by determing whether the underlying assumptions are appropriate, whether accurate, current and relevant information is being used, and whether suitable controls have been incorporated into the operations or programs.

400   Performance of Audit Work

AUDIT WORK SHOULD INCLUDE PLANNING THE AUDIT, EXAMINING AND EVALUATING INFORMATION, COMMUNICATING RESULTS AND FOLLOWING UP

.01 The internal auditor is responsible for planning and conducting the audit assignment, subject to supervisory review and approval.

410 PLANNING THE AUDIT

Internal auditors should plan each audit.

.01   Planning should be documented and should include:

.1   Establishing audit objectives and scope of work.

.2   Obtaining background information about the activities to be audited.

.3   Determining the resources necessary to perform the audit.

.4   Communicating with all who need to know about the audit.

.5   Performing, as appropriate, an on-site survey to become familiar with the activities and controls to be audited, to identify areas for audit emphasis and to invite auditee comments and suggestions.

.6   Writing the audit program.

.7   Determining how, when and to whom audit results will be communicated.

.8   Obtaining approval of the audit work plan.

420 EXAMINING AND EVALUATING INFORMATION

Internal auditors should collect, analyze, interpret and document information to support audit results.

.01   The process of examining and evaluating information is as follows:

.1   Information should be collected on all matters related to the audit objectives and scope of work.

.2   Information should be sufficient, competent, relevant and useful, to provide a sound basis for audit findings and recommendations.

.2.1   *Sufficient* information is factual, adequate and convincing, so that a prudent, informed person would reach the same conclusions as the auditor.

.2.2   *Competent* information is reliable and the best attainable through the use of appropriate audit techniques.

.2.3 *Relevant* information supports audit findings and recommendations and is consistent with the objectives for the audit.

.2.4 Useful information helps the organization meet its goals.

.3 Audit procedures, including the testing and sampling techniques employed, should be selected in advance, where practicable, and expanded or altered if circumstances warrant.

.4 The process of collecting, analyzing, interpreting and documenting information should be supervised to provide reasonable assurance that the auditor's objectivity is maintained and that audit goals are met.

.5 Working papers that document the audit should be prepared by the auditor and reviewed by management of the internal auditing department. These papers should record the information obtained and the analyses made and should support the bases for the findings and recommendations to be reported.

430 COMMUNICATING RESULTS

Internal auditors should report the results of their audit work.

.01 A signed, written report should be issued after the audit examination is completed. Interim reports may be written or oral and may be transmitted formally or informally.

.02 The internal auditor should discuss conclusions and recommendations at appropriate levels of management before issuing final written reports.

.03 Reports should be objective, clear, concise, constructive and timely.

.04 Reports should present the purpose, scope and results of the audit; and, where appropriate, reports should contain an expression of the auditor's opinion.

.05 Reports may include recommendations for potential improvements and acknowledge satisfactory performance and corrective action.

.06 The auditee's views about audit conclusions or recommendations may be included in the audit report.

.07   The director of internal auditing or designee should review and approve the final audit report before issuance and should decide to whom the report will be distributed.

440   FOLLOWING UP

Internal auditors should follow up to ascertain that appropriate action is taken on reported audit findings.

.01   Internal auditing should determine that corrective action was taken and is achieving the desired results, or that management or the board has assumed the risk of not taking corrective action on reported findings.

500   Management of the Internal Auditing Department

THE DIRECTOR OF INTERNAL AUDITING SHOULD PROPERLY MANAGE THE INTERNAL AUDITING DEPARTMENT

.01   The director of internal auditing is responsible for properly managing the department so that:

.1   Audit work fulfills the general purposes and responsibilities approved by management and accepted by the board.

.2   Resources of the internal auditing department are efficiently and effectively employed.

.3   Audit work conforms to the Standards for the Practice of Internal Auditing.

510   PURPOSE, AUTHORITY AND RESPONSIBILITY

The director of internal auditing should have a statement of purpose, authority and responsibility for the internal auditing department.

.01   The director of internal auditing is responsible for seeking the approval of management and the acceptance by the board of a formal written document (charter) for the internal auditing department.

520 PLANNING

The director of internal auditing should establish plans to carry out the responsibilities of the internal auditing department.

.01 These plans should be consistent with the internal auditing department's charter and with the goals of the organization.

.02 The planning process involves establishing:

.1 Goals.

.2 Audit work schedules.

.3 Staffing plans and financial budgets.

.4 Activity reports.

.03 The *goals* of the internal auditing department should be capable of being accomplished within specified operating plans and budgets and, to the extent possible, should be measurable. They should be accompanied by measurement criteria and targeted dates of accomplishment.

.04 *Audit work schedules* should include (a) what activities are to be audited; (b) when they will be audited; and (c) the estimated time required, taking into account the scope of the audit work planned and the nature and extent of audit work performed by others. Matters to be considered in establishing audit work schedule priorities should include (a) the date and results of the last audit; (b) financial exposure; (c) potential loss and risk; (d) requests by management; (e) major changes in operations, programs, systems and controls; (f) opportunities to achieve operating benefits; and (g) changes to and capabilities of the audit staff. The work schedules should be sufficiently flexible to cover unanticipated demands on the internal auditing department.

.05 *Staffing plans and financial budgets*, including the number of auditors and the knowledge, skills, and disciplines required to perform their work, should be determined from audit work schedules, administrative activities, education and training requirements, and audit research and development efforts.

.06   *Activity reports* should be submitted periodically to management and to the board. These reports should compare (a) performance with the department's goals and audit work schedules and (b) expenditures with financial budgets. They should explain the reasons for major variances and indicate any action taken or needed.

530   POLICIES AND PROCEDURES

The director of internal auditing should provide written policies and procedures to guide the audit staff.

.01   The form and content of written policies and procedures should be appropriate to the size and structure of the internal auditing department and the complexity of its work. Formal administrative and technical audit manuals may not be needed by all internal auditing departments. A small internal auditing department may be managed informally. Its audit staff may be directed and controlled through daily, close supervision and written memoranda. In a large internal auditing department, more formal and comprehensive policies and procedures are essential to guide the audit staff in the consistent compliance with the department's standards of performance.

540   PERSONNEL MANAGEMENT AND DEVELOPMENT

The director of internal auditing should establish a program for selecting and developing the human resources of the internal auditing department.

.01   The program should provide for:

.1   Developing written job descriptions for each level of the audit staff.

.2   Selecting qualified and competent individuals.

.3   Training and providing continuing educational opportunities for each internal auditor.

.4   Appraising each internal auditor's performance, at least annually.

.5   Providing counsel to internal auditors on their performance and professional development.

550 EXTERNAL AUDITORS

The director of internal auditing should coordinate internal and external audit efforts.

.01 The internal and external audit work should be coordinated to ensure adequate audit coverage and to minimize duplicate efforts.

.02 Coordination of audit efforts involves:

.1 Periodic meetings to discuss matters of mutual interest.

.2 Access to each other's audit programs and working papers.

.3 Exchange of audit reports and management letters.

.4 Common understanding of audit techniques, methods, and terminology.

560 QUALITY ASSURANCE

The director of internal auditing should establish and maintain a quality assurance program to evaluate the operations of the internal auditing department.

.01 The purpose of this program is to provide reasonable assurance that audit work conforms with these Standards, the internal auditing department's charter and other applicable standards. A quality assurance program should include the following elements:

.1 Supervision.

.2 Internal reviews.

.3 External reviews.

.02 *Supervision* of the work of the internal auditors should be carried out continually to assure conformance with internal auditing standards, departmental policies and audit programs.

.03 *Internal reviews* should be performed periodically by members of the internal auditing staff to appraise the quality of the audit work performed. These reviews should be performed in the same manner as any other internal audit.

.04   External reviews of the internal auditing department should be performed to appraise the quality of the department's operations. These reviews should be performed by qualified persons who are independent of the organization and who do not have either a real or an apparent conflict of interest. Such reviews should be conducted at least once every three years. On completion of the review, a formal written report should be issued. The report should express an opinion as to the department's compliance with the Standards for the Practice of Internal Auditing and, as appropriate, should include recommendations for improvement.

APPENDIX E

Statements on Internal Auditing Standards

SIAS NO. 1: CONTROL: CONCEPTS AND RESPONSIBILITIES

Statements on Internal Auditing Standards *are issued by the Professional Standards and Responsibilities Committee, the senior technical committee designated by The Institute of Internal Auditors, Inc., to issue pronouncements on auditing standards. These statements are authoritative interpretations of the* Standards for the Professional Practice of Internal Auditing.

Organizations, internal auditing departments, directors of internal auditing and internal auditors should strive to comply with the Standards. *The implementation of the* Standards *and these related statements will be governed by the environment in which the internal auditing department carries out its assigned responsibilities. The adoption and implementation of the* Standards *and related statements will assist internal auditing professionals in accomplishing their responsibilities.*

Foreword

The Institute of Internal Auditors issued its *Standards for the Professional Practice of Internal Auditing* in 1978 "to serve the entire profession in all types of businesses, in various levels of government, and in all other organizations where internal auditors are found . . . to represent the practice of internal audititng as it should be. . . ." Experience and success have demonstrated the credibility of the basic principles promoted in the *Standards*.

The Standards state that internal auditing is to assist members of the organization in the effective discharge of their responsibilities by providing them with information regarding control. However, differences of opinion have existed regarding the nature of control and the roles of the participants in its establishment, maintenace and evaluation.

This statement provides guidance on these issues by focusing on Guidelines 300.02 and 300.03 and providing three additional guidelines.

Background

Controls were defined early in the evolutionary process of organizational management as mechanisms or practices used to prevent or detect unauthorized activity. The purpose of controls was later expanded to include the concept of getting things done. Current usage leans toward any effort made to enhance the probability of accomplishing objectives.

Examples of "controls" abound. A partial list relating to protection of cash highlights the diversity of opinions: a safe, a locked safe, a requirement to lock cash in a safe, a procedure directing the storage of cash in a locked safe, restricted access to a safe and its contents, assignment of responsibility for protecting cash, authorizing cash disbursements, a record of cash disbursements and receipts, and unannounced cash counts. This diversity should not be construed as indicating a problem; in fact, the opposite may very well be true. All of these may be regarded as controls, depending on circumstances and the specific activity being reviewed.

As illustrated above, control is used as a noun, a verb, and an adjective; the term is used to describe a physical device, a method of performing an activity, a step in a process, a means to an end and an end in itself.

Differences of opinion exist regarding the term "system of internal control." This term was used in a 1949 American Institute of Certified Public Accountants study titled *Internal Control—Elements of a Coordinated System and Its Importance to Management and the Independent Public Accountants*. From the external auditor's viewpoint, the importance of the system of internal control was "to establish a basis for reliance thereon in determining the nature, extent, and timing of audit tests to be applied in the examination of the financial statement." Since then, the term has been used by auditors to describe the set of controls within a specific system, operation or department; it has also been used in the context of the organization's system of internal control.

It is clear that management* and internal auditors are interested in both specific controls in specific systems and in overall control. It is generally agreed that their scope of interest (and responsibilities) extends beyond that of external auditors. To clearly delineate the difference between the broader control concerns of management and internal auditors and the narrower control concerns of external auditors, the broader concept of control will hereafter be referred to as the "overall system of control."

Differences of opinion exist regarding the specific nature of management's role in the establishment, maintenance and evaluation of control. For example, it is commonly stated that management plans, organizes, directs and controls. Thus, at least conceptually, controlling has been viewed as a separate activity. However, specific actions taken by management to enhance the likelihood that objectives and goals will be achieved, such as the setting of standards, the monitoring for compliance to those standards and the related feedback to those in a position to take corrective action, are ongoing and fully integrated with planning, organizing and directing activities. Therefore, controlling can be viewed as a part of planning, organizing and directing rather than as a separate activity.

There is also diversity of opinion as to how much of the management process is subject to internal auditing's review. Since such diversity of opinion regarding the nature of control and roles played by the par-

---

*As used in this statement, the term "management" includes anyone in an organization with responsibilities for setting and/or achieving objectives.

ticipants may cause or contribute to less than optimum performance by internal auditors, the following concepts were formulated to serve the profession. These concepts guide the interpretations contained in the remainder of this statement:

- Management plans, organizes, and directs in such a manner as to provide reasonable assurance that established objectives and goals will be achieved.

- Internal auditors examine and evaluate the planning, organizing and directing processes to determine whether reasonable assurance exists that objectives and goals will be achieved. Thus, all systems, processes, operations, functions and activities within the organization are subject to internal auditing's evaluations.

- External auditors evaluate "internal accounting control" within the parameters stated in their Generally Accepted Auditing Standards.

- Audit committees have guidance and oversight responsibilities related to internal and external auditings' performance.

- Boards of directors have guidance and oversight responsibilities related to subordinate management's performance.

300 Standard—Scope of Work

THE SCOPE OF THE INTERNAL AUDIT SHOULD ENCOMPASS THE EXAMINATION AND EVALUATION OF THE ADEQUACY AND EFFECTIVENESS OF THE ORGANIZATION'S SYSTEM OF INTERNAL CONTROL AND THE QUALITY OF PERFORMANCE IN CARRYING OUT ASSIGNED RESPONSIBILITIES

(The new interpretive guidelines are in bold print.)

.01   The scope of internal auditing work, as specified in this standard, encompasses what audit work should be performed. It is recognized, however, that management and the board of directors provide general direction as to the scope of work and the activities to be audited.

.02   The purpose of the review for adequacy of the system of internal control is to ascertain whether the system established provides reasonable assurance that the organization's objectives and goals will be met efficiently and economically.

.1 Objectives are the broadest statements of what the organization chooses to accomplish. The establishment of objectives precedes the selection of goals and the design, implementation and maintenance of systems whose purpose is to meet the organization's objectives and goals.

.2 Goals are specific objectives of specific systems, and may be otherwise referred to as operating or program objectives or goals, operating standards, performance levels, targets or expected results. Goals should be identified for each system. They should be clearly defined, measurable, attainable and consistent with established broader objectives, and they should explicitly recognize the risks associated with not achieving those objectives.

.3 A system (process, operation, function or activity) is an arrangement, a set or a collection of concepts, parts, activities and/or people that are connected or interrelated to achieve objectives and goals. (This definition applies to both manual and automated systems.) A system may also be a collection of subsystems operating together for a common objective or goal.

.4 Adequate control is present if management has planned and organized (designed) in a manner which provides reasonable assurance that the organization's objectives and goals will be achieved efficiently and economically. The system design process begins with the establishment of objectives and goals. This is followed by connecting or interrelating concepts, parts, activities and/or people in such a manner as to operate together to achieve the established objectives and goals. If system design is properly performed, planned activities should be executed as designed and expected results should be attained.

.5 Reasonable assurance is provided when cost-effective actions are taken to restrict deviations to a tolerable level. This implies, for example, that material errors and improper or illegal acts will be prevented or detected and corrected within a timely period by employees in the normal course of performing their assigned duties. The cost-benefit relationship is considered by management during the design of systems. The potential loss associated with any exposure or risk is weighed against the cost to control it.

.6   Efficient performance accomplishes objectives and goals in an accurate and timely fashion with minimal use of resources.

.7   Economical performance accomplishes objectives and goals at a cost commensurate with the risk. The term efficient incorporates the concept of economical performance.

.03   The purpose of the review for effectiveness of the system of internal control is to ascertain whether the system is functioning as intended.

.1   Effective control is present when management directs systems in such a manner as to provide reasonable assurance that the organization's objectives and goals will be achieved.

.2   Directing involves—in addition to accomplishing objectives and planned activities—authorizing and monitoring performance, periodically comparing actual with planned performance and documenting these activities to provide additional assurance that systems operate as planned.

.2.1   Authorizing includes initiating or granting permission to perform activities or transactions. Authorization implies that the authorizing authority has verified and validated that the activitiy or transaction conforms with established policies and procedures.

.2.2   Monitoring encompasses supervising, observing and testing activities and appropriately reporting to responsible individuals. Monitoring provides an ongoing verfication of progress toward achievement of objectives and goals.

.2.3   Periodic comparison of actual to planned performance enhances the likelihood that activities occur as planned.

.2.4   Documenting provides evidence of the exercise of authority and responsibility; compliance with policies, procedures and standards of performance; supervising, observing and testing activities; and verification of planned performance.

.04   The purpose of the review for quality of performance is to ascertain whether the organization's objectives and goals have been achieved.

.05   The primary objectives of internal control are to ensure:

.1   The reliability and integrity of information

.2   Compliance with policies, plans, procedures, laws, and regulations

.3   The safeguarding of assets

.4   The economical and efficient use of resources

.5   The accomplishment of established objectives and goals for operations or programs

.06   A control is any action taken by management to enhance the likelihood that established objectives and goals will be achieved. Management plans, organizes and directs the performance of sufficient actions to provide reasonable assurance that objectives and goals will be achieved. Thus, control is the result of proper planning, organizing and directing by management.

.1   **Controls may be preventive (to deter undesirable events from occuring), detective (to detect and correct undesirable events which have occured) or directive (to cause or encourage a desirable event to occur).**

.2   **All variants of the term control (administrative control, internal accounting control, internal control, management control, operational control, output control, preventive control, etc.) can be incorporated within the generic term. These variants differ primarily in terms of the objectives to be achieved. Since these variants are useful in describing specific control applications, participants in the control process should be familiar with the terms as well as their applications. However, the methodology followed by internal auditing in evaluating such controls is consistent for all of the variants.**

.3   **The variant "internal control" came into general use to distinguish controls within a organization from those existing externally to the organization (such as laws). Since internal auditors operate within an organization and, among other responsibilities, evaluate management's response to external stimuli (such as laws), no such distinction between internal and external controls is necessary. Also, from the organization's viewpoint, internal controls are all activites which attempt to ensure the accomplishment of the organization's objectives and goals. For the purpose of this statement, internal control is considered synonymous with control within the organization.**

.4 **The overall system of control is conceptual in nature. It is the integrated collection of controlled systems used by an organization to achieve its objectives and goals.**

.07   Management plans, organizes and directs in such a fashion as to provide reasonable assurance that established objectives and goals will be achieved.

.1 **Planning and organizing involve the establishment of objectives and goals and the use of such tools as organization charts, flowcharts, procedures, records and reports to establish the flow of data and the responsibilities of individuals for performing activities, establishing information trails and setting standards of performance.**

.2 **Directing involves certain activities to provide additional assurance that systems operate as planned. These activities include authorizing and monitoring performance, periodically comparing actual with planned performance and appropriately documenting these activities.**

.3 **Management ensures that its objectives and goals remain appropriate and that its systems remain current. Therefore, management periodically reviews its objectives and goals and modifies its systems to accommodate changes in internal and external conditions.**

.4 **Management establishes and maintains an environment that fosters control.**

.08   Internal auditing examines and evaluates the planning, organizing and directing processes to determine whether reasonable assurance exists that objectives and goals will be achieved. Such evaluations, in the aggregate, provide information to appraise the overall system of control.

.1 **All systems, processes, operations, functions and activities within the organization are subject to internal auditing's evaluations.**

.2 **Internal auditing's evaluations should encompass whether reasonable assurance exists that:**

a. **objectives and goals have been established;**

b. **authorizing, monitoring and periodic comparison activities have been planned, performed and documented as necessary to attain objectives and goals; and,**

c. **planned results have been achieved (objectives and goals have been accomplished).**

.3 Internal auditing performs evaluations at specific points in time but should be alert to actual or potential changes in conditions which affect the ability to provide assurance from a forward-looking perspective. In those cases, internal auditing should address the risk that performance may deteriorate.

SIAS NO. 2: COMMUNICATING RESULTS

Statements on Internal Auditing Standards *are issued by the Professional Standards and Responsibilities Committee, the senior technical committee designated by The Institute of Internal Auditors, Inc., to issue pronouncements on auditing standards. These statements are authoritative interpretations of the* Standards for the Professional Practice of Internal Auditing.

Organizations, internal auditing departments, directors of internal auditing and internal auditors should strive to comply with the Standards. *The implementation of the* Standards *and related statements will be governed by the environment in which the internal auditing department carries out its assigned responsibilities. The adoption and implementation of the* Standards *and related statements will assist internal auditing professionals in accomplishing their responsibilities.*

Foreword

The Institute of Internal Auditors issued its *Standards for the Professional Practice of Internal Auditing* in 1978 "to serve the entire profession in all types of businesses, in various levels of government, and in all other organizations where internal auditors are found . . . to represent the practice of internal auditing as it should be. . . ." Experience and success have demonstrated the credibility of the basic principles promoted in the *Standards*.

The *Standards* establish a basis for the guidance and measurement of internal auditing performance. For Communicating Results, this basis is delineated in the *Standards* by seven guidelines related to the types, contents, and attributes of audit reports. This statement interprets Guidelines 430 through 430.07.

430 Standard—Communicating Results

Internal auditors should report the results of their audit work. (The new interpretive guidelines are in bold print.)

    .01   A signed, written report should be issued after the audit examination is completed. Interim reports may be written or oral and may be transmitted formally or informally.

.1 Interim reports may be used to communicate information which requires immediate attention, to communicate a change in audit scope for the activity under review, or to keep management informed of audit progress when audits extend over a long period. The use of interim reports does not diminish or eliminate the need for a final report.

.2 Summary reports highlighting audit results may be appropriate for levels of management above the head of the audited unit. They may be issued separately from or in conjunction with the final report.

.02 The internal auditor should discuss conclusions and recommendations at appropriate levels of management before issuing final written reports.

.1 Discussion of conclusions and recommendations is usually accomplished during the course of the audit and/or at postaudit meetings (exit interviews). Another technique is the review of draft audit reports by the head of each audited unit. These discussions and reviews help ensure that there have been no misunderstandings or misinterpretations of fact by providing the opportunity for the auditee to clarify specific items and to express views of the findings, conclusions and recommendations.

.2 Although the level of participants in the discussions and reviews may vary by organization and by the nature of the report, they will generally include those individuals who are knowledgeable of detailed operations and those who can authorize the implementation of corrective action.

.03 Reports should be objective, clear, concise, constructive and timely.

.1 Objective reports are factual, unbiased, and free from distortion. Findings, conclusions and recommendations should be included without prejudice.

.2 Clear reports are easily understood and logical. Clarity can be improved by avoiding unnecessary technical language and providing sufficient supportive information.

.3 Concise reports are to the point and avoid unnecessary detail. They express thoughts completely in the fewest possible words.

.4 Constructive reports are those which, as a result of their content and tone, help the auditee and the organization and lead to improvements where needed.

.5   Timely reports are those which are issued without undue delay and enable prompt effective action.

.04   Reports should present the purpose, scope and results of the audit; and, where appropriate, reports should contain an expression of the auditor's opinion.

.1   Although audit report format and content may vary by organization or type of audit, they should contain, at a minimum, the purpose, scope and results of the audit.

.2   Audit reports may include background information and summaries. Background information may identify the organizational units and functions reviewed and provide relevant explanatory information. They may also include status of findings, conclusions and recommendations from prior reports. There may also be an indication of whether the report covers a scheduled audit or the response to a request. Summaries, if included, should be balanced representations of the audit report content.

.3   Purpose statements should describe the audit objectives and may, where necessary, inform the reader why the audit was conducted and what it was expected to achieve.

.4   Scope statements should identify the audited activities and include, where appropriate, supportive information such as time period audited. Related activities not audited should be identified if necessary to delineate the boundaries of the audit. The nature and extent of auditing performed also should be described.

.5   Results may include findings, conclusions (opinions) and recommendations.

.6   Findings are pertinent statements of fact. Those findings which are necessary to support or prevent misunderstanding of the internal auditor's conclusions and recommendations should be included in the final audit report. Less significant information or findings may be communicated orally or through informal correspondence.

Audit findings emerge by a process of comparing "what should be" with "what is." Whether or not there is a difference, the internal auditor has a foundation on which to build the report. When conditions meet the criteria, acknowledgement in the audit report of satisfactory performance may be appropriate. Findings should be based on the following attributes:

Criteria: The standards, measures or expectations used in making an evaluation and/or verification (what *should* exist).

Condition: The factual evidence which the internal auditor found in the course of the examination (what *does* exist).

If there is a difference between the expected and actual conditions, then:

Cause: The reason for the difference between the expected and actual conditions (*why* the difference exists).

Effect: The risk or exposure the auditee organization and/or others encounter because the condition is not the same as the criteria (the *impact* of the difference).

.7 Conclusions (opinions) are the internal auditor's evaluations of the effects of the findings on the activities reviewed. They usually put the findings in perspective based upon their overall implications. Audit conclusions, if included in the audit report, should be clearly identified as such. Conclusions may encompass the entire scope of an audit or specific aspects. They may cover but are not limited to whether operating or program objectives and goals conform with those of the organization, whether the organization's objectives and goals are being met, and whether the activity under review is functioning as intended.

.05 Reports may include recommendations for potential improvements and acknowledge satisfactory performance and corrective action.

.1 Recommendations are based on the internal auditor's findings and conclusions. They call for action to correct existing conditions or improve operations. Recommendations may suggest approaches to correcting or enhancing performance as a guide for management in achieving desired results. Recommendations may be general or specific. For example, under some circumstances, it may be desirable to recommend a general course of action and specific suggestions for implementation. In other circumstances, it may be appropriate only to suggest further investigation or study.

.2 Auditee accomplishments, in terms of improvements since the last audit or the establishment of a well-controlled operation, may be included in the audit report. This information may be necessary to fairly represent the existing

conditions and to provide a proper perspective and appropriate balance to the audit report.

.06   The auditee's views about audit conclusions or recommendations may be included in the audit report.

.1   **As part of the internal auditor's discussions with the auditee, the internal auditor should try to obtain agreement on the results of the audit and on a plan of action to improve operations, as needed. If the internal auditor and auditee disagree about the audit results, the audit report may state both positions and the reasons for the disagreement. The auditee's written comments may be included as an appendix to the audit report. Alternatively, the auditee's views may be presented in the body of the report or in a cover letter.**

.07   The director of internal auditing or designee should review and approve the final audit report before issuance and should decide to whom the report will be distributed.

.1   **The director of internal auditing or a designee should approve and may sign all final reports. If specific circumstances warrant, consideration should be given to having the auditor-in-charge, supervisor or lead auditor sign the report as a representative of the director of internal auditing.**

.2   **Audit reports should be distributed to those members of the organization who are able to ensure that audit results are given due consideration. This means that the report should go to those who are in a position to take corrective action or ensure that corrective action is taken. The final audit report should be distributed to the head of each audited unit. Higher-level members in the organization may receive only a summary report. Reports may also be distributed to other interested or affected parties such as external auditors and audit committees.**

.3   **Certain information may not be appropriate for disclosure to all report recipients because it is privileged, proprietary, or related to improper or illegal acts. Such information, however, may be disclosed in a separate report. If the conditions being reported involve senior management, report disbribution should be to the audit committee of the board of directors or a similar high-level entity within the organization.**

SIAS NO. 3: DETERRENCE, DETECTION, IN- VESTIGATION, AND REPORTING OF FRAUD

Statements on Internal Auditing Standards are issued by the Professional Standards and Responsibilities Committee, the senior technical committee designated by The Institute of Internal Auditors, to issue pronouncements on auditing standards. These statements are authoritative interpretations of *the* Standards for the Professional Practice of Internal Auditing.

Organizations, internal auditing departments, directors of internal auditing, and internal auditors should strive to comply with the Standards. *The implementation of the* Standards *and these related statements will be governed by the environment in which the internal audit department carries out its assigned responsibilities. The adoption and implementation of the* Standards *and related statements will assist internal auditing professionals in accomplishing their responsibilities.*

Foreword

The Institute of Internal Auditors issued the *Standards* in 1978 "to serve the entire profession in all types of business, in various levels of government, and in all other organizations where internal auditors are found . . . to represent the practice of internal auditing as it should be. . . ."

The *Standards* has been widely accepted and remains current despite continuous changes in business, society, and the profession of internal auditing. Promoted widely in management texts and used extensively in professional and technical symposia, such increasing acceptance and use demonstrate the credibility of the principles established by the *Standards*.

Fraud is a significant and sensitive management concern. This concern has grown in recent years owing to a substantial increase in the number and the size of the frauds disclosed. The tremendous expansion in the use of computers and the size of and publicity accorded computer-related frauds intensify this concern.

The internal auditor's responsibilities for deterring, detecting, investigating, and reporting of fraud have been a matter of much debate and controversy. Some of the controversy can be attributed to the differences in internal auditing's charter from country to country and from organization to organization. Another cause of the controversy may be unrealistic expectations of the internal auditor's ability to deter and detect fraud.

While several standards and guidelines directly or indirectly address the issue of internal auditors' responsibilities in cases of fraud, the following directly address these responsibilities:

Standard 280—Due Professional Care

Internal auditors should exercise due professional care in performing internal audits.

.01 **In exercising due professional care, internal auditors should be alert to the possibility of wrongdoing, errors and omissions, inefficiency, waste, ineffectiveness and conflicts of interest. They should also be alert to those conditions and activities where irregularities are likely to occur.**

.02 **The possibility of material irregularities or noncompliance should be considered whenever the internal auditor undertakes an internal auditing assignment.**

.03 **When an internal auditor suspects wrongdoing, the appropriate authorities within the organization should be informed. The internal auditor may recommend whatever investigation is considered necessary in the circumstances. Thereafter, the auditor should follow up to see that the internal auditing department's responsibilities have been met.**

Standard 300—Scope of Work

THE SCOPE OF THE INTERNAL AUDIT SHOULD ENCOMPASS THE EXAMINATION AND THE EVALUATION OF THE ADEQUACY AND THE EFFECTIVENESS OF THE ORGANIZATION'S SYSTEM OF INTERNAL CONTROL AND THE QUALITY OF PERFORMANCE IN CARRYING OUT ASSIGNED RESPONSIBILITIES.

.01 Internal auditors should review the means used to safeguard assets from various types of losses such as those resulting from theft, fire, improper or illegal activities and exposure to the elements.

Characteristics of Fraud

.1 Fraud encompasses an array of irregularities and illegal acts characterized by intentional deception. It can be perpetrated for the benefit of or to the detriment of the organization and by persons outside as well as inside the organization.

.2 Fraud designed to benefit the organization generally produces such benefit by exploiting an unfair or dishonest advantage that also may deceive an outside party. Perpetrators of such frauds usually benefit indirectly since personal benefit usually accrues when the organization is aided by the act. Some examples are:

a. Sale or assignment of fictitious or misrepresented assets.

b. Improper payments such as illegal political contributions, bribes, kickbacks and payoffs to government officials, intermediaries of government officials, customers or suppliers.

c. Intentional, improper representation or valuation of transactions, assets, liabilities or income.

d. Intentional, improper transfer pricing (e.g., valuation of goods exchanged between related entities). By purposely structuring pricing techniques improperly, management* can improve the operating results of an organization involved in the transaction to the detriment of the other organization.

e. Intentional, improper related party transactions in which one party receives some benefit not obtainable in an arm's-length transaction.

f. Intentional failure to record or disclose significant information to improve the financial picture of the organization to outside parties.

g. Prohibited business activities such as those which violate government statutes, rules, regulations or contracts.

h. Tax fraud.

.3 Fraud perpetrated to the detriment of the organization generally is for the direct or indirect benefit of an employee, outside individual or another firm. Some examples are:

a. Acceptance of bribes or kickbacks.

b. Diversion to an employee or outsider of a potentially profit-

---

*As used in this statement, the term "management" includes anyone in an organization with responsibilities for setting and/or achieving objectives.

able transaction that would normally generate profits for the organization.

c. Embezzlement, as typified by the misappropriation of money or property, and falsification of financial records to cover up the act, thus making detection difficult.

d. Intentional concealment or misrepresentation of events or data.

e. Claims submitted for services or goods not actually provided to the organization.

Deterrence of Fraud

.4 Deterrence consists of those actions taken to discourage the perpetration of fraud and limit the exposure if fraud does occur. The principle mechanism for deterring fraud is control. Primary responsibility for establishing and maintaining control rests with management (See *SIAS No. 1,* Control: Concepts and Responsibilities).

Internal Auditing's Responsibilities

.5 Internal auditing is responsible for assisting in the deterrence of fraud by examining and evaluating the adequacy and the effectiveness of control, commensurate with the extent of the potential exposure/risk in the various segments of the entity's operations. In carrying out this responsibility, internal auditing should, for example, determine whether:

a. The organizational environment fosters control consciousness.

b. Realistic organizational goals and objectives are set.

c. Written corporate policies (e.g., code of conduct) exist that describe prohibited activities and the action required whenever violations are discovered.

d. Appropriate authorization policies for transactions are established and maintained.

e. Policies, practices, procedures, reports and other mechanisms are developed to monitor activities and safeguard assets, particularly in high-risk areas.

  f. Communication channels provide management with adequate and reliable information.

  g. Recommendations need to be made for the establishment or enhancement of cost-effective controls to help deter fraud.

Detection of Fraud

 .6 Detection consists of identifying indicators of fraud sufficient to warrant recommending an investigation. These indicators may arise as a result of controls established by management, tests conducted by auditors, and other sources both within and outside the organization.

Internal Auditing's Responsibilities

 .7 In conducting audit assignments, the internal auditor's responsibilities for detecting fraud are to:

  a. Have sufficient knowledge of fraud to be able to identify indicators that fraud might have been committed. This knowledge includes the need to know the characteristics of fraud, the techniques used to commit fraud, and the types of frauds associated with the activities audited.

  b. Be alert to opportunities, such as control weaknesses, that could allow fraud. If significant control weaknesses are detected, additional tests conducted by internal auditors should include tests directed toward identification of other indicators of fraud. Some examples of indicators are unauthorized transactions, override of controls, unexplained pricing exceptions and unusually large product losses. Internal auditors should recognize that the presence of more than one indicator at any one time increases the probability that fraud might have occurred.

  c. Evaluate the indicators that fraud might have been committed and decide whether any further action is necessary or whether an investigation should be recommended.

  d. Notify the appropriate authorities within the organization if a determination is made that there are sufficient indicators of the commission of a fraud to recommend an investigation.

.8   Internal auditors are not expected to have knowledge equivalent to that of a person whose primary responsibilty is detecting and investigating fraud. Also, audit procedures alone, even when carried out with due professional care, do not guarantee that fraud will be detected.

Investigation of Fraud

.9   Investigation consists of performing extended procedures necessary to determine whether fraud, as suggested by the indicators, has occurred. It includes gathering sufficient evidential matter about the specific details of a discovered fraud. Internal auditors, lawyers, investigators, security personnel and other specialists from inside or outside the organization are the parties that usually conduct or participate in fraud investigations.

Internal Auditing's Responsibilities

.10   When conducting fraud investigations, internal auditing should:

a.   Assess the probable level and the extent of complicity in the fraud within the organization. This can be critical to ensuring that the internal auditor avoids providing information to or obtaining misleading information from persons who may be involved.

b.   Determine the knowledge, skills and disciplines needed to effectively carry out the investigation. Assess the qualifications and the skills of the internal auditors and of the specialists available to participate in the investigation to ensure that it is conducted by individuals having the appropriate type and level of technical expertise. This should include assurances on such matters as professional certifications, licenses, reputation and that there is no relationship to those being investigated or to any of the employees or management of the organization.

c.   Design procedures to follow in attempting to identify the perpetrators, extent of the fraud, techniques used and cause of the fraud.

d. Coordinate activities with management personnel, legal counsel and other specialists as appropriate throughout the course of the investigation.

e. Be cognizant of the rights of alleged perpetrators and personnel within the scope of the investigation and the reputation of the organization itself.

.11 Once a fraud investigation is concluded, internal audit should assess the facts known in order to:

a. Determine if controls need to be implemented or strengthened to reduce future vulnerability.

b. Design audit tests to help disclose the existence of similar frauds in the future.

c. Help meet the internal responsibility to maintain sufficient knowledge of fraud and thereby be able to identify future indicators of fraud.

Reporting of Fraud

.12 Reporting consists of the various oral or written, interim or final communications to management regarding the status and results of fraud investigations.

Internal Auditing's Responsibilities

.13 A preliminary or final report may be desirable at the conclusion of the detection phase. The report should include the internal auditor's conclusion as to whether sufficient information exists to conduct an investigation. It should also summarize findings that serve as the basis for such decision.

.14 *SIAS No. 2,* Communicating Results, which expands on Specific Standard 430 and provides interpretations, is applicable to internal audit reports issued as a result of fraud investigations. Additional interpretive guidelines on reporting of fraud are as follows:

a. When the incidence of significant fraud has been established to a reasonable certainty, management or the board should be notified immediately.

b.   The results of a fraud investigation may indicate that fraud has had a previously undiscovered materially adverse effect on the financial position and results of operations of an organization for one or more years on which financial statements have already been issued. Internal audit should inform appropriate management and the audit committee of the board of directors of such a discovery.

c.   A written report should be issued at the conclusion of the investigation phase. It should include all findings, conclusions, recommendations and corrective action taken.

d.   A draft of the proposed report on fraud should be submitted to legal counsel for review. In those cases in which the auditor wants to invoke client privilege, consideration should be given to addressing the report to legal counsel.

APPENDIX F

Partnership Role of the Internal Auditor

The accomplishment of the basic service role of the internal auditor to management starts with understanding management problems and needs, but then goes on to involve a partnership role between the manager and the internal auditor at all operational levels—a partnership role that extends to helping management achieve its managerial goals and objectives to the maximum extent possible. Such an effective partnership role can be achieved in many ways. We believe, however, that the following are essential ingredients of a sound program to achieve the desired results:

Excerpt from *Modern Internal Auditing* by Victor Z. Brink and Herbert Witt, (New York: John Wiley & Sons, Inc., 1982), pp. 76–77.

1. The ability to provide basic protective services but, at the same time, to help management achieve desired improvement. Moreover, the protective contributions often provide an important foundation for making the constructive contribution.

2. Being continuously alert to use the point of detachment from actual operational responsibilities as a special capability to identify, evaluate and support issues of significant management interest.

3. The capacity to interface in a persuasive manner with managers at all levels. This is a combination of operational understanding plus a manner of personal appearance and conduct.

4. Avoidance of the inherent temptation of auditors to use unduly available power with management and other operational auditees. Such actions generate auditee resistance that then blocks ongoing constructive relationships.

5. The strategic focus on control as the credential for the analysis and review of operational areas. Since the technical expertise of the auditee is typically always superior, the focus on control provides a more acceptable justification of the audit assistance offered.

6. The respect at all times during the process of assistance for the responsibility that managers have for operational results. Hence staff recommendations must stand on their own merits, as judged by those who have operational responsibility.

7. The continuing blending of the objectives of assistance at auditee levels with the necessity for upward disclosure within the framework of total organizational welfare. It is indeed the latter focus which neutralizes all lower-level conflict for the upward exposure.

The potential of service to the organization through assistance to management at all levels is a major goal for professional internal auditors. It is these potentials that justify every possible effort on the part of the internal auditor to see the management job through the eyes of management and to render all possible assistance for maximum goal achievement of all managers. The problems of management are very complex and are continually changing in the light of both internal and external environmental factors. This means that management increasingly needs the assistance of internal auditors and will, in most cases, welcome it when the ability and credibility of the internal auditor are established. It is a continuing challenge to internal auditors to render assistance which is in fact made productive through management acceptance and application.

Index